Date due

	FEB 21 '72		
	FEB 23 '72		
	MAR 9 '72		
	MAR 1 '72		
	MAR 1 '73		
	FEB 20 '73		
JUL 29 1976			
JUL 21 1976			
79 10 29			
79 10 15			
02 02 22			
09 08			
83 06 14			

HABITS AND VIRTUES

IMPRIMI POTEST:

John J. Foley, S.J.
Provincial, Wisconsin Province
November 28, 1964

IMPRIMATUR:

✠ Joseph Cardinal Ritter
Archbishop of St. Louis
July 9, 1965

George P. Klubertanz, S.J.

St. Louis University

Habits and Virtues

New York

APPLETON-CENTURY-CROFTS
Division of Meredith Publishing Company

PREFACE

"Habit" and "virtue" are terms that are used frequently today. In writings on education the importance of habit as one kind of learning is stressed. Psychologists often speak of habit, and many of their investigations deal with the effects of training. Moralists and writers on the living of religious truths and ideals are deeply concerned with virtue and vice.

Strangely enough, there is no single, full-dress, contemporary treatment of these topics. In fact, it seems that those who write on one of these aspects do not attend to any of the others. This is unfortunate. When, in a book on ethics, the whole descriptive psychology of habits is left out (as it almost always is), the result is a kind of formal (one could more unkindly call it verbal) treatment of justice, temperance, and courage. In quite a contrary fashion, some writers on asceticism (the practice of virtue) seem to be concerned mainly with techniques, particularly little "actions" to be performed, much as one would describe and advise the practice of setting-up exercises. It is the author's conviction that these limitations cause much good to remain undone, and sometimes cause harm.

The formalism of much writing on ethics is apparent to many persons. The most characteristic contemporary reaction is to discard most of the traditional content of moral doctrine, and to stress instead the major importance of love, the supreme value of the last end, the dignity and freedom of the human person as an absolute ethical value. All these emphases are excellent, and without these principles a real and satisfying ethics cannot be constructed. Therefore, we should be most grateful to those philosophers and theologians who have reintroduced them into psychological and moral discussions.

In the rejection of formalism and legalism, however, we should not imagine that it is enough to "love" (in a vague, general, senti-

mental meaning of this word). St. Augustine's "Love God and do
what you will," is said to the already virtuous man. His love is an
enlightened and ordered love. But how does a man enlighten
and order his love? It was said by the great Apostle of love, "How,
then, can the love of God abide in him who possesses worldly
goods, and, seeing his brother in need, closes his heart to him?
Little children, let us not love merely in word or with the tongue,
but in action, in reality" (I John, 3:17-18, Knox). Is there then
something in addition to love? We must learn concretely what to
do when love is called for. We must know how to prepare ourselves that when love is called for, we are able to respond. These
further determinations of the great principle of love are the
virtues.

There is another, related, and yet different reason for a study
of the virtues. Since the origins of scientific psychology, much has
been learned through this study of man, and this knowledge has
been increased many times over in the past few years. Certainly
some of this detailed knowledge is not relevant to an understanding and direction of human action, but much of it is most relevant. But how is it to be put together with the basic and over-all
principle of love? It would be disastrous if, after such a promis-
ing beginning as we now have, theologians and ethicians would
retreat to the cloudy peaks of general motivation and leave the
details of daily action to be solved on non-moral, subhuman
grounds. Conversely, when the sciences of human action (such as
individual and social psychology, psychiatry, and so on) degen-
erate into mere techniques of efficiency, the manipulation of the
daily behavior of most men becomes a horrifying possibility. Men
need to know the principles by which they can maintain their
own freedom and self-determination.

Let it be said at once that this book will not be a complete
treatment of the doctrine of the virtues. When the task is as
serious as the preceding considerations have indicated, a complete
synthesis is not yet possible. But the limitations need to be recognized, not only by the author, but also by the reader. When a
writer selects as the topic of his presentation the intrinsic, acquired principles of human activity, he does not thereby deny
that there are extrinsic principles necessary for that very activity,

or that there are gratuitous gifts of God ennobling that same activity. One can ask, "What is it *in* a man that accounts for his activity being *observably* thus and so?" without denying the existence of God, the necessity of grace and the infused virtues for meritorious activity, and so on.

Let me also from the beginning disclaim the intention of writing a theological work. But I do not see that this requires me to ignore the contributions that mankind has received from the Christian revelation and the developments contributed by theologians. To illustrate from another area of thought: it is impossible to determine, by philosophical procedures, the spatial structure of the solar system, but it would be ridiculous for a philosopher today to ignore that structure. Nevertheless, the mere recognition of the conclusions reached by the astronomers does not make the philosopher a scientist. Similarly, a Christian philosopher would be a fool—if not worse—either to pretend to prove the data of revelation or to ignore it. But his recognition of certain facts thus made known does not make him so formally a theologian that all his writings are properly theology. It depends on his mode of argumentation; and, if he argues philosophically, not basing his arguments upon the revealed statements or on the authority of the teaching Church, his work ought to be considered a philosophical one. (If someone else wishes to restrict the term *philosophy* to a production of reason that entirely ignores all revelation, he may of course do so, but he and I have no quarrel.)

Some readers may feel that there is a serious theological difficulty involved: Is it possible for a Christian to study virtuous activity except as a theologian? This is a purely theological difficulty. Hence I shall answer here only briefly and without explanation of the evidence behind my statements.[1] First, there are good theologians who think this procedure is valid. Secondly, apart from mystical experience, neither grace nor the infused habit of charity can be experienced in such a way that they can be distinguished and identified. Thirdly, the presence of grace and charity cannot be concluded to infallibly in any given case,

---

[1] For a more technical elaboration of this position, see the article, "Vertus morales 'naturelles' et 'surnaturelles,'" *Revue Thomiste*, vol. 59 (1959), 565-575.

not even in one's own case. Fourthly, there still are theologians who hold with St. Thomas Aquinas that "grace does not destroy nature, but perfects it." A philosophical investigation of moral activity is therefore possible, provided that strictly philosophical procedures are carefully followed. It is indeed preferable that a critical analysis of human behavior be done by a person who has had a good theological training, for in practical matters it sometimes seems that only under the guidance of Divine Revelation can a human being reach the full knowledge and enjoy the full freedom that is needed to be a philosopher.

In spite of the fact that this is a philosophical study, the book is not written primarly for professional philosophers. It is written for people who are interested in the theory of human action, human virtue, human perfection, and for people who are engaged in helping and training others in the practice of human virtue and the pursuit of perfection.

But how can people who belong to different "schools of spirituality" profit from one and the same analysis? First of all, the differences between these various "schools" are often exaggerated. Of course, there are differences of emphasis, of concrete implementation. But the basic insights must be common to all Christians or they are not basic. Secondly, original differences have become smaller over the centuries. Mutual understanding has helped; the development of both theory and practice in all "schools" has brought them closer together. Thirdly, in the perspective of history we can more easily see what is common to all and is therefore primary, in contrast to what is particular. Fourthly, the current revival of the theology and philosophy of love and the renewal of the Catholic liturgy have made it clear that in some sense there is but one spirituality for all Christians. Finally, the philosophical analysis itself will show that there must be various sorts of structures, and will provide the principles through which the particular historically determined structures can be understood.

Because of the special aim of this work, it will not begin with the philosophical principles. The principles will be developed as they are discovered in the course of the investigation; so, no great technical acquaintance with philosophy will be presupposed.

Finally, this book is also not written for professional psychologists and educationists. Material from these fields has been used, but no original research is here presented, nor is there any claim to present little-known facts. Rather, what psychologists will find here pertaining to their specialty will be well known and even trite facts and conclusions. They may, on the other hand, find the philosophical analysis strange, unless they are also somewhat proficient in this kind of work.

In brief, this book is not aimed primarily at a learned audience and is not basic research. Hence, it will not be documented in a scholarly fashion. Instead, the major sources will be given in the form of bibliographies at the end of each chapter. Those who are interested in what the book is trying to do will find in the books and articles referred to much concrete detail that will help them to understand the analysis much better; on occasion, there will be references to more detailed philosophical analyses.

The material discussed in this book has been taught as a graduate course regularly to seminarians and occasionally to others during the last fifteen years. Lively discussions, now on one point, now on another, have often clarified, reoriented, and even changed the opinions presented. To these students this book is dedicated.

G.P.K., S.J.

CONTENTS

Chapter Two: KINDS OF SIMPLE HABITS

Chapter Three: COMPLEX HABITS

Chapter Four: IMPORTANCE, GROWTH AND DESTRUCTION AND GENERALIZATION OF HABITS

Chapter Five: VIRTUE AND VICE

Chapter Six: THE CARDINAL VIRTUES

Chapter Seven: CONCLUSIONS AND CORRELATIONS

HABITS AND VIRTUES

Chapter One

Acquired Modifications

Facts, Descriptions, and Preliminary Distinctions

POINT OF DEPARTURE

Some topics of scientific investigation are entirely outside ordinary experience, and so a knowledge of them is acquired only by means of specialized scientific experiment. This is both an advantage and a disadvantage: because the knowledge is built up scientifically from the start, it can be rigorously controlled and accurately elaborated; but because it is not previously known in common experience, it remains the property of a relatively few specialists.

On the other hand, some things are already known long before the scientific investigation of them is begun, largely because they fall necessarily within ordinary experience, sometimes also because in a given culture (or subculture) they are often written about. This is an obvious advantage in that a discussion of them can begin well in the middle and can be shared by a larger number of readers; but, at the same time, since this knowledge has been acquired piecemeal, from diverse sources, and is mixed with emotion and error as well as symbol and metaphor, a scientific treatment of its objects must correct, purify, and render coherent a whole group of preexisting ideas. It is therefore impossible to proceed in a simple and straightforward fashion.

Now, everyone who reads this book has had some experience of habit in himself and in his acquaintances; indeed, it may be that a great deal of experience has preceded. In addition, he has almost certainly read something about habit and virtue.

In a discussion of habit, therefore, we must begin with some commonly accepted meaning of words, and with a reference to

1

commonly possessed and recognized evidence. This will make for a complicated presentation and some backtracking of the argument. Yet a linear argument from evidence to conclusion would have a deceptive simplicity and a fallacious objectivity, since many unexamined conceptions would in fact creep into the reading and uncontrollably change the meaning of any statement of the evidence.

Because of this complexity of development, it may help to state briefly what is intended. This is to be a *progressive* investigation of habits and virtues. The beginning notion will be vague and elastic, and by means of an extensive survey of human activity, we shall try to pin down just what man does achieve. We shall range from physical activities to mental, from "mechanical" actions to the free and deliberate. Along the way it will be necessary to direct the reader's attention to aspects of human activity that he may not have noted before, to lead him to distinguish where he had been accustomed to take experience as a whole. These are digressions, but they are necessary.

Through an analysis of man's activities and powers, a number of different kinds of habits will be found. In this investigation we will also find that many of these habits are complex, involving more than one factor, and that many of them are grouped together in various ways. This chapter will close with an attempt to give a formal definition of habit.

Next, we will examine the way in which habits begin to exist and to grow, what keeps them alive and influential, how they are lost or destroyed. We also want to see how the influence of habits can extend beyond the original area of acquisition. Really, this is extremely important; if habits were merely specific, they would not be very interesting. As it is, the fact that habits can extend far beyond the original area of acquisition makes their influence of major importance. So we must take very seriously the question of the transfer of habits.

The second major question of our investigation is the nature of virtue. According to the theory of St. Thomas Aquinas, some habits are human virtues. This point needs very serious consideration. How are we to understand habit? What is the nature of human virtue? How is virtue acquired? How is virtue perfected?

How can we make sense of all the various requirements of human goodness? Here the theory of the four cardinal virtues helps to put order into the total field of human goodness.

Finally, our last consideration is the application of all this elaborate analysis to the concrete case of the individual. Each human person is in some way unique; each has his own special requirements. How, from general points of view, can we say anything at all about his personal goodness?

WHAT SORT OF EVIDENCE IS PERTINENT?

In its general use, the term *habit* implies a set of characteristics: that behavior (activity) is modified, that the modification is not part of the substance or nature of the thing modified, that the thing whose behavior is modified remains substantially the same, and that the modification is relatively permanent, not just momentary or for a very brief time. *Habit* does not designate the activity itself, nor the modification of the activity, but rather a qualification of the subject (agent) which is the reason for the modification. For this reason, habits cannot be discovered in themselves, precisely as habits, but only through the activities in which stable modifications show themselves.

A generation ago, many psychologists and educationalists were bitterly opposed to the notion of habit. They were willing to admit only those factors that they could find by means of physical analysis (microscopes, chemical analysis, and so on). Since habit as habit could not be discovered in this way, it was denied. Later on, the uselessness of this restriction was realized, and now scientists admit habits in one form or another.

As a result of this discussion one point was emphasized. Habits are not something like trees or wrinkles on the face; they cannot be found by a simple, superficial inspection of a man or an animal. Their *existence* must be reasoned to, as well as their nature. We can conclude to their existence only on the basis of evidence, and that evidence is not the habit itself.

What sort of evidence will show the existence of a habit? Suppose one and the same thing (a dog, for instance) has acquired or learned a new way of acting, which remains constant over a relatively long period of time. What is implied in this evidence? First, to account for the consistency of the behavior in spite of changing circumstances, we must conclude to the presence of some modification within the thing itself. Second, because this modification was acquired, it is different from the nature (essence) of the thing, since the nature as such is complete from the moment the thing begins to exist. A dog is a dog from the start, though it has to learn to sit up and beg. And third, because it already had some behavior before it learned this particular way of acting, there is a *modification* of behavior. Thus, in a word, the fact of long-term learning is an evidence for the existence of a habit. This evidence need not be the only one, but it is easily discoverable, and so we can begin with it.

In this preliminary account of what we could mean by a habit and how we could find it, we have set down nothing except plain description, and the obvious inference that there is something in the agent which is the source of what we have described. Our definition in no way reveals *what* this source is, and in no way prejudices our later attempt to determine as far as possible the nature of habit.

We want first to discuss whether distinctive modes of acting are acquired by things, and then in what sense this can be said.

THE FACT OF ACQUIRED MODIFICATIONS

Some things, as soon as they exist, have all the distinctive modes of acting they will ever have. The lowest orders of being illustrate this. If a chemical is changed at all, it is no longer the same chemical. Once such things are, they are what they are completely. They do not "learn" (acquire) a mode of activity; they cannot be taught. The typical procedures of physics and chemistry presuppose fixed, objective traits and relations.

Other things do acquire distinctive modes of acting. Some aggregates of nonliving things are capable of modifications of activity. Certain *machines* must be "broken in"; these are mechanical adaptations. Some electronic equipment breaks down; the electronic calculators called "brains" can fall into "habitual" errors, and models now being constructed will adapt their behavior on the basis of the results of previous activity. There are also adaptations in *plants,* of a sort. A plant has to be treated carefully in being taken from a hothouse to the outside. Gradually, it grows stronger, and has adapted itself to a much more variable climate. *Animals* can acquire modes of behavior. Some, for example, an amoeba, respond very little to training; others—fish, dogs, apes— can learn very much more. *Men* are evidently capable of some acquired modes of behavior—this hardly needs proof.

These illustrative instances give us the evidence for saying that there *are* acquired modes of behavior. Therefore, the notion of habit has an objective point of departure, for adaptation does occur.

A QUESTION: ARE ALL ACQUIRED MODIFICATIONS THE SAME?

Seeing that there *are* modifications, can we simply go ahead, examine any one of them, and come up with an adequate analysis of what habit is? We can, if they are all the same. We can compare our situation to that of a student who wishes to know what an animal is. He finds out that fish are animals, and without further question begins to examine a fish. Can he legitimately conclude that animals have scales and live in the water?

We should then take a preliminary look at several different modifications. If they turn out to be basically different, then we will have to investigate the whole ambit.

(1) Though we are not concerned with electronics, not even with plants and animals, but with adaptations in human beings, we can begin with physical modifications in men which are similar to changes in nonliving things. If a man's leg is broken, his way of walking is different. What are the characteristics of such a change? (*a*) It necessarily and by its nature involves a change in the material substance; it is based on a change in the material structure; consequently it can be found by other means of investigation as well as by its effects on the activity. (*b*) It cannot *not* be used—one cannot arbitrarily decide to use it or not. (*c*) It makes no difference how such an adaptation is acquired, whether it is by one's own activity or not—one breaks his own leg, or an-

other man does, or an automobile. Since this is the case, a mechanical (physical) modification is acquired *passively*. (*d*) It makes no difference whether the man who undergoes it is aware of its presence; its *physical* presence is enough to make a change in the activity. For example, if in the course of an appendectomy a doctor finds a malfunctioning gall bladder and takes it out, the change in the patient's activity is as complete and entire when the patient remains in ignorance of what happened as when he is informed. Thus, there is no necessary connection between a physical modification and consciousness, and so no direct connection.

(2) Now, let us take another sort of habit and compare it on these points. We can take as an example a habit of reasoning (such as a habit of mathematics strictly so called, in a skilled mathematician who can easily think mathematically). There was a time when the man could not think in this way; therefore, the modification is an acquired one. Now, mathematics (*a*) is purely abstract and intellectual; it cannot be based on a change in material structure and has no direct connection with any material structure.[1] (*b*) Is it necessarily used? Can a mathematician think otherwise than mathematically? Obviously he can. Can he think of mathematical objects otherwise than mathematically? Must he think of number or figure in the mode of mathematical reasoning? For example, can he treat it historically or imaginatively? Can he ask how it is possible for some one to acquire a mathematical mode of reasoning? That is, can he engage in a psychological investigation of number and of mathematics itself? Can he make mistakes in mathematics?[2] Or, if a person has been first trained in Euclidean geometry, can he deal in a new and different way with geometrical

---

[1] Both epistemologically and psychologically, a habit of reasoning like mathematics is *immaterial*. For presentations of evidence, see Frederick D. Wilhelmsen, *Man's Knowledge of Reality* (New York, Prentice-Hall, 1956), pp. 140-142; and Klubertanz, *The Philosophy of Human Nature* (New York, Appleton-Century-Crofts, 1953), pp. 161-164.

[2] A mistake in mathematics is not made by means of the habit of mathematics. If the mistake is made rarely, by chance, the mistake means that sometimes the habit is not used, or is interfered with, or is not yet completely developed. If the mistake is made consistently, what is operating is not the habit of mathematics (which is aimed at correct reasoning), but a different habit of faulty reasoning (which deals with mathematical elements but is not aimed at correct reasoning).

objects? In other words, even when a man has a habit, and does the same general thing (for example, deals with the same mathematical objects and ideas), he can act in a way not necessarily in conformity with the mode previously acquired. Therefore, an intellectual habit is not necessarily used. (c) Can an intellectual habit be acquired passively? Can a man become a mathematician by just waiting for something to happen to him?[3] Perhaps we might here think of the "Slumber Method" of learning (listening to a recording during sleep). Familiarity with a language can be learned in this way, and it even seems that factual information—or rather the *words* stating such information—can be acquired by mere hearing. In a similar way, we could say that a parrot "learns mathematics" when someone teaches it to recite some formulae. But the ability to repeat formulae is by no means the possession of an understanding of mathematics, as any teacher of that subject can testify. In fact, our own experience shows us that it is impossible to acquire any intellectual habit passively; we have to work at it quite actively. Not only can an intellectual habit not be acquired passively; as passively possessed, it is of no use or profit to us. (d) If an intellectual habit can be acquired only through activity, it must necessarily be acquired consciously. Moreover, a person cannot use an intellectual habit unconsciously. Some habits (such as motor skills, as we shall see) can be used unconsciously. Can a person think scientifically and be unaware that he is so thinking, that he is using his science? Note that a habit of scientific knowledge is by definition not only a way of thinking but one which leads to proved conclusions.[4]

The nature of scientific knowledge requires not only that some-

---

[3] Absolutely speaking, God can produce in an intellect (the technical term is *infuse*) a naturally acquirable habit, for example, of knowledge. But the fact that God is the author of nature does not militate against the causality of nature itself, and a miracle still leaves a natural order of events which in the nonmiraculous cases operates according to its own laws.

[4] By the term "scientific knowledge" I mean to include not only what are called "sciences" in the narrow contemporary sense (such as physics or biology) but also mathematics, logic, philosophy, theology, history—in short, any organized knowledge about a distinctive subject matter, proceeding from evidence, basic insights, and proper principles by way of a proportioned manner of reasoning to conclusions seen to follow with some kind of necessity from the evidence.

thing is known, but also that it be *known* to be *true* (in the way suitable to the particular kind of knowledge). A person has scientific knowledge, not when he merely reaches a conclusion which is true, but when he is certain that it is true. This latter knowledge arises from the nature of the starting points, and also from a clear awareness of the method by which the conclusion was reached. But this requires a continuous and reflective (not necessary reflex) awareness of what is being done.

One can know about mathematics in other than scientific ways. In order that it be known scientifically, the reasoning processes occurring in it must be conscious as reasoning. Therefore, there is a necessary connection between a habit of scientific knowledge and explicit consciousness. In other words, this kind of intellectual modification is necessarily used consciously and cannot be used unconsciously.

Thus there are (at least) two descriptively very different kinds of acquired modifications, the purely physical and the intellectual. In the case of the purely physical ones, we can easily identify and describe not only the change in activity, but also the permanent modification of the subject acting. Purely immaterial modifications of activity, such as science, are also comparatively easy to isolate and describe, at least for anyone who has done some advanced work in some line of intellectual endeavor. But that these immaterial modifications of activity require a modification of the subject is perhaps not so clear and can advantageously be made more explicit.

One cannot suppose a consistent accuracy in reaching conclusions by a series of lucky and unrelated accidents. And even if such a series were supposed—if we were to imagine that an experimenter would accidentally reach correct conclusions in twenty successive cases—there would not be any science in the strict sense of that word, but only the materials of a science. For such an experimentalist would not be certain that he had reached justified conclusions. Nor can we suppose that the sureness and accuracy of scientific reasoning is to be accounted for by deliberate, painstaking effort exercised anew in each case, for the fact that scientific reasoning becomes familiar and easy is well known and undeniable. It remains, therefore, that there is an intrinsic modification acquired in the use of scientific reasoning, that is, that there is a habit of scientific reasoning.

Let us now schematically compare the two modifications we have examined.

Physical	*Intellectual*
a material change[5]	no material change
when present, used necessarily	not used necessarily
no relation to previous human activity as human; not an immediately related consequence of deliberate choice	acquired by personal, conscious, deliberate activity
therefore passive	never wholly passive
no internal relation to consciousness	necessarily related to awareness

We can note that in all physical adaptations there is an interchange, the replacement of one disposition with another. For example, the breaking of a leg is not only the acquisition of a disposition of parts but the loss of the previous disposition, that of the structure of the unbroken leg. A loss is necessarily involved as well as a gain. It is not simply an acquired modification, but the acquisition of a perfection with the loss of another, a replacement. Analogously, in the case of nonliving things, when a machine is broken, there is not the acquisition of a new structure supervening upon a lack of structure; but one structure is replaced with another, one qualitative disposition is replaced by another. Generally, these two belong to the same kind of quality. Hence, the modification always involves a loss.

Contrast this with scientific knowledge. What does the intellect lose to gain a science? We are not considering the case of a person who had a bad habit, one who habitually made mistakes, but rather the case of a person who did not have any habit of reasoning at all. If the intellect has no habit at all, will it go along one path by its nature, even though only in a fumbling way? No, it

---

[5] Note that this need not be a substantial change; often, however, some kind of substantial change or modification may be involved. For example, the loss of an organ (an eye, a hand) is a change of the substance itself. In other cases, there is a change in the structure or quality of a material thing; these structures and qualities are themselves properly called material.

will be acting according to its imperfect (potential) nature and hence be liable to error, but it will possibly reach the truth. Any habit of reasoning—of consistently and surely reaching a definite kind of goal—is an acquired perfection,[6] a gain without a corresponding loss. For ignorance and the absence of a definite habit of reasoning are not positive evils, but, as we say, mere privations.

The philosophical reason for this is: If the nature of a power is indeterminate as it exists in itself in the real order,[7] then there is no determination to be replaced. The new determination is a simple addition. As the habit of mathematics is developed, the learner builds a "structure" in his intellect which does not replace a preceding structure.

In ordinary language, we do speak of a "habit" of reasoning, though the application of the term "habit" to other intellectual activity is less common. We ordinarily do not apply the term to physical modifications. Nevertheless, we cannot be entirely guided by common usage. That is why we include in the scope of our consideration acquired physical modifications, provided only that they influence behavior. We shall see later whether common usage is justified.

For the moment, we have seen that there are two descriptively different types of acquired, permanent modifications. It may be that they have nothing else in common except that they are acquired modifications; it may be that they are only accidentally different. It is possible, after all, to find some clearly distinguishable classes of things, and later on to find that they are nevertheless essentially the same. For example, a person beginning to observe living things might carefully distinguish between caterpillars and butterflies, describe each type very carefully, and only later on find out that they are not only essentially but even individually the same living things. His descriptive distinction will not prevent

6 Even a "bad" habit is good in some sense, for it is the act and perfection of a power. We call a habit "bad," not because it is not a positive perfection in itself, but in relation to desired results or in relation to nature; see Chapter Five.

7 We shall see later in detail that the different powers man has are indeterminate in different ways, either in themselves or in relation to some use. Here we are concerned only with the basic principle and its exemplification in the case of the intellect.

him from finding this out. And, unless he at first distinguished, he could not describe his subject accurately. Two undesirable results could come about: either he would have only a vague notion which could never be defined, or he would involuntarily but quite effectively suppress the differences of one of them, and thereby arrive at a misplaced definition. It is therefore necessary for us to be both inclusive and detailed, concrete.

SCOPE AND CRITERIA OF THE INVESTIGATION

Can we find the kinds of modifications human beings can undergo in such a way that we could later justifiably decide that there is some essential common genus? To answer this question, we must make a complete induction, if we wish to know whether there is a common genus with specific differences. For only through a complete induction of all the species can we establish the nature of a common genus, or be certain that there is more than one kind of modification.

How are we to enumerate all the specific types of modifications a human being can undergo? An attempt to enumerate them in their concrete variety seems foredoomed to failure, for the most superficial glance at psychological studies reveals an inexhaustible multiplicity. We must in some way reduce this multiplicity to a smaller number. One possible way to cover all the types is to examine all the different functions which a human being exercises. We identify a kind of function by describing *what is done*,[8] and this we call the "object" of the activity. Now, different conscious experiences have different qualities: seeing has a different quality than hearing. But when we try to clarify, even to ourselves, what seeing or hearing is, we cannot simply state and restate this quality. What then do we do to analyze these experiences? We try to describe the object of the activity: what it is that the experience concerns. But an "object" in this broad sense has many aspects, and many of them may not be relevant. When we see a guitarist,

---

[8] This is true in the case of immanent (vital) activities. As far as transient activities go, "what-is-done" depends on the nature of the recipient of the action as well as on the nature of the agent. Thus the analysis of transient activity is much more difficult, and in many cases we cannot distinguish the roles of agent and patient. But we are not concerned with such activities here.

we see a human being and a wooden instrument. But this is also what we hear, so merely naming the object will not help us to understand the activity. We need to describe the object precisely in the way in which it is an object. Thus, seeing is directly experiencing something colored (not a human being as human, not the instrument as wooden). Hearing is directly experiencing something sounding. If we completely describe the object of an activity in its relevant relation as object, we completely identify, and thus define, the activity. For example, a complete description of a sounding thing as object (a vibrating body acting through compression waves within certain limits of magnitude and so forth), singles out what we do when we hear. In the order of directly sensible objects, we could say that the proper object of a sense is a thing as providing a characteristic stimulus for a sense. More generally, the *proper* object of any activity is a thing as being relevant to some activity in a characteristic, or formal, way.

The analysis of human experience by means of a consideration of the proper objects involved (a "formal object analysis"[9]) leads to a relatively small number of *kinds* of activity. In the order of sensory knowledge, the different kinds of activity are related to the kinds of organs that we use: seeing specially pertains to the eyes, and so on. But the primary way of distinguishing activities philosophically is through their proper objects.

Now, vital and cognoscitive activities are not continuous, but are interrupted and change. Yet the ability to perform them remains as long as the living thing remains alive and healthy. The ability to perform a definite kind of activity (that is, as distinguished by a proper object) we call a "power." So there will be distinct powers whenever there are distinct kinds of activities.

Powers are distinguished into several levels, and on each level there are several powers. These levels are: physical (including the mechanical), physiological (biological), motor (or, more generally, "executive" powers), sensory, and rational. By an examination of the activity of each power, we will try to find out whether it can be modified, and in what way or ways. We will then be able

---

9 A very complete "formal object analysis" has been made by St. Thomas Aquinas and his followers. We are going to employ the results of that analysis here as a frame of reference for our own investigation.

finally to determine whether acquired modifications are all essentially the same or not. We will be able to assert a complete induction, because the list of powers we will use is an exhaustive one, as far as species or kinds of powers are concerned.

Second, in making this induction, we will need some kind of easily applicable criterion to determine whether there is a modification. We have already noted that the acquired modifications we are investigating manifest themselves in the permanent modification of behavior. How shall we decide that behavior has been significantly modified? The type of activity most easily described, and that which is least involved in theoretical presuppositions,[10] is motor activity, such as a manual skill. The criteria by which we recognize the presence of such a motor habit can serve as general criteria for recognizing any permanent modification of behavior. Now, we say that a manual skill is habitual when it has become:

(a) *sure and successful.* If we want to know whether a person has a motor skill, you ask him to perform the action. If he succeeds exactly, if he gets done precisely what he wants to do, we decide he has the habit. This does not mean that he approves the result; for example, a man in typing might make precisely the mistakes he predicts he will make. In many manual skills, the sureness, the perfect coordination, are manifest in even a single performance.

(b) *consistent.* A person who can type a whole page without a mistake has the habit of typing, though anyone can hit a single key. In many cases we cannot tell a habit from a single action, but we recognize it from the consistency with which an accurate (or perhaps, a slovenly) action is performed.

(c) *easy, facile, pleasant.* The speed of response may be involved, but not necessarily. A person who does not yet have a manual skill finds the action difficult, trying. When it has become habitual, the habitual action is pleasant to perform, all other things being equal. A person may have a "bad" habit, and absolutely speaking he does not enjoy the action; yet, of two actions

---

10 We do not say that the *explanations* of motor skills have no theoretical presuppositions; we will consider some of these explanations later on. We are concerned now only with the criteria by which we recognize the presence of a skill.

equally approved, the one that is relatively pleasant is the habitual one.

Because the term "pleasure" is an ambiguous one, it is necessary to clarify the way in which it is used to indicate the presence of a habit. (1) One meaning of the word "pleasure" is in reference to an appetitive response, which we can call "joy in a good possessed." As an act of appetite, it is distinct from the act and object *in which* we take pleasure. When the appetite concerned is the sensory appetite, this joy is called an emotion if it is strong, but a feeling, sentiment, or attitude if it is weak. When the appetite is the rational one (the will), the act is the act of approval. (2) Sometimes, "pleasure" is used in a special way to designate some kinds of sense experience, particularly those of touch. When we say of someone that he "lives a life of pleasure" we mean that he is excessively[11] given over to the pleasures of food, drink, and sex. (3) The word "pleasure" is also used to name a special characteristic present in some acts of any and every power, or, by transfer, a special quality of the object of such an act. Sometimes an object is eminently suitable to the power: for example, some colors are pleasant, others harsh; a pleasant day is eminently proportioned to man's senses in the ideal balancing of temperature, sunlight, wind, sound, visual appearance. Here, the "pleasure" is a characteristic of the object itself. It is in this sense that we speak of some activities as being pleasant, that is, when they are entirely proportioned to the power. The "pleasure" of such activities is not distinct from the activities themselves.

In setting down the criterion of pleasure as one of the characteristics of habitual action, we are using the word in the third of these senses. Hence, the meaning of the expression "habitual activity is, other things being equal, a pleasant one" is that to the

11 See St. Thomas Aquinas, *Summa Theologiae*, II-II question 152, article 2, response to the second argument. This implies that there is a positive rational use of pleasure. As St. Thomas says, "Everything which is against a natural order is vicious. But nature has attached pleasure to acts necessary for human life. Therefore, the natural order requires that man use these pleasures as much as is necessary for health. . . . Man must sustain his body in order to use his reason (that is, his spiritual powers). But sustaining the body is done by pleasurable actions. Consequently, the good of reason cannot exist in man if he abstains from all pleasure," *op. cit.*, II-II, q. 142, art. 1 and response to the first argument. See below, pp. 166-171.

extent that a power has been modified by the habit, the habitual action is eminently suited to it, and so is pleasant in comparison with other acts to which there is no special proportion, and even more so in comparison to acts contrary to the habit, which have become unsuitable, disproportioned.

Success, consistency, and pleasure are criteria that do not directly give any information about the nature of the habit. If they can be found, a habit of some kind is present. What the habit is will have to be determined from the evidence obtainable from an analysis of the modified activity itself.

MOTOR ACTIVITY

Now we can begin our examination of the powers of man by studying man's motor activity. We have already noted that there are acquired modifications in this realm of behavior. Since it is so obvious, we can use this area to see how our criteria apply, in distinguishing more accurately what everyone already knows from his own experience.

In fact, the existence of motor habits is so well known that there are some unfortunate consequences, which we will do well to be on our guard against. (1) People consider this *the* habit in terms of which all other habits must be explained. We have already considered the fallacy of taking one instance as an adequate representative of the entire group. (2) It is possible to consider a motor habit as only one among many, and yet select the wrong points to concentrate on in developing an idea of habit in general. We have tried to avoid restrictive criteria, for example, the fact that a habitual motor action requires less attention.[12] Our

---

[12] This is the aspect of habit highlighted by William James in his famous discussion of habits in *The Principles of Psychology* (New York, Holt, 1904), Chap. Four. The following selection (pp. 114-115) is typical:

. . . When we are learning to walk, to ride, to swim, skate, fence, write, play, or sing, we interrupt ourselves at every step by unnecessary movements and false notes. When we are proficient, on the contrary, the results not only follow with the very minimum of muscular action requisite to bring them forth, they also follow from a single instantaneous "cue." The marksman sees the bird, and, before he knows it, he has aimed and shot. A gleam in his adversary's eye, a momentary pressure from his rapier, and the fencer finds that he has instantly made the right parry and re-

criteria (success, consistency, ease) are purely empirical and descriptive, and are at least not necessarily restrictive.

What is changed in the acquisition of a motor skill? Primarily
and directly, a motor skill does not consist in a modification of
the members that exercise the motion (hands, legs, etc.) . The
muscles need not be changed, except accidentally. In some cases,
muscles are not strong enough to do the work involved in motor
skills, and then exercise will be necessary to bring about the
needed increase in strength. If a person has developed the strength
of his muscles for one skill (e.g., typing) and the same strength is
required for another (e.g., piano playing) , there is no further development of muscles in the acquiring of the second skill.

Positively, it has been pointed out that in the development of a
motor skill a series of distinct stimuli (for example, the letters *a,
n,* and *d*) must become a single stimulus for a series of integrated
movements. In typing, the words, and even phrases and sentences,
must be seen (or heard, etc.) as a whole; and the movements of
striking the individual keys must become a single continuously
flowing movement. Thus, in the gaining of the motor skill of
typing, several kinds of organization are involved. (1) There is
the organization of perception. We have to see organized units.
There is, as we know, a basic tendency already present in the sim-
plest sensory experience—this tendency is probably innate—of organizing sensory stimuli into wholes or structured groups.[13] But
this is not sufficient; the sort of organization of perception that is
required for rapid typing needs to be learned. We will study this
later when we come to consider habits of knowledge. (2) There is,

---

turn. A glance at the musical hieroglyphics, and the pianist's fingers have
rippled through a cataract of notes. . . . Our lower centers know the
order of these movements, and show their knowledge by their "surprise"
if the objects are altered so as to oblige the movement to be made in a different way. But our higher thought-centers know hardly anything about
the matter. Few men can tell offhand which sock, shoe, or trousers-leg they
put on first. They must first mentally rehearse the act; and even that is
often insufficient—the act must be *performed*. So of the questions, Which
valve of my double door opens first? Which way does my door swing? etc.
I cannot *tell* the answer; yet my *hand* never makes a mistake. No one can
describe the order in which he brushes his hair or teeth; yet it is likely
that the order is a pretty fixed one in all of us.

13 The Gestalt theory of perception has studied this phenomenon in detail.

secondly, the control of movement. Skill, as we can see from examples such as typing, athletics, the playing of musical instruments, and even a habit like walking, consists almost entirely in control of movement. Now, what is involved in the gaining of control? Extensive experiments indicate that improvement in control consists at least partly in the development of kinesthetic images.[14] For example, a person who does not have the habit of typing needs to look at the keyboard and at his fingers so that he knows accurately both where his fingers are and where to move them, and he must continue to watch them so that he can correct the movement when it deviates from the desired direction.[15] In this case, the kinesthetic imagery is deficient and is compensated for by visual perception. But if a person forces himself to attend to kinesthetic sensations, he can learn to know exactly where his fingers are at any given instant (within the scope of his habituation), and exactly how much to move them so that they come to another precisely determined position. In the beginning, it takes a considerable effort of attention, but, as the skill is attained, a minimum of attention suffices for exact knowledge and control of finger movements. And, once perception has been organized, and the kinesthetic imagery has become complete and sharply delineated, nothing else would seem to be necessary to account for what we find even in elaborate motor skills.[16]

For the acquisition of an adequate kinesthetic image, the "span

[14] A "kinesthetic image" is an image (that is, a recalled sensation) of the position and movement of bodily members, derived from the muscle sense, which is one of the pressure or "touch" senses. On kinesthesia and patterned movement, see, for example, Robert S. Woodworth and Harold Schlosberg, *Experimental Psychology*, revised ed. (New York, Holt, Rinehart and Winston, 1954), pp. 648-654; or W. D. Commins and Barry Fagin, *Principles of Educational Psychology*, 2nd ed. (New York, Ronald, 1954), pp. 620-640.

[15] The recent emphasis in the field of engineering on control systems has brought some helpful similarities, notably the notion of "negative feedback." A system can be built so that a movement deviating in one direction from a predetermined pattern is a stimulus for a corrective movement in the opposite direction.

[16] We are here considering only skill, not what might be called the "mechanical arts." A typist who types perfectly what is on the copy rapidly and easily has the *skill* of typing (which is a motor habit); a secretary who intelligently arranges the paragraphs of a letter or the footnotes in a dissertation has a craft rather than mere skill. The nature of craftsmanship will be considered later.

of attention" must be sufficient to retain in memory the first step of the movement until the last step is executed. Only in this way can the various parts of the movement be learned as a *continuous* sequence.

From this analysis, we can digress briefly to consider what animals can do in the acquisition of motor skills. We have seen that the conditions are, first, the organization of perception; secondly, the development of an adequate kinesthetic image; this latter in turn requires a clear kinesthetic sensation, a sufficient span of attention, and an imagination of a fairly high order.[17] Many animals seem not to have any precise kinesthetic sensation and seem to be unable to make precise movements. Such animals could not acquire any elaborate skills. But animals of higher orders would seem to have sufficient kinesthetic sensations. Animals, however, have a relatively short span of attention; it has been estimated that an adult monkey can attend to about as many successive items as a very young baby. This limitation at once restricts the skills animals can learn. Thus, elephants can learn simple routines of movement; monkeys can be taught to ride bicycles, play a short melody on a simplified piano; dogs can learn tricks of jumping, and so on. There is, however, an accidental limitation. Not all animals are interested in learning motor skills; some are docile, easily moved to attend to the actions; others are uninterested, even hostile. Obviously an animal which is bored or is fighting will not learn. Animals cannot learn motor skills by being passively moved, any more than a person can learn to type by having someone else repeatedly move his fingers.

In summary, we have found in our examination of man's motor activities that the habitual modifications of behavior manifested in this area are due not to any intrinsic modifications of the physical members concerned but to (1) organization of perception and (2) kinesthetic images. We can tentatively conclude that motor habits are special types of imagination habits, since the organization of perception and kinesthetic learning are both functions of

----

[17] From the scientific point of view, this would be a hypothesis; as such it would seem to be capable of at least partial experimental investigation. It might be interesting and profitable if someone would make such an investigation.

this sensory power of man. Further study of these habits will have to come after we have discussed the imagination in general. It is important to remember that there are no habitual modifications of the motor (or "executive") powers themselves in a motor skill. Their performance is improved because of improvements in the imagination, to which they spontaneously respond, in a fully determinate way. Motor powers respond to whatever stimulus they are presented with, unless some extrinsic factor interferes with that response. Therefore, habitual modifications of behavior involved in motor skills must be due to a habitual modification of the stimulus presented to the motor powers: this points to a habit of the imagination, not of the motor powers themselves.

PURELY PHYSICAL LEVEL OF ACTIVITY

Examples of purely physical activities are: gravitational attraction, electrical conductivity, the galvanic reflex. They can be defined as such activities as are capable of being studied by the methods of the physical sciences, or as such activities as man has in common with nonliving things.

Are there acquired modifications at this level? We have already referred to structural changes, such as broken legs, loss of organs, transplants. We could also notice here the temporary modifications brought about by the injection of chemicals; here, behavior is also modified at the physical level; for example, the amount of calcium in the blood is determined by the proportion of certain chemicals. We might also consider the variability of the red blood corpuscle—it has two levels at which it can hold CO_2: one in the capillaries and veins, one in the lungs and arteries. But this variability is present from the beginning; it is not an acquired ability to hold and then release CO_2, but a structural consequence.

As another type of acquired physical modification, we can consider the increase in physical strength resulting from sheer muscle growth. This is obviously an acquired modification, but it is purely quantitative; it does not change the *way* of acting. Other physical modifications, such as growth, obesity, change in bone structure (as in some diseases), are not directly related to activity at all.

All these modifications are acquired, in the sense that they are not present from the beginning, nor an immediate and inevitable consequence of maturation. Those which are not directly related to activity would not fall into the consideration of habit at all. To those which relate to activity, we can apply the criteria of habit. Are activities made more successful or accurate by these modifications? Purely quantitative modifications extend the scope of an activity, but do not make the original activity more accurate. Other chemical and physical changes bring about a different activity, not a more successful form of the preceding one. Since this is the case, activities at this level are not modified after the fashion of a habit.

To understand the nature of the modifications which are acquired, we can consider their relation to the material components of the agent. Given a particular structure and composition of parts, certain activities immediately follow, and follow in a determined way. These activities are not modified unless structure or composition are changed, and this not by a simple acquisition of a structure where none was before, but by an interchange, a gain-and-loss. Modifications of this kind we will call "dispositions" rather than habits.

PHYSIOLOGICAL (BIOLOGICAL) LEVEL OF ACTIVITY

These are the activities which are at the level of vegetative activity, for example, digestion. Is a digestive process modifiable? Yes, within certain limits. Some things which are not nourishing foods for man can become so if a person continues eating them; for example, during the Second World War experiments with chemically modified wood fiber showed that human beings could subsist on such "Ersatz" foods, but that it took about two weeks before the organism was able to assimilate them even partially. Likewise, specially prepared grasses can be quite edible, but again a short period of adaptation is necessary.

Another modification of physiological processes is found in drug addiction. Drug addiction is ordinarily not a merely physiological modification (though in rare instances of incautious medication it may be just that). Usually it is a complex state involving both physiological and psychological factors. We will consider these two kinds of factors separately, taking the physiological ones now. Repeated use of certain drugs (the so-called "habit-forming" drugs) brings about a need for them. Therefore, drug addiction is an acquired modification. The body becomes accustomed to the presence of the drug, so that its continued presence is necessary for its functioning, and its absence brings on pain, discomfort, uneasiness, and other malfunctions. Along the same line of modification, it has been observed that the body can be accustomed to the presence of some poisons, so that after some time, doses which formerly would have been lethal can be tolerated by the body.

On examination, the physiological modifications occurring in drug addiction are found to be changes, either temporary or permanent, in material structure. Definite biochemical changes at the molecular level are assumed by most researchers; in some cases there seem to be some changes also at the level of larger structures.

The changes involved in the adaptation of digestive processes are ordinarily temporary. It is thought that "new" enzymes appear to break down the formerly undigestable food. Again, the precise mechanism involved is not well understood. Similarly, a change in the ability to tolerate poisons seems to be an adaptation of the same kind, perhaps biochemical.

This evidence is corroborated by the treatment given to a drug addict. In general, it has two phases: correct nutrition and rest to bring the body back to normal functioning, and improvement of the psychological state.

Are these changes *habits?* According to linguistic usage, we do speak of habits in the case of drug addiction. To find out whether this usage is justified, the criteria of habit need to be applied. First, the body does successfully accommodate itself to drugs and to some Ersatz foods. Second, it uses (and needs) these things regularly, consistently. Third, what was first done with difficulty becomes relatively easy for the organism. From a negative point of view, our third criterion of ease or pleasure is also verified in that the drug addict feels less uncomfortable with his drugs than without them. Thus, the three criteria of success, consistency, and ease or pleasure are all verified in some sense or other.

Nevertheless, physiological habits are very closely allied to dispositional changes rather than to behavioral modifications directly. The evidence which we have examined shows that losses and changes in material structures are involved which are then necessarily followed by behavioral changes.

EXTERNAL SENSATION

Here, our question is put with respect to the external senses alone, not with regard to the perception of sensible things, which is a complex act into which many factors enter, some of them non-cognitive.

Is perception improved in success, ease, and pleasure? Let us take the example of the ability to estimate distances. Psychologists have conducted extensive experiments on the visual perception of distance, and their accounts make interesting reading. But the facts are readily available, and can easily be verified. A hunter or an athlete can learn to estimate distance very accurately. Another evident example can be found in the training of observers for the ground observer corps. After a period of training, observers can rapidly identify airplanes at great distances and very accurately. Again, people can learn a great deal in listening to music. A trained conductor can tell at once which one of a hundred instruments is off key. An educated listener can hear and distinguish themes and counterthemes, the component notes in a chord, and the rich overtones, though to an untrained hearer there are only pleasant, rhythmic sounds. Tactile perception can be trained; for example, the professional safecracker can tell by touch when the tumblers of a lock are in place. Most persons can distinguish a handful of colors; department store buyers can distinguish and identify hundreds. Experienced persons, such as cooks and teatasters, can distinguish many tastes and odors that ordinary people cannot. Therefore, it is clear that sense perception is capable of very considerable modification.

Our first problem is one of analysis. Our direct knowledge (experience) of sensible things is subject to modification, habituation. But the question is, what is the part played in this experience by external sensation? Sensation is not a term describing a kind of experience. Our immediate experience, as it concretely presents itself to us, we call "perception" or "sense perception."[18] Sensation is a constitutive element of perception, so it can be considered separately only by analysis. By "sensation" we will henceforth mean the experience gained through one of the special senses, such as sight or hearing—what I get with my eyes or ears alone—in abstraction from all other factors which may be present. More strictly still, sensation may be defined as the direct cognitive response of a sentient organism to a special sensible object, such as color, sound, odor. Sensation thus defined is not found as a separate experience in a normal adult. Whether mentally defective persons or infants have "pure" sensations cannot be found out from them, and external observation gives very little information. The only way we can speak of pure sensation is by an analysis of perception and an *abstraction* from all other component elements.

What happens when sense perception is habitually modified? In the training of airplane spotters, one of the first things done is to teach the students to pay close attention to detail. It is pointed out that the position of the rudder, the presence and location of a bulge or blister, the relative positions of wings, engines, and nose, are identifying characteristics. Observers must know what to look for, and must observe precise detail. These are first of all matters of *attention*. Similar improvement of attention can be found in the other instances reported above. Attention thus is one of the factors responsible for the modification of perception; it admits of increase; but it is not the act of the external sense.

Secondly, a great deal of the modification introduced into sense

---

[18] By "perception" is meant the entire experience of a present sensible thing. By "sense perception" is meant the same experience, abstracting from the part normally played in it by the intellect and will.

By making this distinction, I do *not* mean to say that we distinctly experience sensations as such. I would most emphatically insist that perception is immediate, not taking place through a prior conscious process. The distinction, therefore, is analytic, not descriptive. Nevertheless, it is necessary for an accurate philosophical analysis of the nature of habit.

perception is an improvement of discrimination. Now, discrimination between sensory objects is made possible by the application of a common standard to them (when they cannot be directly compared in sensory presentation). The standard is not a third sensory object, but a memory image. Thus, discriminating and identifying colors involves a memory of color. If the standard is a vague one, a person will find it difficult to distinguish objects that differ only slightly, for the image will match equally well with many colors. The same is true for the estimation of distances, the recognition of shapes, the analysis of tones. If the standard image is made more accurate, more detailed, then a much greater number of objects can be distinguished. However, the memory image itself, which is changed, does not belong to external, but to internal sense.

Thirdly, an experiment on odors will bring out another factor in the improvement of sense perception. Two psychologists became interested in the discrimination of odors. Ordinary people do not discriminate odors very carefully, and have a very poor vocabulary for their identification; most often we name them by their sources: the odor of frying bacon, roses, coffee, and so on. The psychologists worked out a complex scale and rated various odors according to components like "sweet," "sharp," and so on. By practice, they became able to specify an odor in terms of fixed coordinates on these scales. They found that they could discriminate and identify a great number of odors and describe them to each other in terms of their standard and its artificial language.

This process is very like the use of the color pyramid, with its three values of hue, brightness, and saturation. By this mentally constructed tool, people can analyze colors and compare them with each other very accurately. The color pyramid and the odor scale show that improvement in perception can be, and often is, brought about by the use of a method of analysis of experience, a method that is constructed by reason, and used in internal sense.

Moreover, the use of the tools of analysis just mentioned usually involves the invention of an artificial language whose carefully distinguished terms serve to fix images precisely. When this language is a numerical one, employing quantitative scales and coordinates, the fixing of images becomes much easier, and accuracy is relatively easy to establish.

But perhaps we have been choosing evidence in a one-sided fashion. After all, many people believe that the senses can be improved by practice. In support of this, they refer to the popular opinion that the loss of one sense (especially sight) brings about an improvement in the sense of touch or of hearing. But experiments with sighted persons have shown conclusively that the finding of one's way about by means of hearing is a matter of paying much more attention to sounds, learning to discriminate between direct sounds and echoes, learning to notice on which side sounds are louder, and so on. The same is true of touch. A sighted person does not need to pay much attention to touch or to remember its deliverances accurately, because he can always glance at the object. But the blind person must pay attention to touch and must remember accurately, and so he learns to "sense" much better. There is an improvement in auditory and tactile perception, but no evidence of an improvement in the direct sensations of touch and hearing.

Again, there have been claims that various exercises could improve the eyes. On occasion it has been necessary to invoke the law against false claims, because the things advised were injurious; for example, the allegation that looking at the sun strengthened the eyes led persons to injure their eyes permanently. There is thus evidence that organic injury can be received from an excessive stimulation, but no evidence of resultant habituation.

On the other hand, some eye exercises do bring about improvement in seeing. Crossing of the eyes is a muscular defect, and it can sometimes be corrected by carefully supervised exercises. This, however, is not strictly an improvement of the sensation, but of a motor activity necessary for effective seeing. Similarly, some cases of astigmatism are due to unbalanced tensions of the muscles by which the eye is turned. These cases can sometimes be cured by exercises which train the muscles to a more evenly balanced tension. This again is a motor activity, not one strictly at the level of sensation itself, though it has effects on sensation.

In addition, sensation is affected by the condition of the organ as a physical compound. Opaque material, such as a cataract, obviously will interfere with vision; a detached retina brings about blindness; lack of the proper chemical composition will lessen the effectiveness of vision; for example, a deficiency in vitamin A_1 lessens the ability to see light and darkness (the so-called "night blindness"). All of these are real changes. But, even though they occur in a sense organ, they are *physical* dispositions rather than habits.

The evidence may be summarized thus. There is clear evidence that there are habits which modify sense *perception*. But the trained perception of the airplane spotter, the music conductor, the odor expert, the teataster, the safecracker, the buyer of colored goods, can be explained by better attention and by sharper, more clearly discriminated images. This conclusion is reinforced by the need for glasses or hearing aids instead of training; and reinforced again by an analysis of the alleged improvement of hearing and touch on the onset of blindness; namely, that this also is a matter of attention and discrimination. Thus, though sense perception is modifiable, there is no evidence that sensation itself is changed.[19]

THE LEVEL OF INTERNAL SENSATION

In the investigation of motor skills and in the modification of sense perception it became clear that sensory activity is habitually modified, even though this modification does not occur in the external, or special senses. We must therefore turn to a study of those sensory elements which are not due to the external senses.

In general, we must make clear what is meant by "internal" sensation. We do not mean that part of the sense of touch by which we feel pain, or by which we sense our own body—its position, its functioning, and the like. All these activities, though they are directed "inward" or toward our own body, belong more accurately to the sense of touch, which is classed with the "external" senses. Though this "internal" touch is a knowledge of

[19] This is by no means the same as saying that there is evidence that sensation is not changed. The certain negative conclusion cannot be reached from an absence of evidence, but only after we have seen how and why habituation occurs in man's operative powers. Then we can argue that there can be no habits in the external senses.

ourselves, it is still knowledge of our own body as an *object*. For convenience, we will designate all those sensations which are concerned with our own body as "propriosensation."

But there are other activities at the sensory level which do not belong to the special senses at all. Most obvious among these is the activity of imagination when this is carried on in the absence of the sensible object. Because the image then seems to be "inside" us—we can close our eyes, turn our attention "inward"—the act of imagination and related sensory functions are traditionally called "internal sensations."

If it was impossible to find in experience an isolated sensation, it is even more impossible to separate physically and consciously the activities of the internal senses. We will have to be even more careful, then, in the analysis of internal sensation, and we will have to devote attention to each "part" of this internal experience.

The Unifying Sense[20]

The argument for the existence of the first distinct function of internal sense is primarily analytic. First of all, it is evident that all my sensations are unified as *mine*, on the side of the sensing subject. Though the external senses are quite distinct, they are all, and concretely, referred to one and the same sensing subject. Secondly, and most conclusively, we can sensitively compare the proper objects of the special senses. Just as it must be by one and the same pair of eyes that colors are directly compared with each other, so the direct comparison of sounds and colors must also be done by a single sense—it cannot be done by the senses of hearing and sight as distinct. The evidence for this is that we immediately and concretely know the similarity of some colors and sounds— "bright" sounds, "quiet" or "loud" colors; so, too, there are "soft" and "hard" colors, and "sharp" or "dull" sounds. These comparisons are not made by intellectual reflection, but sensitively; we sense them before we can explain them.[21]

[20] This power is often called "the common sense." This expression, a translation of the Latin *sensus communis,* is too ambiguous in English.

[21] Because the scientific explanation of light and sound as "waves" is unknown to many who do compare the sensations, as well as unnecessary for the comparison.

Now, when we ask how it is possible that the various special sensations can be unified, we see that this occurs inasmuch as all of them are sensations. Hence, we can say that the object of this unifying sense is "what the other senses know."[22] As a result, we can say that the unifying sense is the power of sensory awareness.

Can we discover the fact of a sensory awareness? One way to approach this is to eliminate the intellectual element by reflection. Let us take, on the one hand, an extraperceptual experience, such as we have when engaged in abstract reasoning (for example mathematical reasoning) , and, on the other a highly concrete perception, such as occurs in aesthetic experience. Next, we can try to single out what is common to both experiences at the level of intellectual activity. Thirdly, we must subtract this common element from the concrete perception. What is left by such reflection is the external sensation itself and the sensory awareness. This latter cannot be described verbally nor understood except abstractly—one can only "point" to it with words which might help to evoke the experience in the reader.

What we mean by "sensory awareness" is something that is both concretely and immediately presented; it cannot as such be defined or verbalized.[23] One can express and define in words only what one can understand. This means that awareness (consciousness) is neither purely rational nor purely sensory as it actually occurs in us. In the direct phenomenological description of awareness we must express the unity that we find there—a unity which includes both sensory and rational aspects.

The fact of sensory awareness in man is confirmed by the evidence that an animal also must have some kind of sensory unification, for in the animal we also find a unity—the dog barks when

22 This phrase is a translation of St. Thomas's *intentio sensus,* which is "Englished" by some authors as "the intention of the senses." We can also translate it as "that which is sensed," or "presence to the knower."

23 Two well-known attempts to describe the perception of self are almost descriptions of *sensory* self-awareness, though it was not the intention of the authors to give such a restricted account. William James in *Principles of Psychology* (New York, Holt, Rinehart and Winston, 1904), vol. I, pp. 298-305, 322-342, explains self-awareness as arising from proprioception, the "warmth" of experiences relative to each other, and the "appropriation" of prior experiences by the later ones. David Hume in *Treatise of Human Nature,* Bk. I, pt. iv, sec. 6, beginning, explains the self by relations of "causation" or continuity.

"its" tail is stepped on. Though we certainly have no complete understanding of an animal's sensory knowledge,[24] we do have the fact of unification. And the only unification they could have would be at the sensory level.

Do we need a power distinct from the external senses for this awareness? At the level of immediate introspection, a person finds that he is understanding, but also that he is sensing. At such a level of immediacy, one does not know which powers precisely are involved in consciousness. There is not even a distinction between intellectual and sensory awareness; concretely, there is but one awareness. The same ego understands and senses, and we can say "the *same* ego" only if there is but one awareness. This awareness takes place in time and space and "has" a body, and so it cannot be purely rational. Neither can it be purely sensitive, since it includes the nonsensible components of thought and volition.[25]

Analysis of what is involved in a power of sense as material and embodied in an organ, shows that reflection upon its own activity is impossible for an organic power. Hence, none of the special senses as distinct is aware of its own activity. So, if there is a sensory knowledge of the activities of sensation, this can be accomplished only by a power distinct from the other senses, whose function is precisely the sensing of the activities of the other sensory functions.

Thus, the unifying sense apprehends sensory activities as activities of sensing; and, since all the actions of the various senses have this common character, the unifying sense unites them all into one common concrete subject of sensing. Hence, the functions of unifying and being aware are not two functions; unification takes place through awareness. In the order of discovery, we find the fact of unification before we realize the distinct element of sensory

[24] It is even difficult to imagine what many animals' external sensations are like. For example, a horse has two eyes independently governed—what would it be like to have two independent visual pictures? And what about the multi-faceted eyes of a fly?

[25] On the intellectual awareness itself, see below, habits on the intellectual level. That we are intellectually aware of our extraperceptual thinking is evident; that rational consciousness enters into perceptual consciousness is proved from the nontemporal, nonspatialized element of permanence and unification of the perceptual consciousness.

awareness; in itself, awareness is the source of unification, as well as its explanation.

Are there any acquired modifications of activity of the unifying sense? There are certainly variations in sensory awareness. Let us examine them to see whether they involve a modification of unifying awareness as such.

Our perceptual awareness of ourselves (proprioception) is evidently subject to habitual modification. First, there is variation, often notable, in the intensity of awareness. Some days we feel sluggish, and our awareness of everything, external and internal, is not very sharp and clear. On other days, our awareness is quite lively. This is a variation in the excellence of the general all-around sensory functioning; it is due to physical factors: fatigue, illness, poor nutrition, depressing weather. As such, this is a physical disposition, not a habitual modification.

Proprioception is also changed in that the person who knows himself changes, and he is the object, the "what" of which he is aware. Changes in the object of proprioception elicit corresponding changes in a person's attention. Consider the sudden self-consciousness of an adolescent: he always knew he had hands and feet, but with rapid bodily changes perception and control are modified, and with increased attention to his bodily movements he becomes even more awkward. Such variation in sensory awareness is adequately explained by changes in the object of awareness and in attention.

We know from experience that attention is determined in two ways. First, there is "object-directed" attention. Examples of this are sudden sensory stimuli, such as loud noises, bright flashes, and so on. A strong sensory stimulus draws the attention to itself involuntarily. Second, there is the so-called "subject-directed" attention. This attention is sometimes voluntary, as when we deliberately concentrate our activities on some object of perception, or of science, and the like. Sometimes subject-directed attention is guided by sensory appetency, as in daydreaming, emotional distractions, and so on. As we shall see later, subject-directed attention is always a function of appetency, either rational or sensory. Hence, the variations of attention are to be ascribed either to sensory stimuli or to the appetites, not to sensory awareness itself.

We know that our proprioception (perceptual knowledge of ourselves) includes propriosensation (the immediate knowledge of our body), which can be modified. This latter knowledge is strongly influenced by our "body image"—the image we form for ourselves through experience and interpretation. Many apparent changes in sensory awareness are actually modifications of our "body image" which we will consider later.

Does growth in self-knowledge involve a modification of unifying awareness? Self-knowledge, it is often said, is very difficult to acquire. This does not mean that it is hard to have a *perception* of ourselves—we cannot escape this perception. What is meant is reflective self-knowledge: for example, the ability to distinguish the motives of our actions. This development of ability to analyze and discriminate internal experience is largely a development of intellectual cognition, not of sensible cognition. Most of the variations in self-reflective introspection are along the lines of discrimination, and this is a slow process. These changes, however, do not involve any modifications of direct sensory awareness, and provide no evidence for the existence of habitual modifications of behavior in the unifying sense.

In summary, we have seen these variations in sensory awareness: (1) greater or lesser intensity; (2) changes in direction and concentration of attention; (3) changes in propriosensation and body-image; and (4) variation in degree of self-reflectivity. The first of these is due to physical factors, temporary or dispositional. The second is a function of appetency. The third reduces to sensation and imagination. The fourth is a matter of knowledge, discrimination, and attention. So, in all these cases, the source of the descriptively discovered variation (change) in awareness can be in some other power whose functioning has an effect upon the unifying sense. Hence, there is no unequivocal evidence that there is any intrinsic habituation of the unifying sense itself. This is as far as we can carry our investigation at the present time.

The Imagination

Under this term we wish to include also a large part of what in English is called "memory"; that part, namely, which consists in the retention and recall of past experience at the sensory level (but not including the recognition of the past *as past*). The imagination is the power of retaining what has been received through the special senses, and of re-presenting what has been retained upon suitable stimulation. Since this retention and recall is precisely the nature of this power, it is not an acquired ability to retain or recall a particular image, but a natural one. Now, one of the meanings of the verb "to learn" is precisely this: to acquire and retain information (which at the level of sensory cognition is a matter of images—of things and/or of symbols). Consequently, not all the cases of learning at the level of imagination will involve habits.[26]

Are there any acquired modifications of activity of the imagination? The easiest and most evident example is that of a person who knows several languages fluently. When he talks English, the only words that occur to him to express his ideas are English; if he switches to French or German, he can continue the same line of thought, but his memory (imagination) supplies only the French words, and the English terms no longer are recalled. When the languages are well learned, the shift from one to the other can be made easily, and one habit will act in complete independence of the other. Moreover, it is clear that the memorization of a vocabulary is a sensory function, since the understood meanings can be simply identical even though expressed in entirely different sensible signs. A language is possessed as a habit, not merely when words are retained and are able to be recalled, but when there is a patterned recall: when the words learned fall into language groups. Obviously the criteria for habit—success, consistency, and ease (pleasure)—are verified in this case.

There are also other types of habits in the imagination. For example, there are typical ways of imagining that can be learned. Thus, a poet has a distinctive way of imagining, one that is both extremely concrete and characterized by attending to unusual similarities. Now, a certain liveliness of imagination is an individual characteristic that cannot be learned; yet, the merely innate

---

[26] This is not to say that such learning is unimportant, but only that it is not a habit. However, it is possible to speak of an image retained and not now actually used as present "in the state of habit." On this use of terms, see below.

excellence of imagination provides only the possibility of poetry. Actually to be a poet requires exercise, practice, skill. Again, different people have characteristically different images: some remember and express themselves through predominantly visual images; for others, the images are mainly verbal; for still others, audile or tactile. It seems that individual inborn differences are partly operative here; yet cultural traits which influence learning and expression accentuate or minimize individual differences, so that we can speak of habit formation in this area also.

Images can join together in complex ways that involve emotion as well as knowledge; these we will consider below.

In addition, there are patterns of remembering attached to rational processes. For example, a science is, strictly speaking, a pattern of reasoning. Nevertheless, a reasoning cannot be carried out without objects, and the supply of data, terms, and so on, must be provided so that the reasoning can go on. For this ordered recall of facts, symbols, information, a disciplined imagination is necessary. All of us have found that when we first attempt to pursue a rational activity (study, prayer, and so on), we are beset with distractions. This means that the imagination is functioning as a distinct sensory power, recalling its images according to sensory laws (similarity, contrast, continuity). But we need to have the imagination present objects according to the proper laws of our rational activity. This means that the sequence of recall must become modified to follow rational patterns rather than imaginational ones. A person who can keep his imagination working along a rational pattern easily, successfully, and consistently has evidently a habit of the imagination.

Can the memory be trained in general—as a power? We can learn to remember better, it is true. We can learn, for example, that immediate repetition of the item to be remembered (for example, someone's name) makes recall easier. Then there is care in knowing the item accurately. In some cases, mnemonic tricks (such as arranging items spatially, connecting them with already familiar sequences, writing and speaking as well as hearing or seeing the word) will be of advantage. In other cases, the intellect can greatly assist memory, as when the items can be put into an understood logical pattern. This, however, is not an improvement of the power, but an acquisition of particular habits. Laboratory investigations conducted by psychologists show no evidence that the memory itself can be improved. For example, the notion that memorizing something every day for a year will produce a generally stronger memory is baseless.

The Discursive Estimation

By this term we refer to the power of making concrete sensory evaluations of "good" and "evil," of suitability and unsuitability, of the immediately and concretely pleasant, unpleasant, useful, and harmful. To see that there is a kind of evaluation which we make, and which is not simply a rational activity, an intellectual judgment, and yet at the same time not a mere matter of actual or retained sensation, we can consider what we mean by *tact*. What tact is cannot really be explained in words; it can be observed in action and can be cultivated by a careful application. But it definitely is not a matter of universal rules and general principles. Nor, on the other hand, is it reducible to external sensation (the experience of color, sound, and so on) nor to any combination or manipulation of sensations. It is a delicate appreciation of what is suitable in word, gesture, inflection, and so on, to express the most subtle human relationships. This is an example of the kind of "evaluation" made by the discursive estimation. Our further study of the modifications of this power will clarify the notion of "estimation."

There is a very complex problem in the study of this power, for in adult experience there are very few if any nonhabitual responses. By the time we begin to reflect on them, almost all our evaluations are modified by habits, so that there are no purely innate responses, but only "learned" ones. Secondly, the activity of discursive estimation is hard to isolate because it occurs along with a directing activity of the intellect in a normal human being. There is not only a copresence of other activities blended into one single experience, but also the presence of intellect *as* directing, and this makes the intrinsic modification of the estimative power hard to discover.

Let us try to get a clearer idea of what sensory estimation is in itself. To start, there are two approaches: (1) animal activities and (2) extreme cases in human activity.

What validity and what advantage is there in the transfer from the knowledge of animals to that of man? The main advantage is that in animals things are much simpler. For example, one might not hit upon the notion of instinctive activity from human beings, but one finds it unmistakably in animals, and so can look for it in man. One can find purely instinctual activity in man only in abnormal states, such as panic fear, as we shall see. We would ordinarily dismiss it as simply abnormal except that we find it also in animals and so come to see that there is an instinctual basis of activity in man.

When we try to understand the sensations of animals, we do something similar; yet there is also a major difference. We begin with our own experience of consciousness and with the unification of distinct sensory experiences brought about by it. We see the fact of the unification of experiences in animals, and argue to sense activity and to consciousness in them.[27] In ourselves we get to both unification and awareness directly, and at sensory unification distinctly. We find sensory awareness in the midst of a complex sensory-rational awareness, and distinguish it out by comparison with rational self-consciousness. Then we can work back to animals to discover the unifying power in them. If we were not conscious ourselves, we could not even find out what consciousness is.

In the case of sensory evaluations, the advantage of investigating animal activity is that their evaluations must belong to the

[27] How do we know that animals are sentient things? Obviously we do not have an immediate, direct intuition of their sensations and appetitions. We observe only their qualitative structure and their external behavior. Yet we conclude—some philosophers excepting themselves from the almost universal persuasion of mankind—that at least the larger, freely moving living things have sensations somewhat like ours. The basis of this conclusion seems to be (a) the similarity of animal structures to those of men (for example, eyes, nervous system); and (b) their behavior, especially their ability to "respond" to environmental stimuli in a selective and goal-oriented fashion, their ability to "learn," and the indications they give of feeling and emotion. The sort of "knowledge" we can reasonably assign to animals and the nature and limits of their "learning" will be discussed incidentally later.

sensory order (since they have no higher, spiritual powers). We can find the presence of these evaluations in animals by studying instinctive activity.[28]

By defining instinctive activity as *conscious* and *unlearned,* we distinguish it from reflex activity, for reflexes, though unlearned, are not conscious. Starting with this simple distinction, we can analyze the designated activity to find its specific function. The conscious aspect of these activities is not the precise point, nor the motor response that follows, since the motor activities are either random or learned. What is unlearned in instinctive activity is the affective link between cognitive experience and the ultimate external response. That affective link is the specific unlearned element. In animals, there are some sensory experiences which as sensory do not *immediately* excite the response which in fact we find, and the eventual response has a special teleological importance. This link is unlearned and yet necessary, because it is manifested in the direction of the response which is not determined precisely by the nature of the object known.

If instinctive activity is unlearned, how can it be eliminated by training? For example, cats and mice (or cats and dogs) have been brought up as friends. The point is not what the animal would have to experience at either the level of external sense or rational judgment. The cat does not have any instinct to eat *rats.* A kitten jumps at anything which makes sudden movements. The thing which is judged to be suitable for eating or for being avoided in a given concrete experience is partly learned, and can be therefore subjected to various kinds of training. There is no problem if we are careful not to humanize the brute. What a mother cat has to do is to show the kitten what to do—that is, to kill and eat the mouse (or the kitten learns by random movements and the taste of the meat). The kitten jumps to anything that moves; but what to do next is not given in this natural impulse.

[28] The term "instinctive activity" can well be used to point to behavior that is conscious and unlearned. It is better not to use the noun, "instinct"; there are very many controversies over the meaning of this word and disputes over what it refers to. The descriptive adjective "instinctive" can be used without entering into these controversies; in fact, in our explanation, we do not use the term "instinct" as a technical term at all; if it had to be defined, we would give it the vague meaning of "natural impulse."

In any given case we must speak very carefully of what is going on. The often quoted statement, "The sheep fears the wolf and flees," is correct if we understand it correctly. We cannot suppose that the sheep fears the wolf as *wolf*—the sheep has no notion of wolf, for this is an intellectual understanding. A chick does not follow its *mother;* at the right time it follows anything that moves, including the man who brings it its food; it might just as well follow a mechanical device. If we take it away from its mother and do not put before it anything that it can follow for about three days after hatching, it will never follow anything, not even its mother. Similarly, a chicken runs not only from hawks, but from anything that swoops above—kites, airplanes, and so on. Thus, "The sheep fears the wolf," is not to be understood formally; "wolf" in this statement designates the thing the sheep fears, not the object of the sheep's fear as the sheep knows it. For the cat-and-mouse relation, the little-furry-object-that-runs-away is to be jumped on; the little-furry-object-that-nestles-alongside is to be played with. In these and similar cases, the instinct is not modified by training; but the material identification of the object of the instinctive reaction is learned, and so can often be learned differently, and sometimes changed.

What then is unlearned in the instinctive behavior? The sensible object is given in experience. The action taken—for example, running away—is also (previously) learned. The external behavior is learned, either as a whole, or as put together out of random movements (and the random movements themselves are explained by structure). What is unlearned is the order, or direction, of running away in such a situation, and the tendency to exercise such activity—that is, the composition of the object and the activity through appetency. In all instinctive behavior, there is an emotion or appetition leading to the activity. Since the appetition naturally, of its very nature, leads to such behavior (for example, fear leads to running away, desire to approach, and so on), there is nothing special to be explained in this link. What needs to be explained is why this object would lead to this appetition—for example, fear. An object which is immediately repulsive to sense as such leads to dislike. It makes no difference (as some experimentalists have mistakenly thought) whether it is by sight or by smell that the animal "senses" danger—the point is that *danger as such* is not *sensible* at all. There is no indication that the smell of a wolf is painful to the sheep, or the sight of a flying object painful to the chicken. And, if it were, it would not arouse the emotion of fear, but of sadness. What then is actually the case? There must be something in the object as known; a mechanical explanation will not do, since appetite is moved by the *known* good (as we shall see later). Therefore it must be something in the object *known as impending, threatening evil*. The knowledge which bridges between the object as sensed by external sense and as responded to by the appetite must be a knowledge of good and evil.

Therefore, in the animal there is a knowledge of good and evil; this knowledge is evidently not identifiable with external sense (and so not with imagination, either), and in many cases could not have been learned. It is therefore the work of a distinct power at the sense level, which we call the "estimative power." This power in animals is incapable of modification, and its evaluations ("estimations") are specific to given kinds of animals. This analysis of instinctive behavior isolates what we want to talk about: a sensory appreciation of good or evil leading to an affective response which brings about an ordered specific external activity.

Secondly, we referred above to cases where innately determined estimations can be found in men. (*a*) There are certain activities of infants which flow from emotion prior to the possibility of their having learned the good or evil through experience. These cases are few in number, and ordinarily they are extremely indeterminate and so not practically useful. They are, generally speaking, fear, rage, and love. We must be careful not to think of these in adult fashion as being connected with specific situations or responses. In a general way, this trio of affective responses is verified, provided we do not misinterpret them. The original situations innately linked to the fear response seem to be "something wholly unexpected," and "being without support." Stand an infant on its feet, and even before he has ever fallen and bumped himself he shows a violent fear reaction. Or bang something unexpectedly near his face; he cannot have learned that this means danger, and yet he immediately is frightened. Rage seems to be involved with being closely confined, even if the infant has never suffered pain by being confined. The love response is more complex. First of all, the human persons around him come to be recognized quite early in the infant's life, and from then on are attended to with a particular interest.[29] Secondly, there is a response of love toward these human beings, especially when the baby is handled affectionately (gentle patting and fondling) . These responses of recognition and love are universal, and seem to precede any grasp of the connection between their objects (the appearance of human beings and the loving attention) and the benefits experienced by the child (being fed, kept dry, and so forth) . The external expression of this knowledge and emotion can be found in sounds of appreciation, embracing, and the like.

In all these cases, the response is relatively indeterminate. The baby does not know any specific thing to do. In fear he grabs at anything. In rage he flails about in all directions without orientation. In expressing love, his gurgling, cooing, and hugging are meaningful only to those who already interpret them as expressions of love.

(b) Another type of case that shows the innate linkage between situation, emotion, and action, without reasoning, is in the extreme case of panic fear, for example. When the Coconut Grove dancehall in Boston burned down, the people present were panic stricken. The descriptions of eyewitnesses are shocking—the responses were violent, heedless, and foredoomed. It was an automatic sense response rather than a rationally guided one, and this kind of response does not work advantageously for man.

In man, the pure estimative[30] shows up only in extreme situations, as in this panic fear. The explanation of such activity is now analogous to that of the brute: sense knowledge leads to ac-

---

[29] Much of what has been written about the priority of the human person in human experience seems to be referable to this instinctive recognition and interest.

[30] We speak of the *pure* estimative power in man when the power of sensory evaluation acts without rational guidance, but of the *discursive* estimation when the power of sensory evaluation acts under the guidance of reason (not necessarily, of course, of *right* reason, nor necessarily of the reason belonging to the man who is acting here and now; it can also be reason-as-expressed-in-culture).

tivity via emotion and the evaluations of the estimative power
(not the *discursive* estimation). Analysis shows that the human
estimative power has a certain number of broadly general evaluations by its nature: certain things are to be loved, feared, got
angry at. Moreover, in the concrete case of an adult, things are not
just to be loved, feared, raged at, in a vague sort of way, but with
very specific responses. The object to which we have an immediate
emotional response becomes very definitely distinguished by learning. As one grows up, he likes to be petted only by specific people
to whom he has a definite (intellectually understood) relationship. The objects are no longer general, but become narrowed
down; the thing becomes determined. If such distinctions are not
made, the response is spoken of as an "immature" (disproportion-
ate or irrelevant) reaction; this occurs when all sorts of things are
lumped together with one general emotion and external reaction.

In adults we do not often find temper tantrums—purely sensory
rage, sheer violence which merely boils, without coordination,
without effective goal-directed activity, compulsive and unordered
passion. These cases give some light about a factor which is present but usually habitually modified in all emotional responses.

Panic fear is not reasoned, nor ordinary. The response is total;
it cannot be explained from any point of view as learned, or reasoned, or due to external sensation. Therefore there is in man
this power which sometimes acts by itself according to its bare
nature.

It may be helpful to compare the reaction of panic fear in man
to some animal reactions—a horse "freezes" at the sight of fire, a
herd stampedes. In animals, there is a scope for the natural estimative which is specifically determined and which is goal directed. Within this scope, the estimative leads to entirely determined action which is for some good. But note that the animal
estimative acts after the manner of a nature; it is restricted in its
scope; there will always be an area which is not within this field;
and outside its limited range it will usually be unsuccessful, often
harmful. But reason has no limits to its area of work. A man can
always act rationally if he keeps his head—this is one of the most
basic differences between nature and reason. For example, horses
sometimes founder. In a field of oats in the wild condition there

are a lot of other plants, and a horse can eat his fill and still be all right, because the food is naturally mixed. But if we let him eat his fill of oats unmixed—a situation which is not the product of nature but of reason—he will founder. Nature cannot take care of all, including the rare, situations. Outside of what it is determined for, nature will lead the animal into difficulty.[31] Another example: a horse avoids poisonous weeds in its native habitat, but when it is taken from there by man and put into a locale for which it has not been structured, it fails to distinguish and may get sick from locoweed. In such situations—which are accidental to nature—the impulse of nature is no longer goal directed. We must therefore consider not only the rarity of the situation, but also the necessary limitation of nature. Universality is not the characteristic of nature, but of reason. Moreover, the scope of nature cannot be widened by training. However, a structure may evolve; but that is another matter, for then a new nature comes into being.

In ordinary adult experience, the estimative power is not acting alone but in the copresence of other activities and under rational judgment, and so it is hard to find. But using what we have just considered as a background, we must try to isolate the habitual response to situations.

We experience in ourselves not only direct intellectual judgments about good and evil, but also concomitant concrete sensory judgments—not of course as separate acts. In judging a thing desirable, we can find ourselves in three states: (a) we rationally judge one way, but our sensory appetite tends the other; for example, I take a medicine I find repugnant. The rational judgment here runs counter to sensory desires; sensory appetite is going contrary to the rational. (b) Our rational judgment is made in the absence of sensory response; for example, when the object is sensorily indifferent. I find the medicine neither pleasant nor unpleasant, but I know it is good for me. For most people, study is neither particularly likeable nor positively distasteful. With regard to such objects, our "attitudes" consist almost solely of rational desires and choices. (c) Sense and rational appetite go together and concur in the same object. We discover we can learn

---

[31] St. Thomas Aquinas makes this point effectively in *On the Virtues*, art. 1.

to like things which of themselves are not directly attractive. A person can learn to read and to get pleasure out of reading; this is not merely a rational appreciation, but a concrete appreciation of it as a good thing for the agent. And man can learn to like almost anything.

Another example of learning in emotion and its expression will bring out a different aspect of habituation. In an infant, loving and liking are very generic responses. A baby does not differentiate between persons nor recognize the significance of times and circumstances. But in a mature adult, the objects of loving and liking are distinguished, and different responses are given to friends, marriage partner, children. This is not simply a control externally imposed by reason. If a baby wants to kiss everybody in sight, this is the kind of lack of differentiation that is expected; if a grownup has the same desire, he is running for office, or drunk, or mentally sick. In a well-developed person, the control is just there—normal, expected; the proper sort of response is not reasoned out explicitly each time. The behavior itself is rational (participatively, as we shall see), immediately, consistently, and easily.

The specificity of objects relates not only to the external behavior, but also to the emotion. Therefore, the modification is a modification of the presentation of the object. Now, as we already know and shall see more explicitly in a later section, the object of conscious appetite is the *known* good. But the knowledge which is modified is not the knowledge of external sense (and consequently not of the imagination either), and so it is intrinsic to a distinct internal sense power, namely, the discursive estimation.

Thus, a baby wants to put anything pleasurable into its mouth. As a person grows up, he loses the desire to put all things into his mouth; coins, for example, go into one's pocket. This difference is not one of intensity of emotion—it is not the case that we still, but weakly, want to put them into our mouths. Nor, in a normal person, is the pocket a substitute mouth. Really, there is no desire at all to eat money. Therefore, it is a question of the specificity of the object of emotion; that is, it is a question of determinate knowledge. The pleasurable-in-this-way is loved with this kind of love, the pleasurable-in-that, with a different kind of love.

Moreover, this specification of knowledge is not purely from the side of the intellect, not simply an act commanded by reason. There is an education of the sensory powers themselves, not externally imposed control each time. In situations which are familiar, a man does this without any deliberation about it. There are years of education of emotion. A mother does not rationally force herself to love her children; she does it with an immediately consequent sensible affection. The response should of course be in harmony with reasonable judgment.

Where then is the habit to be precisely located? We are not now concerned with the investigation of habits in appetitive powers— either with discovering their presence or absence or with making them unnecessary. The argument by exclusion will not work if we expect to find a case where such a judgment would exist in the absence of other sensory cognition. We have already seen that the internal senses work together. But we can use the argument from exclusion if we find, upon analysis, that neither the external senses, the unifying sense, nor the imagination can account for one of the factors present and undergoing modification in full perceptual experience: namely, the concrete knowledge of the sensibly good or evil. Will the external senses account for the modification of knowledge of the good? In this area there is nothing pertinent; we have already seen that there is no habit in the external senses, and we also seen that the knowledge of good (except for that sort which is pleasing or painful to the sense itself) is not an act of the external senses. There is likewise no relevant modification in the unifying sense. Can the imagination account for the change?

Certainly, the imagination enters into all perceptions, and it is even more particularly the power by which we present absent objects to ourselves. Now, some modifications of perception can be accounted for by association. If, for example, what is effective in the modification of instinctive behavior is a natural repulsion to one object bound up with another, then the modification is adequately explained by the association of object with image (or image with image). This can be illustrated with a typical experiment. A child is shown something which it would ordinarily grab, and, just as it grasps it, a sudden noise is made very close by, causing the child to jump. If this is done often enough, the mere seeing of a teddy bear will make the child cry or shrink away. This reaction is partly explained by the fact that through repeated experience a frightening association has been built up. The sight of a teddy bear arouses the image of teddy-bear-horrible-noise. It is this complex memory image that arouses fear.[32] Thus, through the natural links between some elements of the complex image and corresponding emotion, emotive and external behavior can be influenced and changed.

At some point of such modification, all that is involved is a modification of the imagination. When an association has become fixed, the experience is not that of a sensed object together with the usual perceptual phantasms[33] together with the newly associated phantasm, but rather this: there is a unified perception of an object which is experienced as a single object, in which what is only incidentally sensible seems as clearly inherent as what is directly sensed. Thus, the apple "looks juicy"; not: the red apple "calls the juice to memory." Similarly, suppose a boy has been forced to attend Mass; in later life, Mass may present itself to him as a boring or confining experience to be avoided. The image and the external sensation blend into one single object of perception.

But not all changes of emotive behavior are explained by habitual modifications of the imagination. Some behavioral changes indicate changes in the estimation itself. Let us contrast the two types of modification. A person visits the home of a friend. A noisy little girl enters the room, and the visitor feels exasperated. Then he realizes that the girl is his friend's daughter. This is now a new object: brat-who-is-daughter-of-friend. The visitor's exasperation changes, lessens, because of the association. In contrast, imagine a person who gets angry at children. One day he reflects that this is the way children are. This is the way they act in the process of growing up; they cannot be expected to make mature judgments, etc. Because of this reflection, the person's attitude to-

32 We can call an image a "memory-image" when it is still descriptively distinct from the present perception. For example, I see *and* I remember.

33 A "phantasm" is the presentation of the internal senses; it is conscious and available to intellectual activity. We can call "perceptual phantasms" those items from past experience which unite with present sensation to form a single, actually undivided sense perception. Thus, perception is normally an indistinguishable blend of present experience and images of past experience.

ward children changes; he is less impatient with them. When we examine these two instances of behavioral change, we see that both involve an acquired modification of emotive and external behavior. In the first instance, a new object is added to the visitor's knowledge: daughter-of-friend. In the second instance, the person realizes he should not find children exasperating; he changes his appreciation without adding any external object. This involves additional knowledge but not knowledge external to the first experience. The person sees the behavior of the child in its proper perspective, as a promise of future maturity. Such a change is not explained simply by a modification of the imagination; it indicates an acquired modification of the discursive estimation itself, a habitual change in the person's concrete sensory judgments.

We should note that although this second change arises from a reasoned reflection, it is not simply a case of self-conquest. It involves a real change of appetitive reaction on the sensory level: the person no longer *feels* angry with children. The discursive estimation is knowledge in a concrete sensory way, although not independent of the intellect. (When the power does act independently of the intellect, it is called the simple, pure estimative power.) This distinction implies that there are concomitant judgments of the intellect about the same real object. But a purely rational judgment does not affect the emotions; they go their own way as before. If a special exasperating situation arises only once or twice, we control ourselves; that is, we feel the emotional reaction but do not let it externalize itself. This is a good way to handle rare cases, but it will not work over a long period of time for common situations. The person who cannot spend ten minutes with children without becoming angry with them should do more than simply control his anger; he should learn to like children, both on the intellectual and on the sensory level.[34]

Other instances of changes of concrete evaluation show the distinctive way in which man's discursive estimation is modified. If

[34] We should note that changes in sensory evaluation are not explained by changes in attention. We are not thinking of situations in which a person learns to *ignore* children or even to ignore their annoying characteristics. Rather, he still sees that children are rude, noisy, and changeable, but he learns to judge them differently. Attention may help us isolate or ignore elements; it cannot change our judgments of what we do actually attend to.

an adult decides that he ought to like an activity (e.g., studying),
he can bring himself to a point where he *feels* good while performing that activity. He can bring himself to enjoy studying, for
example, without bringing any extrinsic associations into the picture. Similarly, he can bring himself to enjoy praying. He can
find total satisfaction (sensory as well as rational) in the act of
prayer. He need not use distinct associations; there need be no
blending of past experience (images) into present experience
(perceptions).[35] He can work on a rational basis directly down
from the intellectual and volitional acts involved in rational approval. He can bring his sensory judgment to correspond with his
rational judgment. Thus we see that we are not dealing with
purely sensory knowledge when we investigate man's discursive
estimation. We are dealing with a compenetration of reason into
sense knowledge, for which there is no counterpart on the brute
level.

A special instance of modification of the discursive estimation
begins with a modification of the imagination, a habitual association of images. For instance, the child is made to fear the clanging-
teddy-bear. Because of the associated image, the child habitually
judges that there is something fearsome about a small furry object. Once this judgment becomes fixed, the associated image (the
original reason for it) can fade out without changing the concrete
sensory evaluation: small furry objects are fearsome. This indicates an acquired modification in the discursive estimation.[36]

If the evidence we have cited is true, then what is involved in
the modification of the discursive estimation is a change in the
object apprehended. It is now known as appealing or repugnant.

[35] This is not to say that such associations ought not or cannot be used with
great success. Yet it remains true that some concrete evaluations can be modified without using associated images external to the object of evaluation.

[36] Another possible explanation is that the associated image has not actually
faded away but is still present below the level of consciousness. This is especially likely if the habitual judgment seems to resist change. For instance, if
the child's mother tries repeatedly to show him that there is actually nothing
fearsome about the teddy bear (the consciously known object) without any
change in the habitual sensory judgment (teddy-bear-is-fearsome), it may well
be that the fearsome associated image (clanging-teddy-bear) has not faded
away at all but merely slipped below the level of consciousness. For a description of how objects may be present in sense knowledge without conscious
awareness of them, see pp. 82-85.

This is not a change in the appetitive reaction to what is pleasant or repugnant; it is a change in knowledge. We cannot change the nature of the appetite; we can change the presentation of the object to the appetite. Since the known good is the proper object of the sense appetite, a change in the object of knowledge will produce a change in the sense appetite. Some things are not spontaneously known as good, but rather as repugnant. They can become known as good. A new way of knowing, a new structure of knowledge is acquired. A change of appetition follows, because a change of appetite's proper object (the known good) has taken place. Finally, since what is involved is a change precisely in the sensory knowledge of *good,* the modification must have occurred in the discursive estimation.[37] If this change has become habitual, then there is a habit in that power.

Is there any way to distinguish whether the change (adjustment, evaluation) in emotional response is due to imagination or to the discursive estimation other than by reflection? It would seem not. It would be nice to have either an immediate apprehension of the change or perhaps some physical evidence that a neurologist could find, but this is not the case. We have to analyze operational factors in a given experience. Yet, although experience is the only starting point, this is not excessively restrictive. We can use the experience of others; to a certain extent, empathetic observation is possible. We try to put ourselves in the position of the person reporting the experience. This takes great care, but it is possible. There are enough common elements in experience so that we can understand an act we have never performed, provided that it is still comparable to our own experience. Of course, if there is a basic lack of continuity between our personal experience and the reported experience, then empathetic observation is impossible.

Memorative Power

A fourth internal sensory cognitive power is often spoken of, a power of retaining estimations previously made. The evidence

[37] This presumes that we are discussing here a real change in the discursive estimation, a change in the sensory knowledge of good that is not accounted for by a change in the imagination, by the association of images external to the original object of evaluation.

that estimations are retained is obscure and problematical; it seems that imagination, association of images, and modifications of the discursive estimation are sufficient to account for all the alleged evidence. Hence we will not discuss this hypothetical sense power any further.

HABITS OF SENSORY APPETITE

We have all experienced appetition on the sense level. Analysis reveals that such appetition is of two kinds. One type centers around sensible goods and its most characteristic act is desire for pleasure; this type involves the pleasure passions (the Freudian libido). The other type centers around anger or attacks on evil; this type involves the aggressive passions. These two kinds of passions (or emotions, to use the nontechnical term) spring from two distinct operative powers: the desiderative appetite and the aggressive appetite. Sensory appetition consists of (1) conscious tendency (2) determined by a known good. The structure of the appetite itself is a tendency toward a good; appetition takes place when this appetite is presented with an object known as good. Sensory appetition is not knowledge, but it involves knowledge: the external senses and/or the imagination, plus the concrete evaluation of the estimative power.

We have already considered an area of activity in which appetite is involved. Any time there is a change of object of appetition, this change is accounted for by a change in the power which presents the object. This then is a modification which actually affects the appetite, but it is not formally a modification *of* the appetite. Any change in *direction* of appetition is adequately explained by a change in the object of appetite, which is a function of the cognitive powers. Such a change in direction of appetition provides no evidence for any intrinsic determination of the appetite itself.

Is there a modification of the appetite itself? How would appetite be intrinsically modified? Appetite is tendency, "motion-towards." Is there a modification of tendency precisely as such? Considered as motion-towards there is in the basic notion of appetite an element of "degree" or intensity, just as there is velocity in locomotion. A fast locomotion is a violent locomotion. Similarly, when we throw a projectile harder and harder, it gets closer and closer to the goal, and sometimes even overshoots the mark. This is a modification of motion-towards, without any change of direction, with only change of strength.

Is it proper to speak of the "strength" of an appetition? In some way acts of appetition can be compared with one another, and of two acts about the same object, one will be found to be "stronger," "more ardent," "keener." If the word "strength" seems too materialistic, a better term has not yet turned up. We shall use it to describe the variations of motion-towards in appetition which involve no change in the object of appetition, only change in the degree of appetition.

Once we know that intensity of appetition can vary, we can look for examples of this on the brute and human level. In a nature which is strictly determined (so that its knowledge of the good is fully determined by its nature, including its estimative power) there is a definite degree of appetitive response called for under the various concrete conditions for which the nature was structured. A horse may founder when he is placed in an unnatural, man-made situation (i.e., a field of oats unmixed with any other plants), but he will not founder grazing on the open range. A horse does not have to learn temperance in the natural surroundings for which his nature is designed; it is determined by his natural powers, especially by his estimative power, that he act in a way which is suited to his nature and which enables his nature to achieve its natural goal. His appetitive reactions cannot be too weak or too strong; it is determined that he react to a definite degree under definite conditions. There is no discoverable variation of strength of motion-towards in animal appetition except such variation as is accounted for by the concrete conditions of the subject and object.

What about human appetition on the sensory level? Can we discover in desiderative or aggressive human appetition variations of intensity which are not adequately explained by the determinate nature reacting in a determinate way to a concrete situation? We are not looking for changes in appetition which can be explained by changes in the object of appetition. Neither are we looking merely for variations of intensity in human appetitive reactions, since these are present in animals and can be explained by the determinate structure of a nature and its operative power. We are looking for *consistent modes of tendency* in human appetition. If human beings are not naturally determined to react to a definite degree to definite circumstances, do they acquire consistent ways (habits) of reacting strongly or weakly to various objects of appetition?

Nor are we concerned with the variations of sensory appetition inasmuch as these variations might be caused by the *external* control of the will. If a particular desire is the act of a person, surely it makes a difference whether he is willingly or unwillingly desiring. But let us suppose that the consistency of sensory appetition is at least partly due to the will. In that case, intellect-and-will would be like a moving power, and the sense appetite like the power which is moved. If there is no intrinsic modification in the power which is moved, then the resulting act is an act of self-control in the sense of violence done to one's self. Such an act cannot be firm and pleasant, and will hardly be consistently performed over a long period of time. If there is to be a consistent mode of tending on the sense level, there must also be a modification in the sense appetites themselves, so that they may harmoniously be moved in accord with their own intrinsic perfection.

Desiderative Appetite

Since there are two powers of sensory appetition in man (desiderative and aggressive appetites), we shall examine each of them separately. The desiderative appetite is that power in man which tends toward the pleasurable good of sense.[38] Are there consistent modes of tendency in the desiderative appetite? Certainly

[38] By the "good of sense" we understand "that which is suitable *as sensed.*" Some goods are sensed directly by an external sense; namely, the sense of touch. The sensations of having one's hunger satisfied with food (not the flavor of the food) are the sensing of a good for the organism. So, too, to a lesser extent, are the other pleasures of touch, warmth, and softness. In general, the processes concerned with nourishment, maintenance of life, and reproduction are pleasurable when they find a proportioned object (and saddening or painful if they do not find such an object). In regard to all other sense objects—visible, audible, and so on—the judgment of the estimative power is required before these objects are known as good.

some people desire sensible things excessively.[39] For example, a person may consistently overeat out of fondness for food (not out of boredom, loneliness, or insecurity, as is perhaps most often the case). At the moment we are not going to determine what the norm is for "excessive" or "deficient" amounts of food. We merely point out that here is a consistent mode of tendency, in the line of temperance. Our example showed a consistent tendency to overdo, to go beyond, to eat to excess. Another extreme would be apathy with regard to food, i.e., the lack of a proportioned and adequate response to the sensibly pleasant good of food. The virtuous mean would be a consistent tendency to proportioned and adequate response to the object of appetition, food. Thus we see that the desiderative appetite can and does acquire in man consistent modes of response, ranging from deficiency to excess.

But does this evidence unequivocally point to a habitual modification of the desiderative appetite itself? Perhaps all that has changed is the object of appetition, which has become more desirable or less desirable. We should note first of all that there is no question of a change in the direction of the tendency. It is still a tendency toward food. Neither has food suddenly become excessively desirable. We are not talking about starving men or about those for whom food is taking the place of something else. That is why we exclude from consideration persons who overeat out of boredom or loneliness or insecurity, not out of fondness for food. We are discussing only people who let their appetite get into a consistently patterned response of excessive (or apathetic) desire. This modification of tendency will not take place in the absence of all other modifications, but we are not discussing here the efficient causes of such a modification. The "known-goodness-of-the-object-itself" need not vary with the acquisition of a consistent mode of tending toward that object. This shows that the acquired modification of behavior is in the desiderative appetite itself.

Could we explain this modification merely by a change in the extent of the good itself? At one time an object looks better, more desirable, than it does at another. "Hunger is the best cook" is ob-

[39] "Excessive" here does not necessarily imply a moral qualification, at least from our present preliminary point of view.

viously a true statement. An estimation of the goodness of food involves an apprehension of the organism and its state, but this very real fact is not the reason for consistency of desire. If they are intemperate, men consistently desire not more food, but more than the proper and proportionate response to the object of appetition. The proper and proportionate response takes into consideration such factors as the needs of the organism and the nature of the food. To eat more food on one occasion than on another does not necessarily involve eating to excess; the consistent mode of tendency (whether proper, excessive, or deficient) involves motion towards a relative quantity, not an absolute quantity.

Some writers (like the famous Father Rodriguez, with his descriptions of the disgusting nature of eating, digestion, and excretion) try to get people to avoid sin and practice virtue by changing the known object of appetition. They try to convince people that food is bad. Now, whatever this may be, it is *not* temperance. If the process were entirely successful, it would lead people not to eat at all; if it is partly successful, it leads to guilt feelings and personality problems, as well as to a saving of food. While it is legitimate to correct misapprehensions concerning an object of appetition, nothing is gained by falsifying or distorting the known object of appetition.

Can change of attention substitute for developing a consistent mode of tendency in the desiderative appetite? For instance, we might listen to exciting reading while we are eating and as a consequence eat just what is necessary and no more. However, the description "just what is necessary" refers to the external act of eating, which may be the effect of an intrinsic appetitive modification or may be merely its external equivalent. Such substitution is dangerous. A person can "make do" with a substitute for some time, but he will finally fail. An adult working with children may control his anger much of the time, but he will often lose his temper too, at least until he learns not to *feel* angry at children's antics. Studies of collapses in adult life confirm this position. Persons who suddenly go to pieces after long years of apparently virtuous behavior do so not because they have suddenly lost all their former good habits but because they never had these good habits and for years had been depending upon external factors to keep control of themselves. When these external factors are removed or weakened, "virtue" disintegrates.[40] A phenomenon that was of somewhat common occurrence in the United States will illustrate this. There have been many cases of apparently good Catholics who practiced their religion in their homeland; after they arrived in the United States, with hardly any struggle they rapidly abandoned all these practices. Among them were many actions which should have been acts of virtue: of religion, faith, fasting, and so on. Deprived of social support and the connection with other long-standing behavior patterns (native dress, language, and so on), what habits there were (if there were any at all) were too weak to bring about action. Therefore, it is important to remember that a habit can be developed only by proper acts of that habit, not, for example, by constant attention to objective quantity in eating but rather by trying to respond in a manner properly proportioned to the concrete object of appetition, i.e., by trying to *want* just enough food and no more or less. This consistent mode of reacting according to a stable proportion is what constitutes the intrinsic modification of the desiderative appetite.

The commonness of substitution of external control for intrinsic modification of tendency makes it difficult to judge moral behavior. A person can give the impression of being highly virtuous without having any virtues at all. We must try to isolate the relevant factor: how much modification is there of the (excessive or deficient) mode of tending toward the object of appetition? We can determine this best in people who go to extremes, who exceed or fall short of the proportioned response. The factors are easier to discover in cases of lack of proportion than in cases of proportion. We can also make use of careful conscious reports, either from our own reflection or the reported reflections of trained subjects. Empathetic understanding can find material for analysis both in dramatic presentations of a character whose appetites

---

[40] Cf. Ernest R. Hull, *Collapses in Adult Life*, 2nd ed. (Bombay, Examiner Press, 1920). This book gives a number of factual accounts of such collapses but provides no detailed explanation.

are disproportioned and in actual case studies of such characters.[41] In reading this material we must try to feel ourselves into
the emotions of the characters; we cannot simply read the words.
This is especially true of a dramatic presentation (e.g., Macbeth
and ambition).

Perhaps we can now discuss the various consistent modes of
tendency it is possible for man to acquire. We shall make use of
Aristotle's classification of human character, but for the sake of
completeness we shall add a few types of our own. With Aristotle,
we shall classify men according to temperance:

1. The *temperate* man does not overeat and has no desire to do so.
2. The *continent* man does not overeat but desires to do so.
3. The *inconstant* man has no consistent mode of tendency or of behavior.
4. The *incontinent* man overeats in accord with excessive desire but
   against his rational approval.
5. The *intemperate* man overeats in accord with excessive desire which
   he rationally approves.

We should note that Aristotle provides no classification of a person who rationally approves of overeating in the absence of excessive desire; Aristotle does not think that disorder can be willed for
its own sake. One other classification has been omitted: that of a
person who is sensibly repelled by a good which he rationally approves, and which is not of itself sensibly repulsive. For example,
a married person may find that he (or she) has acquired a sensory
repugnance to all use of sex because of the way in which he has
observed premarital chastity. Because his sensory responses are
askew, modified by learning, we cannot classify him as acting
according to nature or as against nature, simply. If he acts rationally, he is like the continent man, forcing his actual feelings, and
yet in accord with nature as it should be. If he follows his impulses, he is like the incontinent man, acting against reason, and
yet he is also acting against his sense *nature*. However, in either
case he is in a violent state.

Because continence and incontinence are violent states, they

41 Cf. T. V. Moore, *The Driving Forces of Human Nature* (New York, Grune
& Stratton, 1948).

cannot be a permanent and satisfactory solution. The temperate man not only quits when he has had enough; he is satisfied with it. The intemperate man overeats and rationally approves what he does. But the continent man merely holds his excessive desires in check, and the incontinent man gives in to his excessive desires against his better judgment. These are violent states and tend to break down. The continent man collapses easily in adult life under the pressure of his desires. He can become temperate or intemperate or suffer a mental breakdown. The incontinent man tends to become either intemperate (i.e., give rational approval to his excessive desires) or to become continent and finally temperate.

We ought to distinguish the continent man from the hero. Being a hero is not a habitual condition: heroism is primarily a matter of fortitude and of individual acts. When heroic virtue becomes an enduring condition, this is beyond the natural powers of man.[42]

Thus we have seen that direction to the object is determined by the known-goodness of the object but that the strength of the motion-towards depends upon the appetite itself and whatever habitual modifications the appetite possesses. Tendency follows on the known good, but the known good's degree of goodness does not entirely determine (in man) the degree of desire. For example, we say of some people that they are generous (not in the pecuniary sense) ; we do not mean that they are necessarily endowed by nature with more responsive powers but that their appetitive responses are wholehearted. Other people "hold back"; they do not make close friends because they never give themselves to a friend; they take part in causes, but they do not wholly commit themselves to anything. There is really no "reason" for this, if by reason we mean some assignable difference in their bodily disposition or in their external situation. There is a "cause" of such a difference, and that cause is precisely the personality going out to-

---

[42] Only when we know we are receiving special helps should we put ourselves in a situation where heroic virtue is necessary. Without that knowledge there is presumption. Sometimes a person may happen to put himself in a spot where heroic virtue is demanded: e.g., a man gets married invalidly, has three children, cannot get the marriage situation straightened out; if he wants to do his full duty, he must practice heroic virtue. This, as we said, is a violence to nature.

ward goods through the various appetites-as-modified-by-habits. The generous and the mean-spirited persons have made themselves such by frequently responding fully or halfheartedly.

We must remember, of course, that the known good is a "good known to be suitable *to me*." Thus the physical presence of the object (e.g., a drink for an alcoholic) or any of a number of conditions in the subject may change the estimation and consequently the proportioned response of the appetite. But our analysis of the modifications in the desiderative appetite in man has revealed consistent modes of tendency apart from any variations in either the subject or the object of appetition. The following diagram illustrates the material we have discussed on the desiderative appetite:

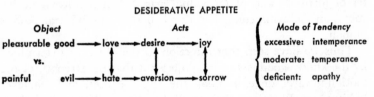

Here we see the habits of the desiderative appetite we want to study further. The principal evidence for the existence of such consistent modes of tendency is our experience of regularly excessive, apathetic, or proportioned responses of the desiderative appetite to its objects.[43]

Aggressive Appetite

The aggressive appetite is the second of the two sensory appetites. To understand the habits of this power, it is advantageous to reflect a bit on the existence and nature of this appetite, since its distinction from the desiderative appetite is not easily discovered. The basic evidence for the existence of the aggressive appetite is

---

[43] We have not discussed such physical modifications as glandular disturbances. Are these possible explanations of the evidence of consistent modes of tendency? The subject is complicated, but this much can be said. Some cases of mental illness respond well to medication, but purely physical therapy does not normally cure a person who has an emotional disturbance. Both physical and psychological therapy are often needed. This proves that acquired modifications of the emotions are present.

this: if there are appetitive reactions which are in conflict both with sensory desires (or aversions) and with the will, there must be a power which is the source of these reactions. Now, we find that fear is sometimes in conflict with sense desire—fear of illness or fear of being caught in a crime often keeps people from carrying out deeds which they strongly desire. Fear is also at times in conflict with will—people compel themselves to do something which they are afraid of. We find the same conflicts in the case of the contrary of fear, daring.[44] Sometimes daring is in conflict with aversion, as when the thrill of a contest leads a man to ignore the natural dislike of pain or weariness. Again, daring is sometimes in conflict with will; for example, a pugnacious individual may rationally choose not to get in a fight and so by his will act contrary to his sensory aggressiveness. Therefore, there is an appetite distinct from both the will and the desiderative appetite.

Now we must try to find out more about the nature of this appetite. It is the appetite which moves one to engage in a serious struggle, for instance, to preserve one's life by bravely attacking an enemy. The object of this act is an imminent evil: as evil, it needs to be removed; as imminent, it can be removed by positive action. We sensibly incline to attack even though our will and/or our desiderative appetite is repelled by the risk of being overcome by the evil which is imminent. If, on the other hand, there appears to be no chance of eliminating the evil, there is neither fear nor daring, but only aversion.

Contrary to the notion of imminent evil is that of a difficult good. When a good is not yet present, but is considered as simply possible, the appetite that comes into play is the desiderative appetite with its most obvious response, desire. But sometimes a not-yet-present good is not merely possible nor automatically future, but possible-with-difficulty. As such it is neither simply good nor simply evil, nor is there simply a relationship of unpleasant means to end. The object itself is at one and the same time difficult and good (as its contrary was at one and the same time evil and avoidable). "Difficult" does not simply imply the presence of an unpleasant thing (e.g., a humid day), for this merely produces

[44] The term "daring" is used as a neutral term to designate the movement of the aggressive appetite toward an imminent evil.

the feeling of sadness in the desiderative appetite. It refers rather to the likelihood of a sensible good not yet present and requiring effort. In the face of such an object, two contrary reactions are possible: the person can incline to exert the effort—and this is called *hope;* or the person can so be repelled by the difficulty that he no longer is inclined to make the effort to gain the good, and this is *despair.*

There is an additional act of the aggressive appetite. When the difficult good is obtained, the difficulty ceases and there is only the good to be enjoyed—an act of the desiderative appetite. Similarly, when the imminent evil is successfully overcome, the aggressive appetite again finds no further act. If, however, the good is not gained or the evil does come upon us, there can be a reaction: an inclination to take revenge, to inflict evil upon the one who caused the evil to us, or upon the evil itself; this response is called *anger.*

From a consideration of these acts of the aggressive appetite, its relation to the desiderative appetite is made clear. Acts of the desiderative appetite come first and lead to acts of the aggressive appetite, and again in turn are followed by acts of the desiderative appetite. Thus the aggressive appetite is an instrument of the desiderative, and serves it as a means.

Now we must find out whether the aggressive appetite is modified by acquired habits. Are there consistent modes of tendency in the aggressive appetite, as there are in the desiderative? Our own experience tells us that there are. If a man's sensible inclination to overcome an imminent evil or to gain a difficult good is proportioned to the circumstances, he is courageous, maintaining his balance between fear and daring, hope and hopelessness. If his reaction is less than suitable, if fear or hopelessness unduly predominate, he is cowardly. If he overreacts, if daring or hope unduly predominate, he is rash, foolhardy, heedless, reckless, and so on. The passion of anger is somewhat similar to daring. It differs from daring in that the evil is present or the good lost, yet still an attack can be made on an evil. In this way, anger, too, can be proportioned to the circumstances, be less than is suitable, or be more than is suitable.

Once we see that the passions of anger, fear, daring, and hope (which figure so largely in human experience) are rooted in the aggressive appetite, it is easy to see that there are consistent modes of tendency and therefore habits in that appetite. Men can and do respond to the objects of these passions either in a proportioned manner, an excessive manner, or a deficient manner. When their sensory response is *consistently* proportioned, excessive, or deficient, we know they have acquired an intrinsic modification of the aggressive appetite. This is the evidence for the existence of habits in the aggressive appetite.[45]

The following diagram illustrates the material we have discussed on the aggressive appetite. Note that the diagram reveals daring and fear as contraries, paralleled by hope and despondency. The proportionate balance between fear and daring in regard to an imminent evil and between hope and despondency in regard to a difficult good is the same kind of structure; there is therefore a single set of habits for both sets of passions. Anger

AGGRESSIVE APPETITE

Object	Passion	Mode of Tendency	Habitual Determination	
			extended period	single action
	daring, hope (motion towards)	excessive:	boldness	recklessness
	fear, despondency (motion away from)	moderate:	confidence	bravery
Difficult		deficient:	anxiety, pusillanimity	cowardice, flight
Sensory Good				
		excessive:	irritability	fury, rage
(Imminent Evil)	anger (redress evil already suffered)	moderate:	mildness of temper	reasonable indignation
		deficient:	apathy	spiritlessness

[45] Some people seem to have innate bravery (confidence). Is this quality the same kind of acquired modification which is present in a *habit* of the aggressive appetite? At this point of our investigation there is really no way to distinguish "innate bravery" from the acquired virtue of bravery. This will not be possible until we have developed a much more accurate notion of habit and have also studied the virtues. Descriptively, we can at least say that it is much easier for some people to be brave than for others. Of course, we do not demonstrate the existence of habits by comparing one person with another, but by comparing one person before and after he has acquired a distinctive modification of behavior.

however has no contrary. Another feature of the diagram is that
it shows two modes of response for each grade of intensity in the
aggressive appetite, and so it includes habits whose acts are sustained over an extended period of time and habits which elicit
briefer and more vigorous acts of the aggressive appetite.

INTELLECTUAL HABITS

One of the two obvious places to find and identify habits is on
the intellectual level (the other, as we saw, is on the level of motor
activity). Before we do this, however, it will be helpful to state
briefly what is meant by intellect and intellectual activity.[46]

Descriptively, intellectual activity is a kind of knowledge, and
thus it is distinguished from appetency (sensory as well as rational). Human knowledge, even at the most primitive level of
awareness, has a double aspect, is composed of two factors or
levels. One is that of certain "felt qualities"—the color, warmth,
resistance, and so on; the other that of consciously and self-con-
sciously possessed recognition.[47]

When we know something sensitively, we know it insofar as it
affects us concretely, or through various elaborations of memory,
imagination, and sensory evaluation. But in all cases, sensory
knowledge, as such (that is, as a deliberately distinguished aspect
of perceptual knowledge), is relative to the concrete situation of
the one sensing. It is partly subjective in that our own reaction
(of seeing, feeling, and the like) is included in the knowledge of
the object.

On the other hand, when we know something intellectually, we
grasp what it is, at least minimally, in knowing that it is something existing, something objectively presented, and so on. We
cannot *feel* or *see* that it is a *thing*, an *object*, much less that it is

[46] "Intelligence," as that term is used today, is very ambiguous, especially in
its adjectival form. It can be applied to animal and even mechanical activity.
It is thus useful for behavioral analysis, but for the purposes of the present
book, it is best avoided.

[47] For a brief phenomenological presentation of this difference, see Robert J.
Henle, S.J., "A Phenomenological Approach to Realism," in Charles J. O'Neil,
ed., *An Etienne Gilson Tribute* (Milwaukee, Marquette University Press, 1959),
pp. 76-82.

a man, a desk, a voltmeter. We sum this up by saying that the object of intellectual knowledge is *being*.

We can now further analyze the object of intellectual knowledge. As being, it already transcends the limitations of sense: it is directed to the object as distinct from our personal, private activity of knowing. From another point of view, intellectual knowledge is always at least in some way universal. The potential applicability of the concept to many distinct individuals has always been recognized as a property which the concreteness of sense knowledge excludes. Our experience shows us that material things are always particular, individual; the object as intellectually known can be freed from particularity. The object as known is not an existent, and its universality is not an ontological attribute. But universal knowledge *is held within an activity,* the conscious, personal act of knowing which is at least as existentially real as the objects of immediate perception. Intellectual knowing, therefore, as an existential activity, cannot be such as to particularize, *materialize,* its object. It cannot, therefore, directly be the act of an organ (a structured part of a material thing which has a proper function) . To express the fact that intellectual knowledge is simultaneously immaterial and existential, we call it "spiritual."

Another characteristic of intellectual knowledge is that through it we are capable of complete reflexivity: we can make ourselves and our own acts the objects of our own acts. Now, material things act on each other, or, at least, parts act on other parts. For an activity to be its own object, that activity cannot be temporally and spatially distended. In material things, we may have difficulty in fixing the exact location of some particles on spatial and temporal coordinates, but we do not think of them as existing independently and also without quantity (extendedness, tridimensionality) . If, then, something is actually given as unextended, we must say that it is existentially immaterial, spiritual. The intellectual knowledge of self-reflection is therefore a spiritual activity. And since powers are proportioned to their acts, the human intellect is a spiritual power.[48]

[48] For a more technical and fuller analysis of the nature of intellectual knowledge and the intellect, see my *Philosophy of Human Nature* (New York, Appleton-Century-Crofts, 1953), pp. 158-204.

It is among acts of this kind that we will look for instances of habitual determination. Among the easiest habits to find are those of *science*—certain and organized knowledge. Scientific knowledge is found anywhere there is a characteristic mode of reasoning which is certain, demonstrative, and successful in reaching its end. That there are such modifications of intellectual knowledge in man is shown by the mathematicians, physicists, and others who show characteristic modes of reasoning. We have already described the habit of the science of mathematics earlier in this chapter and isolated some of its characteristics. For clarity's sake, it may be helpful to consider some examples of the other habits of the intellect. Other scientific habits include the various natural and social sciences and the different branches of philosophy. These scientific habits of reasoning all rest on the understood *general* relationships of the objects themselves. But objects are not only related in general to each other; in the concrete they are also related to the knowing-feeling subject. The mode of knowledge which progresses from one point to another by means of such subjective and concrete relations used to be called "poetry" because poetry eminently embodies this type of thought; today we might call it "humanistic knowledge." Other habits of the intellect are those of judging about complex objects (which are neither evident in themselves nor proved from evidence). Opinion is a habitual determination of the intellect according to which a person consistently judges about an object or a class of objects in a determinate but non-scientific way; such knowledge bulks large in the normal person's life, since included in that category are not only such things as political opinions, prejudices, and superstitions, but also the "layman's knowledge" of medicine, law, and the countless other areas of reality with which modern man is expected to be familiar but in which he is not scientifically proficient. Some special habits depend upon habits of the will which regulate the way people accept as true what they believe or hear. Some people habitually believe all gossip, advertising, etc.; others habitually believe certain types of gossip or advertising. Some students are incredulous, some are docile, some lack all critical sense, are completely gullible. Such attitudes develop habits of the intellect, opinions; but they are themselves habits of the will which modify the will's tendency toward a complex good (i.e., assent to propositions without direct evidence, on the authority of others) .[49] Two other areas in which the intellect acquires important habitual modifications are the areas of art and prudence. The nature of these habits will be discussed in Chapters Three and Five. We mention them here merely to illustrate the *diversity* of intellectual habits.

Since the sciences have objects of greater or lesser generality, they can be placed in an order such that the more general is "higher" and "includes" the lower.[50] In the realm of natural knowledge, the "highest" and "most inclusive" scientific knowledge is the philosophy of being, metaphysics; if Revelation is taken into account, it is sacred theology. These knowledges order and arrange other knowledges. The intellectual habits which are the source of such ordering-judgments are called "wisdoms."

The act of wisdom is principally a judgment ordering and relating things and activities to each other and to the ultimate goal of life. Now, all order has a principle according to which the ordered series unfolds. In wisdom, it is the ultimate goal which is this principle. Since the ultimate goal is both known and loved, and since knowledge and love are of various kinds (reason and faith, natural order of the will and supernatural charity), there can be different kinds of wisdoms. When wisdom derives principally from a knowledge of the last end, it is speculative in character (thus, metaphysics and sacred theology are speculative wisdoms) ; when it derives from an order to the last end, it is practical (deriving from supernatural charity there is infused wisdom, deriving from a long exercise of the natural virtues there is the wisdom of experience). Nevertheless, all wisdoms have a relation to action, since they deal with the ultimate goal, and so the possession of wisdom is one of the greatest enrichments of action as well as of knowledge.

All these intellectual habits deal with objects which are not evident in themselves. But man also knows some things which are

[49] The nature of habits of the will will be discussed in the next section of this chapter.

[50] There are many ways of understanding what is meant by "higher" and "inclusive," though any explanation which destroys the autonomy of the "lower" orders of scientific knowledge is self-defeating in that it leaves nothing for the "higher" knowledge to order. The task of investigating this problem of order among knowledges and guarding against disastrous misunderstanding belongs to the philosophy of knowledge, epistemology.

evident in themselves. Thus, when I am in the presence of an object which is influencing my cognitive powers, I know that that object exists. Similarly, when I understand the intelligibilities involved in the proposition, "A thing cannot both be and not be at the same time and in the same way," I simultaneously understand the truth of that proposition.

These are judgments which are said to be known "in themselves"; that is, they are such that no evidence outside the elements of the judgment itself is necessary. Is there any evidence that there is a habit involved in the making of such judgments?

It is a fact that these judgments are easy, provided only that the terms are understood. As far as success or firmness is concerned, scarcely with the greatest violence do men make mistakes in these judgments (though they can apparently become confused about them). The criterion of pleasure is hard to apply here because of the simplicity of the acts.

Now, our question is, do the ease and success in making these judgments require a habit, or have we here the simple nature of a potency entirely determined by its object? In the case of the external senses, we saw that these powers, being entirely passive to their proper objects, did not need a habit and, because of their passivity, could not acquire one. How does the intellect stand by comparison? We will presuppose here the Thomistic analysis of the nature and object of the intellect. According to this analysis, the proper object of the intellect, the intelligible, is "whatever-is," or "being." That which the intellect aims at in its activity is truth, that it will be conformed to what is, and in this way come to possess the perfection of what is. The act in which truth can be reached is the judgment, which for human beings is a complex act, for there is always the complexity of *what* is and that it *is*.

Is there any way in which the intellect can be said to be purely passive, that is, as passive as an operative power can be? First, we can consider the intellect insofar as it is specified to one object rather than another, which is insofar as it grasps *what* something is.[51] This is a grasp of an absolute nature; and in this act, grasping

---

[51] On the various acts of the intellect, see Quentin Quesnell, S.J., "Participated Understanding: The Three Acts of the Mind," *The Modern Schoolman*, vol. 31 (1954), 281-288.

an undivided unity, the intellect can only act according to the way it has been impressed. In this act, then, the intellect is passive, and so there can be no habit. This holds for all acts of this kind, so that we can say that there can be no habits with regard to the act of "simple apprehension," as we have just described it.

What about the act of judgment itself as a complex act? There are purely perceptual judgments, in which the intellect expresses only what is actually and contingently given here and now. From what we have already seen about the role of habits in our experience, we should not expect to find that adults can easily make a purely perceptual judgment. An adult's perception is very largely influenced by habits, and to free himself from this influence is quite difficult. But if a man did this, he would find that his judgment, in being determined by what is contingently given, has only the consistency and pattern of the given objects. And in this case, too, there would be no special determination on the part of the intellect.

Nonperceptual judgments fall into different classes. The judgments which pertain to scientific knowledge are determined by the reasoning that led to them and so are habitually determined. Other complex judgments are not determined by antecedent necessary reasoning, and these are "opinions." That opinionative judgments can be consistent and easy to pronounce seems to be evident enough not to require further discussion. There remain the judgments which are said to be "known in themselves."

We have already noted that these judgments known in themselves are as a matter of fact consistently true. They are not merely perceptual judgments, and so are not entirely passively determined by an object; they go beyond perception. They are not determined by antecedent reasoning, since they are known in themselves.[52] The intellect must be in some way determined to make these judgments.

Because man's intellect is made for truth, and because nature

[52] Some try to explain the first principles by saying that they rest on the evidence of being itself. It should be noted that to relate the evidence of being itself to the first principles is a task of metaphysics (and such an act is one of the reasons why metaphysics is a "wisdom"). But this is a scientific knowledge of first principles, not the direct and immediate judgment made prior to all scientific analysis.

always has all the necessary principles to perform its natural activities and reach its natural goals, it must be possible from the beginning for man to reach truth. But all other truths in some way rest on the truth of the first principles, and they cannot rest on any other truth, evidently enough. Nor can they be gained simply by trial and error, since prior to their discovery error could not be recognized. On the other hand, the intellect as a power must be open to all being and cannot be determined to just one kind of truth. And, properly speaking, there is nothing like completely innate knowledge. In view of all these conditions, we can conclude that there must be a habit of first principles; yet it cannot be acquired by a judgment about first principle made without it; and from another point of view it cannot be innate as a habit of judging with a determinate content. Therefore, it can only be innate as a tendency or inclination. Once the judgment has actually been made, then the habit of first principles is present in its full perfection as a habit.

These very general considerations do not seem to lead with inescapable necessity to the conclusion that there is a distinct innate habit of first principles. Here, it appears that it is better to say, "Very probably there is a really distinct innate habit of first principles."

HABITS OF THE WILL

The will is an appetite, not a cognitive power. Its natural object of tendency is good-known-intellectually. We must now investigate will-acts in man to determine whether the will acquires habitual modifications. In the course of this investigation we should remember that a man may choose one object rather than another because of a modified intellectual judgment about that object rather than because of any modification in the will itself. (For example, the will in constantly choosing the right course of action refers back to the intellect, to prudence, which is concerned with finding what is concretely suitable.) So our question in this section must be: can we find any modifications of the will as rational appetite, modifications which directly qualify its acts in the very line of tendency?

In the case of the sensory appetite, we found a triple modifica-

tion of the tendency as motion-towards: too much (too violent),
just right, too little (too weak). At the level of sensory appetite,
these and only these modifications are possible, since the sensory
appetite has a particularized nature, directed to a definite kind of
object. Because it is a particularized good, there can be no *habitual* distinctions of objects for the sensory appetites; all distinctions of objects are distinctions of nature or of the knowledge of
the object. Yet the sensible object can be desired too eagerly, and
so forth.

The object of the will (that to which it is directed as will) is
that-which-is-simply-good. This object does not have any particularized, specific, or limited nature such as the objects of the sensory appetites have. This object and therefore the will as rational
appetite have a kind of infinity about them. Therefore, unlike the
sensory appetites, the will cannot acquire consistent modes of motion-towards its proper object. A man cannot acquire a habit of
moderately, excessively, or deficiently willing that-which-is-simply-
good, which is the proper object of his will. That-which-is-simply-
good cannot be desired too much by rational desire; it is only adhered to or not adhered to, chosen or not chosen.[53] Moreover, the
distinction of appetible objects at the sensory level into "pleasurable goods" and "difficult goods" does not appear at the level of
will, because the intellect is able to cut through all the differences
such as "sensibly pleasant" and "difficult" and see "the good as
such" simply. Hence, there can be only one rational appetite.

To suppose that the will could "become stronger" as a power
would be (1) to imagine that it can act like a muscle, blindly
exerting more or less force, or (2) to treat it as a limited nature,
instead of as an "open" power.[54] In the first case, we must remem-

[53] "That which is simply good" is never rejected by the will; it is "chosen"
or "not chosen" only in the sense that if an act of the will is elicited at all, the
object of that act is chosen under the aspect of "good as such." Practically all
human will-acts have limited goods as their objects, but these objects are
willed not because of their limitations but because of the goodness which they
do possess. This is what it means to say that an object is willed under the
aspect of "good as such." "Goodness as such" is not *an* object of man's will,
but rather *the aspect* under which all the objects of man's will (including God,
infinite goodness) are willed.

[54] On reason as essentially an *open* nature (contrasted to all subrational natures which are "closed"), see, for example, Anton C. Pegis, "Nature and
Spirit," *Proceedings of the American Catholic Philosophical Association,* vol.
23 (1949), 69-73.

ber that the will is a rational appetite, a tendency toward *what-we-understand-to-be-good*. It is not a mechanism which develops certain operational patterns as an automatic result of repeated activity. The shift in modern psychology from a mechanistic treatment of the will to a study of motivation, autonomy, ego-development, and the like, represents a return to a better balance and (in many cases) a return to the equivalent of doctrines on the will which practical wisdom never abandoned.[55]

In the second case, only if the voluntary response of man's will were already fixed by its very nature to a particular object or class of objects could we think of a "general habit of intensity toward that object." But in fact the will is not determined to any particular class of objects. What is "indeterminate" about the will is precisely the very adherence to a given object or class of objects. Now, it is indeed true that a person can have more or less of a habit. Thus, it is possible to will *justly* with more or less intensity. But this is growth in a specific habit of the will, not a general habit of "willing intensely." Men do not build up "will power in general." A man may be admirably just, and so in the area of relations to others may will the good-of-another most intensely; but it does not follow that he wills with the same intensity in other areas of volition or even with rectitude. So experience bears out what we have concluded to as a result of the analysis of the will's objects: because that-which-is-simply-good does not have a particularized nature, there can be no proportional mode of tendency toward it.

We need to make one more observation on the object of the will before we investigate whether there are any habits in the will itself. "Goodness" is always a relative term, expressing a relation between an object and an appetite. "Good" when predicated of an object means not only reality (actuality) but also relation to some appetite or nature. To attempt to consider goodness as nonrelational is to attempt to consider a relation as if it were an absolute quality. Evidently this cannot be done. Therefore, when we speak of "the good" as the proper object of man's will, we must be talk-

[55] Cf. Johannes Lindworsky, S.J., *The Training of the Will* (Milwaukee, Bruce, 1929), pp. 50-79.

For detailed references on this and related points, see G. P. Klubertanz, S.J., "The Psychologists and the Nature of Man," *Proceedings of the American Catholic Philosophical Association*, vol. 25 (1951), 66-88.

ing about an object which has relevance to man, to his nature and powers; and therefore concretely the good is "good for the one who is willing."[56]

With this point in mind, we can return to our original question and ask whether there are any acquired modifications of the will which directly qualify its nature as rational tendency. This is not a question about modifications of the object, which properly pertain to the intellect. Nor, as we have seen, are we looking for acquired modes of tending toward the will's proper object. Rather, we must ask about particular kinds of objects. It would seem that the will itself as a natural tendency would not need any modification to tend perfectly toward whatever object is presented as "good for me as man," for example, "food" when I am hungry. Are there objects which are not so simple, which are not presented only as "good for me"? There are in fact several types of complex objects of the will. In such cases there might be a possibility of acquiring a facility of willing which does not flow immediately and naturally from the power-presented-with-its-proportioned-object.

Let us examine the case of willing a good which is "good for another as other." We often will good for a person distinct from ourselves, inasmuch as he is distinct (that is, even when his good deprives us of something). As distinct from us, he is not by that very fact good for us, precisely because of the distinction between us. For example, when a man pays his debts, it is good for the creditor to receive the money due to him, for this is his right; but the money comes out of the debtor's pocket. There seems to be a semilatent conflict here, so that the will does not spontaneously move toward what is good for another as it does toward what is good for itself. Of course, it does not tend to the *evil* of another either. In other words, neither justice nor injustice is a spontaneous tendency in man. Both are habitual modifications of man's will which must be acquired.

What if a man pays his debt to keep from going to jail? In this case he is not willing the good of another (that the creditor get

---

[56] This is by no means the same as saying that all love is necessarily self-love, but the far different statement that a person simply cannot will an object which he thinks is entirely unrelated to him. These considerations will be discussed at considerable length in Chapter Six.

the money due to him) but rather his own good (freedom) ; he obtains his own good by a mere means (paying his debt) . If this is the will act, then the debtor is willing a good for himself, but he is not exercising the virtue of justice, although he is avoiding the sin of injustice. We must note that in the payment of debts out of justice, we directly will a *good* (therefore an end, not a means) which *is in fact* and *is known* to be the good of another. This can be done, but it is not easy. Such a habit must be acquired. If one moves toward the good-of-another consistently, easily, and with pleasure, then he has a habit of justice.

We should observe that a habit of the will involves a special kind of "determination." It is not a determination of the object, as is the case with habits of the imagination, discursive estimation, and the intellect. Neither is it simply a matter of more or less, as is the case with the habits of the sensory appetites. It involves acquiring a consistent appetitive reaction to complex objects which do not *simply* fall under the proper object of the will. When we practice justice, we will the good-of-another-as-other; this is an added determination of willing that-which-is-simply-good-for-me-as-man.

It is noteworthy that willing the good of another is not spontaneous for man even though man is by nature a social being. The tendency to society is a tendency to the *common* good and thus, implicitly, to what-is-good-for-me. Since society is first constituted by a common good (which, as common, is also *mine*) , there is a natural tendency in the will toward it. When a man acquires a full knowledge of society, he realizes that it is constituted by others besides himself, that the common good is the good of others as well as of himself, and that therefore justice is necessary. Moreover, when one studies society, one also finds that it needs a structure and that this involves certain sets of opposites (such as leader and led) . These distinctions set up new relations of justice.

To make it clear that justice is not the only habit of the will, and in order to obtain a better understanding of the nature of a will habit, it will be advantageous to consider one other special relation. It is possible to consider goods, not only as suitable for me, but as due to and proper to me. We have often heard it said of some people that they act as if the world owed them a living. St. Thomas takes it that the will can become disorderedly attached to goods in this way. This is more than a mere assertion that I have natural rights, for rights are rights to actions and to opportunities. But what is in question here is the result of action, claimed without the effort of action. This affection of the will for goods (possessions, but especially honors) as due to a presumed personal superiority, St. Thomas calls *pride*. On the other hand, the direct and realistically based movement of the will toward the goods which are the proportionate results of achievement is called *humility*.[57] The opposite vice, of undervaluing the results of my labors, has no special name. Possibly we could call it "self-abasement."

These, of course, are not bare and plain will habits; there is a whole complex context of sensory images, discursive estimations, and sensory appetitions without which pride or humility could not be formed in the first place, and without which they would not have their present experiential character. We will consider this whole complex later; for the present, we are concerned only with the will habit, which shows how the movement of the will is determined.[58]

---

[57] Distinguish this carefully from the fear of responsibility which is the vice opposed to magnanimity.

[58] There is also the matter of a good which is not the good-of-nature, and therefore neither the good simply as convertible with being, nor the "good-for-me" (as rightly or wrongly willed in humility or pride), because these goods —since good is relational—are proportioned to the *nature* of man. If, then, there is a good above the nature of man—which we know from the Christian faith—then the will must be perfected by a supernatural, infused habit in order to tend to that good in the proportioned way. The reason this habit is supernatural and caused only by God is that the natural habits of the will must be proportioned to the nature of the will itself. And the structure of the will, in turn, inasmuch as it is a nature, is determined by the nature of man. Just as the nature of man as nature is not ordered to a supernatural good (but requires the elevation known as sanctifying grace), so the corresponding structure (*pondus*) of the will does not suffice to tend to the supernatural good. An added "infused" habit is necessary, and this is usually called supernatural "charity." Though we are not going to treat of this habit of charity here, it is extremely important, indispensable in a complete analysis of the principles of human activity as it *should be* in the concrete order of elevated human nature.

SOURCES FOR CHAPTER ONE

Note: The books and articles listed here give the basic experimental and observational evidence which is made use of in the chapter. In many cases, they themselves are summary presentations, and provide more detailed bibliographies to which the final appeal is to be made.

General Sources

Hilgard, Ernest R., *Introduction to Psychology*, 2nd ed. (New York, Harcourt, Brace & World, 1957) , pp. 232-280; on learning.

Hilgard, Ernest R., *Theories of Learning*, 2nd ed. (New York, Appleton-Century-Crofts, 1956) ; pp. 1-14, on the nature and kinds of learning and the basic theories offered; pp. 460-479, on the basic problems of learning.

Siwek, Paul, S.J., *Experimental Psychology* (New York, J. F. Wagner, 1959), pp. 333-342; on learning and habits.

Woodworth, Robert S., and Schlosberg, H., *Experimental Psychology* (New York, Holt, Rinehart and Winston, 1954); the most inclusive and best balanced of the general textbooks; it contains extensive bibliographies. Learning and habits are treated, pp. 541-732, 814-848.

The Point of View of the Educational Psychologist

Commins, W. D., and Fagin, Barry, *Principles of Educational Psychology*, 2nd ed. (New York, Ronald, 1954), pp. 125-218, 479-551, 615-776; on learning.

Cronbach, Lee J., *Educational Psychology* (New York, Harcourt, Brace & World, 1954), pp. 44-66, 73-111, 245-403, 521-575; on learning.

Dunlap, Knight, *Habits: Their Making and Unmaking* (New York, Liveright, 1949); this text is directly concerned with the ways to acquire or break habits; it includes data from animal behavior. It has an excellent critique of merely mechanical explanations, though in his turn the author seems to be rather deficient in sensitivity to moral implications. There are detailed bibliographies for the individual chapters and a comprehensive bibliography on habit formation (1937-1949) by J. E. Morsh.

Witherington, H. Carl, *Educational Psychology*, rev. ed. (Boston, Ginn, 1952); one of the few books in this area that specially talks about development of the imagination, pp. 122, 143.

Particular Aspects of Learning

Ammons, R. B., and Willig, Leslie, "Acquisition of Motor Skills," *Journal of Experimental Psychology*, vol. 51 (1956), 118-126; deals with the effects of "massed practise."

Arnold, Magda, *Emotion and Personality* (New York, Columbia, 1961), vol. I; vol. II, pp. 309-330; on the distinctively human emotions.

Benzaquin, Paul, *Holocaust!* (New York, Berkeley Publishing Corporation, 1960); the story of the Coconut Grove disaster, very graphically told.

Blake, Robert R., and Ramsey, Glenn V., *Perception: An Approach to Personality* (New York, Ronald, 1951), p. 107; the authors hold that space is learned and that tactile space has to be related to visual space by learning.

Downey, June E., *Creative Imagination, Studies in the Psychology of Literature* (New York, Harcourt, Brace & World, 1929), pp. 105-116, 135-148, 162-174; some detailed attention to (acquired) patterns of imagining.

Estvan, Frank J., and Elizabeth W., *The Child's World: His Social Perception* (New York, Putnam, 1959); perception is highly individualized; development of spatial perception precedes that of time; attitudes tend to become consistent.

Gibson, Eleanor J., "Improvement in Perceptual Judgment as a Function of Controlled Practice or Training," *Psychological Bulletin*, vol. 50 (1953), 401-431; this article presents evidence of improvement in acuity, discrimination, and recognition; discusses the amount, distribution, and sequence of practice; has a bibliography of 221 items.

Gibson, J. J., and Mowrer, O. H., "Determinants of the Perceived Vertical and Horizontal," *Psychological Review*, vol. 4 (1938), 300-323; organization of spatial perception and the influence of experience.

Harlow, Harry F., "Motivational Forces Underlying Learning," in *Kentucky Symposium, Learning Theory, Personality Theory and Clinical Research* (New York, Wiley, 1954); experimental evidence (using monkeys as subjects) is presented and discussed to support the contention that above and beyond the visceral-need appetitive motivational mechanisms and the emotional mechanisms, there is a third category of motives, a category of motives which are elicited by external stimuli and which have been described by such names as manipulation, exploration, curiosity, and play.

Hilgard, Ernest R., "The Role of Learning in Perception," in R. R.

Blake and G. V. Ramsey, eds., *Perception: An Approach to Personality* (New York, Ronald, 1951); emphasizes the role of learning in the development of perception and the function of memory in present experience.

Himwich, H., "Psychopharmacologic Drugs," *Science*, vol. 127 (1958), 50-72; a fine survey of the present situation.

Hoch, Paul H., and Zubin, Joseph, eds., *Problems of Addiction and Habituation* (New York, Grune & Stratton, 1958); recent material on habit formation in the use of drugs.

Hull, C. L., *A Behavior System* (New Haven, Yale, 1952); the final statement of his system, stressing the notion of habit.

Hull, C. L., "Knowledge and Purpose as Habit Mechanisms," *Psychological Review*, vol. 37 (1930), 511-525; this presents Hull's basic reasons for his theory of habits and also gives a view into his meaning of that term (formation of internal substitute stimulus and anticipatory goal reaction).

Jersild, A. T., Markey, F. V., and Jersild, C. L., "Children's Fears, Dreams, Wishes, Daydreams, Dislikes, Pleasant and Unpleasant Memories," *Child Development Monograph*, No. 12 (1933); material on unlearned emotional responses.

Katz, David, *Gestalt Psychology, Its Nature and Significance* (New York, Ronald, 1950) perhaps the best introduction to Gestalt psychology. Chapters 7 to 9 and 13 to 24 are especially relevant to habit formation.

Lowes, James Livingston, *Road to Xanadu* (Boston, Houghton Mifflin, 1927); a remarkable study of the imagination of Coleridge, exemplifying in a concrete instance some possible developments.

McClelland, D. C., *Personality* (New York, Holt, Rinehart and Winston, 1951); there are four basic reactions, which can be grouped around these points: safety, affiliation, achievement, and frustration reduction. This can be interpreted as related to the same basic appetitive responses spoken of in this book: fear, love, and anger.

McGeough, J. A., review of Thorndike's *The Fundamentals of Learning, Journal of General Psychology*, vol. 8 (1933), 285-296; good evaluation of a well-known theory of learning; stress on habit systems, which are brought about by repetition and effect.

Maritain, Jacques, *Creative Intuition in Art and Poetry* (New York, Pantheon, 1955), pp. 184-185, 242-243, 310-312; on poetic knowledge and experience.

Miller, Neal R., "Learnable Drives and Rewards," in S. S. Stevens, ed., *Handbook of Experimental Psychology* (New York, Wiley, 1951); experiments so far have dealt mainly with fear, and this study presents a good summary of the work done.

Morgan, C. T., *Introduction to Psychology* (New York, McGraw-Hill, 1956), p. 144; has a very good account of "memory-span" or "span of attention." Has material on very early, unlearned emotional responses of infants.

Rahner, Karl, S.J., *Theological Investigations,* vol. I, Cornelius Ernst, trans. (Baltimore, Helicon Press, 1961), pp. 347-381; this treatment of "concupiscence" aids in an understanding of the nature of the desiderative appetite.

Reymert, M. L., ed., *Feelings and Emotions: The Mooseheart Symposium* (New York, McGraw-Hill, 1950); excellent collection of contemporary information and views about emotion.

Senden, M. von, *Space and Sight,* Peter Heath, trans. (London, Methuen, 1960); this recent and very complete discussion of the perception of space discusses the cases reported by earlier authors concerning the experience of congenitally blind patients after operation. Perceptive in seeing the weaknesses of the arguments proposed by others, he himself sets up some false dilemmas and concludes that blind people have no perception of space. The three appendixes by A. H. Riesen, G. J. Warnock, and J. Z. Young make up for some of the deficiencies of the text.

Vinacke, W. Edgar, "The Investigation of Concept Formation," *Psychological Bulletin,* vol. 48 (1951), 1-31; concludes that very little had been done, and that from a very limited aspect. There is a bibliography of 76 items.

Instinct and Animal Behavior

Lorenz, Konrad Z., *King Solomon's Ring* (London, Methuen, 1952); on animal instinct and training; most interesting first person account. Some of the chapters are a bit romantic.

Thorpe, W. H., *Learning and Instinct in Animals* (Cambridge, Harvard, 1956); after dealing with the general concepts of drive, goal-directedness, and so on, the author takes up learning and habituation in animals and gives comparative abilities of eight groups of animals.

Chapter Two

Kinds of Simple Habits

ARE THERE ANY ESSENTIAL DIFFERENCES AMONG HABITS?

In the first stage of our investigation, we adopted a descriptive criterion (success, consistency, pleasure) for the existence of habits and applied it to the various powers of man. We have already noted in passing that the meaning of the criterion varies somewhat from power to power; we can therefore conclude that habit is not an utterly undifferentiated kind of reality. Of course, we have not yet determined the nature of habit. We have not even raised the question of its essential definition; we cannot do this before we have completed our inductive investigation.

So far in this investigation we have found habits in many different powers. Is it possible to begin to divide and classify these habits? Of course, we can admit in passing that anything can be classified and that many classifications are arbitrary and subjective. But it is also possible for classifications to be objectively based and significant.

Now, we are engaged in a study of the habits of *man,* and we can agree that intelligence and freedom are characteristics of man. In our inductive study of man we may have noticed that some habits are directly related to intelligence and freedom, and others are not so related. We have not asked whether this is a difference of degree and emphasis or whether it shows a real difference in the types of habit. But we can see at once that if such a real difference were to appear, it would be a significant one for an analysis of the nature of human habits.

In Chapter One we examined each of man's operative powers to determine whether there was any evidence for the existence of an acquired modification in that power. Now we will reexamine each of those powers in which we discovered habits to determine whether intelligence and freedom are characteristics of some habits and not of others. This would establish the existence of different types of habits in man.

We can ask two related questions about the habits in each power: (1) what is the relation of this particular habit group to the activity of consciousness and (2) what is its relation to volition and/or choice? The first question can be amplified to read: Can one *acquire* this habit without being aware of it? Can one *use* this habit without being aware of it? Is there, in other words, any necessary dependence of the habit on knowledge? If so, what is this dependence? In our investigation we will sometimes use the criterion of acquisition and sometimes the criterion of use. Whichever criterion is more readily available will be used. Similarly, with respect to the habit's relation to volition, it will sometimes be easier to consider whether a given habit is voluntary, sometimes whether it is free.

MOTOR SKILLS

What is the relationship of motor skills to consciousness? We do not wish to discuss mechanical or manual arts at the present time but merely the motor skills which sometimes accompany such arts and sometimes are found by themselves. Can these motor skills be used without our being conscious of them? In our ordinary experience we have a minimal awareness of motor activities and skills. Yet we also have experience of motor activities outside the scope of consciousness: for example, tapping fingers or feet, scratching, etc. If we move into more abnormal activities (such as automatic writing), we find a complex use of motor skills without any awareness on the part of the person performing them. Thus, a doctor can block off the vision of the patient so that he cannot see his arm and then block the sensory nerves in the arm so that they do not report its movements. As a result, the patient can write lengthy productions without any awareness. He has no notion of what he is writing, nor even that he is writing at all. The work may be quite legible (as good as his ordinary handwriting) but is sometimes of a weird content (like dream material) and often recounts events which the person could not previously recall. Of course, during this writing there must be activities going on in the imagination, since language is involved. But our question is about the conscious use of this motor skill, which appears to be started by the simple stimulation of the pencil put into the hand and the position of the arm At any rate, such automatic writing shows that motor skills can be exercised without our being conscious of them. Not only is the patient unable to *reflect* on his automatic writing; he is not even conscious of his activity by direct awareness.[1]

Indirectly, such automatic behavior proves a defect in the patient's personality; he does not have complete integration and control in an area where such control is desirable.[2] However, since even normal people do things absentmindedly, the personality flaw is a question of degree. The point of unconscious motor activity could also be established with normal people. Besides the evidence of absentminded behavior, it is also true that normal people can get to do automatic writing (though not while remaining normal, not without bordering on dissociation of personality).

It should be clear that such automatic writing cannot proceed from the intellect; intelligence cannot be separated from its own awareness. Moreover, although the written material often contains good sentences or at least phrases, it need not make good sense.[3] Since the intellect is not concerned in the production of such writing, there is no more truth in it than in a tape recorder.

[1] By the term "consciousness" we do not imply fully reflective awareness. If a person has understanding and acts rationally, he is not acting like a brute, even though he does not have the reflective awareness necessary for freedom at the time. He still has direct consciousness of himself as an agent actually performing an activity; an animal has only awareness of ongoing activity, not of himself as the source of that activity.

[2] Of course, the dissociation of personality involved in automatic writing need not be total. The patient is still rational in other areas and has sufficient judgment to report on his mental states. The fact that some of his activities escape his consciousness does not necessarily impair his other activities.

[3] Psychologists might object to this analysis on the score that dreams and automatic writing are related to repressed material which is revealed in pictures rather than logical dialogue; symbolism is thus involved, and it is ingenious and to the point. But the kind of symbolism involved does not seem to require a *present,* actual influence of intellect, since it is concrete rather than abstract. It could well be that an intellectual grasp was involved *at one time.*

What have we established concerning consciousness and the motor skills of man? We have shown that motor skills can *sometimes* operate independently of consciousness. This is not the same as saying motor skills can *always* do this; they cannot. But the fact that they sometimes do run on independently of consciousness proves that consciousness is not essentially involved in the use of motor skills.

The conclusion we have reached on the basis of this extreme case can be approached from an analysis of quite ordinary motor skills. It seems that in the early stages of the acquisition of a skill we need to pay explicit attention to our movements (of hand, foot, and so forth). But as the skill improves, we pay less attention to details; often we are conscious only of the final result or of the movement as a whole. For example, the skilled golfer keeps his eye on the ball, whereas the beginner has to see to it that his hands and feet are in the right place, his elbow is still, and so on.

A complete analysis of the changes that go on as a skill becomes more perfect is not possible. We know that the central nervous system is active in the control of skillful movements, though there is considerable doubt about the extent to which the brain is involved. We know that the activity of the striped muscles is initiated and governed by the motor centers in the brain. Some physiologists think that in the beginning impulses travel through roundabout paths before they reach the motor centers and that as a skill grows these paths become shorter—as it were, new circuits are set up. This, however, is a theory that is not very solidly established. All that we are sure of is that skilled responses are more rapid, and that we do not pay explicit attention to detailed sensations of the object and the act-in-progress. The details can therefore be said not to be sensed, as details. It does not follow that they are simply and completely unconscious, but it does follow that knowledge as formal and explicit knowledge is not an essential element in a perfected motor skill.

An experiment with sensory discrimination shows that the motor effectiveness of a sensation or image is not simply the same as knowledge. A subject is trained to make two different responses to two notably different shapes. When the responses are entirely habitual, the shapes can be made more and more similar. At a cer-

tain point, the subject can no longer visually tell which shape is
being presented, yet if he lets the motor response go without both-
ering about recognizing the difference, he finds that his motor response still discriminates in the way in which he was formerly
trained.[4] Similarly, a good driver responds to distance and speed
more rapidly and more accurately than he is aware of knowing
these factors. The awareness as such does not govern the details of
the response, though it seems to be important that a person be
aware in general of the whole situation.

What is the relation of motor skills to volition? It is obvious
that none of the unconscious motor activities are free; consciousness is a prerequisite of freedom. Of man's conscious motor activities, some are free and others are not. Consider the case of persons
who are fully aware of what they are doing and yet cannot stop.
The compulsive behavior of the melancholic who cannot stop
wringing her hands is an example of such activity. Some motor
activities of which we are normally minimally aware are usually
independent of volition but under special circumstances can be
controlled. Often such control requires special training. Some of
these activities always operate independently of volition; we cannot acquire control over them. For instance, the autonomic nervous system is generally automatic. Some of its functions can be
directly controlled (e.g., breathing); others cannot. The rate of
the heartbeat, the amount of sweating under emotional strain,
etc., ordinarily do not submit to conscious control; a well-known
form of the lie detector is based on the supposition that a person
cannot control the amount of sweating. Yet yoga shows that control can be acquired over automatic actions (probably by association of these centers with contiguous centers which are subject to
control, possibly only in a very indirect fashion by controlling centers which themselves control the activities of the so-called autonomic system). We shall ask later whether such control is normally
advantageous to man;[5] here we wish only to establish that in the
exercise even of those motor activities which are conscious, voli-

---

[4] It is clear that sensory organs can initiate reflex responses which are actually sharper than the associated sense knowledge, as is clear in the case of the
iris reflex.

[5] See pp. 96-97.

tion controls only some and these often only after special training.

As a final question in the area of motor skills we can ask whether consciousness and rational appetency are necessary in the acquisition of such skills. Both seem to be necessary, but to a very minimal degree. In the acquisition of motor skills, we have to go through the motions; it is doubtful that we would ever acquire a motor skill if someone just moved our limbs for us. We know from our previous analysis that the habitual modification present in a motor skill concerns the organization of perception and kinesthetic imagination, both of which are functions of the imagination. There is no intrinsic modification of the executive powers involved; all modification lies in the imagination. Because of this it is easy to see that if a person is totally unconscious, he is unable to act and thus cannot acquire the motor skill. His imagination cannot acquire a habitual modification under such circumstances. All that is necessary, however, is that he be awake and minimally active. A person does not have to know what he is doing or why. Manual skill (not manual arts, of course) can be taught without any explanation other than a demonstration. We can also explain first, but if we start a man acquiring a skill mechanically and then switch to a method involving instruction and understanding, we normally confuse him. For example, a good gymnast need not know the principles of balance at all. If we begin to teach him gymnastics by simply putting him through the proper motions and then change to teaching him various rules and general techniques, his learning will be impeded and imperfect.

We can note here the (partially) passive nature of motor skills, both with regard to their acquisition and exercise. It is true that motor skills involve habits of the imagination which actually produce modified human behavior; they are the source of operations and in that sense active. But motor skills are in man the most passive of his habitual modifications. Either intellect-and-will or external circumstances or both set up a situation in which the proper habitual modifications of the imagination are *almost automatically* acquired and used. This *extrinsic* openness of man's imagination in the formation of motor skills is like the openness of a tool which is determinable in various ways in the same extrinsic sense. In the acquisition of motor skills, man can both manipulate external factors (for example, rearrange the typewriter keyboard) and modify his own acts of intellect and will which control his activities. If a person decides to type differently each day, he will never learn the habit; neither will he acquire the habit of typing if he uses a different keyboard each day. Either the person himself or someone else or external circumstances sets up a routine-situation. Then a habit can be developed and will be developed almost automatically. It will operate in the same routine-situation just as automatically.[6]

To summarize: Consciousness and rational appetency are required to some minimal degree for the acquisition of motor skills in man, but both may be absent in the exercise of certain types of motor skills. This shows something significant about the nature of such motor habits. Since we know from other sources that it is metaphysically impossible for an act of the *intellect* to be unconscious, the occasional independence of motor skills from consciousness shows that they are not intrinsically dependent upon intellect in man. This conclusion is reinforced when we note the passive, semiautomatic nature of most motor skills.

IMAGINATION

What is the relationship of the imagination to consciousness? Are there activities of the imagination occurring without con-

[6] Animals develop such "automatic" motor habits through training by man, because through man's reason there is a similar extrinsic openness in animals with respect to the formation of motor skills. Man must set up the proper conditions (of reward or punishment, for instance), but under these conditions animals can acquire habitual modifications of motor activities, at least if they possess the necessary level of kinesthetic sensation and sense memory. Can there be acquired, learned modifications of motor activity in animals apart from training by man? We should first notice that many things which at first sight seem to be learning really are something else in animals. For example, proficiency in running is more a maturation process than a learning one, as tests show. The natural rhythm of vegetative life is controlled by factors such as light and darkness and temperature, not by learned habits. By and large, there is little learned activity in the motor activities or the vegetative and sex life of animals. Much of this is determined entirely by the concrete situation and the nature of the animal. A relatively difficult question to handle is that of what an animal's imagination can do. Even here, mere retention and association account for a lot of "learning." It is not necessarily true that a new way of acting has been acquired.

sciousness?[7] This is hard to discover in normal experience, though there are fringe experiences which we shall discuss later. In strictly abnormal behavior, however, we have already seen that automatic writing involves the actual use of images without consciousness. Another piece of evidence for unconscious imagining comes from certain appetitive experiences. We know that sense appetites can be put into act in only two ways: by direct material stimulation of the organ and by its being presented with a known good. As for organic stimulation, experimentation shows that it results in an experience which resembles "feeling angry," for example, but which is not actually that emotion (although it may form a predisposition to real feelings of anger). Now, some people experience an act of sense appetition which does not have the artificial appearance of chemically stimulated emotion; nor in the concrete case is there adequate evidence of chemical stimulation or of other (nonproper) organic material stimulation. Yet these people are unable to find in their conscious experience the object of this sense appetition. This type of experience is commonly called a "free-floating" feeling. For example, a person feels anxious but has no idea what he is anxious about. The emotional experience may become very strong and trying without his being able to identify the source of the anxiety. Since the appetitive reaction is genuine, there must be a known object which is functioning as a known sensible evil, but this object is not known consciously.[8]

When anxiety or some other feeling arises from a completely unconscious image (or from one which is almost completely unconscious), people normally hunt out an object to be anxious about. They are here and now really anxious about this new ob-

[7] We are not discussing here the special modifications of the imagination which regulate motor activity. We have already shown that such habits can be exercised under certain conditions without intellectual awareness.

[8] It seems that any explanation of unconscious imaging involves some real distinction between the function of consciousness and that of imaging.

For completeness it will be helpful to distinguish four ways in which the imagination presents images. (1) Normal controlled, or at least controllable, recall. (2) "Over-fixing," when an image remains conscious and will not go away; we experience this when "a tune runs through our heads," when we cannot forget an insult, and so on. (3) Repression; this occurs when we not only do not want to recall an image, but we cannot; there is some "block" which prevents its "rise" to consciousness. (4) A neurotic free-floating feeling,

ject; but it turns out that when this cause for anxiety is removed, they speedily find another and still another. Psychiatrists therefore conclude that the objects alleged by the sufferers are not really and completely the causes; the feeling seems to exist prior to any object on which it later fastens, and to float from one to another. That is why it is so often called "free-floating anxiety." We can also think of this movement as a kind of transfer, which we will discuss later. Similarly, an anxiety can be "generalized"; that is, a feeling caused by one object can attach itself to other objects which have a greater or lesser similarity or proximity to the original object.[9] Free-floating anxiety is a second instance of imagination operating independently of consciousness.

Furthermore, we have all experienced certain fringe states which indicate the presence of unconscious images, especially after we have established the fact of unconscious imagining in abnormal states. For example, we have a problem which we cannot solve. We forget it, go on with other business. When we return to it, it is solved. This happens frequently in devising mechanical gadgets. What happens in such activity? Can it be due simply to forgetting a "blind alley" type of image or to the disintegration of a "blocking image?" This supposition does not explain this precise experience. It is not simply that what we could not solve at one time we can solve at another; forgetting a false start would explain such

---

where the image is actualized but is blocked from consciousness. We can schematically diagram the last two cases.

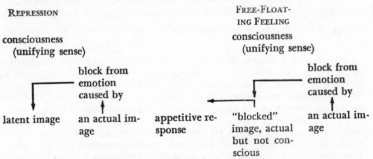

[9] Anxiety and other feelings are sometimes caused by very vague and ill-defined objects. The image can be indistinguishable from a lot of other things; in such a case there could also be a floating or transferred anxiety.

an experience. Rather, our experience involves returning to an abandoned problem and finding it already *solved*,[10] as it were by itself. There must therefore have been some unconscious activity.

Unconscious images may or may not be habitual. Some of our evidence has been from isolated cases, but the facts of repression, free-floating anxieties, and guilt feelings show the presence of habitual modifications of behavior. Of course, we do not say that we find the habit directly and immediately. We argue to its existence through consistency and constancy. We *conclude* that there is a determination in the power. This is not inborn but acquired; often the disturbed person was all right a few years ago, often he can be cured. The habits manifest themselves in their results. The Freudian techniques of free association and projective techniques like the Rorschach tests are designed to uncover habits, not just isolated activities.

The evidence for unconscious images shows that the imagination can at least sometimes operate independently of consciousness and, a fortiori, of volition. From this we conclude that habits of the imagination are not intrinsically dependent upon intellect in man.

DISCURSIVE ESTIMATION

What is the relationship of the discursive estimation to consciousness? Are there habits in this power which are independent of consciousness and therefore of the intellect? When we first approached the question of habits in the discursive estimation, we worked out of conscious experience. We found that people do get into concrete ways of estimating sensible goods; the examples we used occurred under intelligence and freedom. Because of the special role of man's *discursive* estimation (i.e., to develop from a relatively indeterminate power under the guidance of reason), we should expect to find most of the habits of this power dependent upon intellect and therefore conscious. But our question is: are

[10] Not intellectually; there is a new organization of the relevant data which was not made deliberately, or even consciously, and when we return to the problem in its new formulation we grasp the intelligibility we were previously unable to discover.

there any habits in this power which are independent of consciousness?

When we raised the question of unconscious habits of the imagination, we went to conscious activities of the sensory appetite for
which there were no consciously known objects. Now, the discursive estimation works with images presented by the imagination
and presents them to the sensory appetite. Hence, the same evidence that proves unconscious habits of the imagination proves
unconscious habits of the discursive estimation. Just as in unconscious imagining, here, too, there is no awareness of making an
estimation. As far as awareness goes, one seems to begin with appetition as the first *conscious* act, as we saw in our discussion of
free-floating fears and anxieties.

To review the evidence, free-floating anxiety presents itself as a
feeling of being anxious. What are we anxious about? The object
is undiscoverable. Therefore there is an unconscious image. In
normal fear and anxiety, one can state the object and the judgment involved. But anxiety concerns a difficult sensory good and
requires the concrete sensory judgment of the discursive estimation. For an act of the aggressive appetite, one needs sensation
(normally) and imagination, discursive estimation, and sensory
appetitive response. Just as the image is undiscoverable in free-
floating anxiety, so is the judgment of the discursive power. It cannot be directly found in awareness by introspection; therefore it is
not conscious. We know it is there because we experience appetency which does not arise from chemical or other nonproper stimulation and for which we can find no consciously known good.
Since appetency requires a known good, the object must be known
(imagined and estimated) unconsciously.[11]

11 This argument proves the *fact* of unconscious imagery on the sense level;
it provides no *explanation* of how this knowledge is acquired or actuated, or
why it is unconscious. Briefly, we can consider the matter in this way. There
are some images which are habitually estimated as repugnant (or, even more
strongly, as evil). The actual presence of such an image to consciousness seems
irreconcilable with the rest of life, especially with the individual's other needs
and desires. Instead of working out realistically the apparent conflict, a person
sometimes finds it easier to turn his attention away from the disturbing image,
particularly if the image or image-complex arouses fear or anxiety. If such
turning-away-through-fear becomes habitual, the image escapes from sensory
consciousness (i.e., the unifying sense). Yet the emotions playing around the

Another indication that there are unconscious images and estimations is the success of therapy. There are known processes of reducing the image to consciousness, correcting the estimation, or at least localizing it, and so getting the sufferer out of his anxiety state. For instance, a man badly wants his mother's approval but knows that he will not get it in the concrete situation. He tries to put it out of his mind, but does so without ever straightening out his ideas and the values involved. He succeeds in "forgetting"; but a feeling of anxiety remains, and he does not know what it is about. He eventually goes to a psychiatrist and after much work discovers that the image in his imagination is that of his mother disapproving of what he is doing. The judgment of the discursive estimation is that his mother's disapproval is something to worry about. Since this has been going on over a long period of time, there is evidence for the existence of a habit not only in the imagination but also in the discursive estimation. Before therapy, both these habits were operating independently of consciousness.

It is clear that unconscious habits of the discursive estimation are independent of volition as well as consciousness. Are there also conscious habits of the discursive estimation which are independent of volition? Experience shows that there are. The activity of the imagination can generally be controlled if sufficient attention is paid to the task; at least undesirable images can be rejected as soon as they appear in consciousness and as often as they appear in consciousness. But if a person has developed habits of concrete estimation, he cannot change his estimations directly and immediately. He cannot simply will not to feel that way. For example, if a person becomes afraid of the dark, he cannot, by a single act of the will, become unafraid of the dark. His estimative habit, once developed, goes into act independently of direct volition. Of course, because his estimation is a discursive estimation, over a

---

image keep it active in the imagination. (If we recall that the imagination is an extended organ, we can see how it is possible that one part of it be blocked off from another.) The habitual turning-away-through-emotion is sometimes called "repression." So, in brief, the repressed image is a product of originally conscious experience. Emotional reaction keeps attention turned from this image, yet at the same time keeps the image active. So the emotion continues to appear in consciousness without any consciously known good (or evil) to which it corresponds. See pp. 84-85.

period of time he can change his estimation and eventually get to the point where he no longer *feels* afraid of the dark without rational grounds. This process takes time precisely because it involves breaking down an established habit and replacing it with a new habit.

Even the evidence of traumatic experiences does not prove that the habits of the discursive estimation are free. Rather, it supports the conclusion that they are independent of volition except to the extent that a man can will to work at changing his estimations over a period of time. Traumatic experiences are shocks resulting in new estimations which remain like habits. They seem to be sudden and entirely new experiences, but actually they require previous preparation and the proper disposition, so that the climactic experience penetrates deeply. Moreover, they need at least some repetition to become "fixed." What happens in psychotherapy when a person gets an insight in one flash and his troubles immediately disappear? Actually the facts are not so dramatic. First, there has been a long period of preparation and a gradual process of breaking down the old habit. Second, even after the habit is changed, more work is needed to make the reorganized phantasms and the modified estimations permanent.

In summary, unconscious estimations prove that the discursive estimation sometimes operates without consciousness and so is not intrinsically dependent upon intellect. Unconscious estimations also show that the discursive estimation can operate independently of volition; and an analysis of experience shows that even conscious estimations often operate in partial independence of volition, though volition can influence them indirectly over a long period of time.

SENSORY APPETITES

What is the relationship of the sense appetites to consciousness? First, do they ever act without our being consciously aware of the appetition? Freud says bluntly that it is impossible to have unconscious emotions. It does seem rather difficult to set up an argument that would clearly show the act of emotion to be unconscious in some particular case and yet to be a real act of emotion.

We have just seen that people can be frustrated or anxious without knowing why; that is, they have unconscious images which are
the causes of conscious emotions. We noted earlier that emotions
are accompanied by what is commonly called "bodily resonance"
—special physiological reactions. There is some evidence that the
bodily resonance commonly associated with anxiety, rage, aggressive feelings does occur, though the people are not aware of
having such feelings. These bodily reactions may in time bring
about ulcers, tension headaches, and so on. Many authors seem
willing to accept this as evidence of unconscious emotion. It does
not, however, seem to be a logically compelling argument. Perhaps we can only conclude that we do not know for sure whether
there are or can be unconscious acts of the sense appetites.

Do the sense appetites ever operate independently of will? On
the one hand, we have all experienced voluntary emotion and
therefore know that our feelings can sometimes be willed. On the
other hand, the same evidence which establishes that some habits
of the discursive estimation are not directly dependent upon volition also shows that sensory appetition can be independent of
volition, except insofar as volition over a period of time is able to
effect a change in the known sensible good and thus influence the
appetitive reaction to that good. We still feel afraid of the dark
even when we *will* not to be afraid. A man who develops bad
habits and then reforms still experiences sensory desires contrary
to his strong rational volition. We know that when the reformed
drunkard passes a tavern he still desires to go in for a drink. Only
after years of effort have changed the object of his estimation can
the drunkard *feel* good about not drinking to excess.

Thus we see, although we do not know for certain that the
sense appetites can act independently of consciousness, that there
are some acts and habits of these appetites which are only very indirectly dependent upon rational volition.

INTELLECT

What is the relationship of intellectual habits to consciousness?
We can evidently be conscious of the acts of intellectual habits.
The question is: Can we ever be unconscious of them? Can there

ever be a nonconscious act of the intellect? Since an act of the
intellect is an actual intelligible, actually present to the intellect
and thus necessarily known, it is impossible that any such act be
unconscious. Indeed, consciousness is the distinguishing mark of
intellectual beings; they possess both direct and reflex self-consciousness. Since no act of the intellect can be unconscious, no
habit of the intellect can be used unconsciously. To use habits of
the intellect, one must actually know, actually be aware that he
is acting in a definite way (though this awareness may be merely
direct, and minimal even in the line of direct awareness). Otherwise, one will not actually be using the intellectual habit in question but doing something else. For instance, one may understand
each proposition in an argument but never understand the argument itself. Until a man understands the argument as such, he is
not performing an act of the science to which the argument belongs. Similarly, unless a person knows why he likes a poem, he is
not exercising an act of literary appreciation. One can go through
the steps of a science without thinking scientifically; one can go
through the stages of an art without thinking as an artist does. A
habit of science is operative only when the person consciously
(though not necessarily *self*-consciously) employs the proper operations of that science.

The conclusion of this analysis is not only that intellectual
habits are used consciously but that they can be used only consciously. In other words, a man must be explicitly aware of what
he is doing in some concrete case of the habit. If he does not argue
scientifically, if he links individual propositions together by their
position on a printed page or the kind of type in which they are
set, he is not exercising his intellectual habit of science. A person
must be aware of the precise character of the habit he is exercising. He does not have to say, "I am going to think in terms of
the canons of scientific method." He does have to apply these
canons as he thinks; otherwise, he is not exercising his habit of
science. The name of the habit need not occur; that is irrelevant.
But the habit must be used consciously, or it is not used at all.
There are no automatic intellectual habits.

We may ask whether sometimes the scientific method is not used
automatically, even in cases to which a person does not think it

applies. What would "automatic" mean in this instance? It may mean "without a lot of self-reflection and deliberation." If it means "without conscious awareness," then we must repeat that there are no automatic activities of the intellect. There is no scientific conclusion unless a person knows that he is reasoning not by surface similarity but by essential relationships. The alternative is to reason according to art or opinion or some other intellectual habit, or to reason without any formal structure at all. In the latter case, of course, one is not using an intellectual habit.[12]

Now that we have established that intellectual habits can never be used unconsciously, we can ask whether they can be acquired unconsciously. We have seen earlier that in the acquisition of motor skills it is absolutely unnecessary that we be aware of what we are doing; the only thing that is required is that we be sufficiently awake to move around and follow the demonstrator. We need not be aware of the mode of activity nor of the connection between steps; there is no need of any understanding. Now, at the level of intellectual activity, can one go through that which is reasoning without understanding it as reasoning? Obviously one can. What happens? Nothing happens except that one understands each proposition separately. A student may understand a proof sentence by sentence; he may go over the proof hundreds of times as a series of propositions which *de facto* follow one another in such and such a series. From such repetition he will never learn the proof; the connections are mechanical, external, and not reasoned. In geometry, a student may understand part of a proof but not the whole of it. He does not have a scientific knowledge of geometry, though he may have some geometrical knowledge. We cannot simply go through the motions to acquire an intellectual habit. Intellectual habits are not acquired unless there is in the process an awareness of what is being done, an awareness of the process itself (the reasoning as such).

Finally, we may ask how intellectual habits are related to volition. Reflection upon our own acts of intellection shows that the exercise of understanding must be willed. One has to will to rea-

12 This may well be. Many people have no scientific habits of mind, and few artistic habits. Most people have a large number of habits of opinion, however. Life is too complicated to think things out afresh every day.

son or not to reason, or to reason in this way or that. In this sense, the exercise of intellectual habits remains dependent upon the will and cannot be carried on independently of the will. It is true that the intellect's act must come first in any given series of intellect-and-will activities, but this priority of nature only serves to give the will an object for its activity. Continuing to think is due to the will. The will is also necessary in the acquisition of intellectual habits, for the intellect is not merely passive as far as its object is concerned. True enough, the intellect must in the first instance be informed from the thing which it knows, and in this stage the intellect is really passive. But once the intellect has been put into act, it can perform different activities. For example, given the information it needs to form premises, the intellect can move itself according to its own laws to various conclusions. If this were not so, the succession of acts of the intellect would be determined by the succession of experiences or images, not by logical connections. True, what is concluded follows from the premises when they are arranged in a certain formal way. But the intellect is not compelled to arrange its judgments as premises, nor is it limited to a particular arrangement or a particular selection of premises. In the choice of way of reasoning, man is free. Once he has chosen to reason, and to reason in a certain way (scientifically, philosophically, poetically, rhetorically), his will does not determine what he will find, but it does really determine him to start and to hold to this course of action.

Given that the intellect has a plurality of operations: to define, to judge, to reason, and to reason in different ways about the same matters, neither the nature of intellect nor the special characteristics of its object entirely determine what it will do in a given case.[13] Hence, many of the acts of the intellect are freely commanded. Consequently, the habits produced by acts of intellect which are freely chosen will themselves depend on free choice in their use (as they did in their acquisition).

In addition, there is a particular exercise of freedom if we are

[13] This has nothing to do with the per se infallibility of the intellect. The objects of that infallibility are per se known propositions and essences, *not* reasoning, ever. In the area of reasoning, the only infallibility is the infallibility (*certitudo*) of virtue.

trying to correct bad intellectual habits. We must will to destroy our old habit and acquire a new one. For example, a person may believe that "the scientific method"[14] is the only method of arriving at truth. Then he discovers other ways to reach truth. To develop proper intellectual habits employing these ways he must lose his previous bad habits of applying restrictive scientific canons where they do not belong and acquire new habits which correctly employ the new ways to truth. He cannot do all this automatically: he must will it.

In summary, we have seen that intellectual habits must be acquired and exercised in strict dependence upon consciousness and volition. They cannot be used unconsciously or without being willed.[15] Furthermore, an intellectual habit is acquired and exercised not by merely going through the motions but by consciously applying the proper procedure of the habit to suitable material. Otherwise some other habit or structureless thought is the result, not the precise habit being aimed at.

WILL

What is the relationship of the habits of the will to consciousness and volition? Is one consciously just? Is one voluntarily just? Evidently one could be both. The question is: Is one ever unconsciously or involuntarily just?[16] Can a man will to give another what-is-due-to-him without knowing or intending that? This is a contradiction in terms, since tendency is to the known good,

[14] Most people who talk about *the* scientific method mean "the method used in the natural sciences, especially physics," and they imply that it is to be used in exactly the same way in other areas of investigation.

For a penetrating analysis of the equivocations committed by writers, see Robert J. Henle, S.J., "A Philosopher's Interpretation of Anthropology's Contribution to the Understanding of Man," *Anthropological Quarterly*, vol. 32 (1959), 29-31.

[15] Such will acts are not necessarily free acts, nor do they always involve moral responsibility. But this is not the point at issue here. We must try to exclude the question of moral responsibility (and moral praise or blame) at this preliminary stage of our investigation.

[16] Of course, we are talking here of the internal human act. I may intend to defraud an employee and yet mistakenly give him a ten dollar bill instead of a one dollar bill. Actually I pay him a (materially) just wage, but my action is not (formally) an act of justice, since I did not intend it.

which, as object, is what specifies the act of the will itself. Therefore, it is impossible to will justly without knowing and intending it.

Moreover, we can also establish that habits of the will are exercised only when they are *freely* intended. They are intrinsically
dependent not only upon volition but upon free volition. We
know that there are necessary acts of the will: whenever the will's
object is presented as good-without-qualification ("simply
good"), that object is willed necessarily, not freely.[17] The objects
of the habits of the will are never goods-without-qualification;
we have seen that habits are not developed in the will except
where the natural tendency of the will towards the "good as such"
is not sufficient to insure consistent adherence to a complex object, a qualified good. For instance, the object of the virtue of justice is not the good-without-qualification but rather the good-of-
another. If this object is willed at all, it is willed freely, since the
will is free to choose or reject qualified goods. Therefore, freedom
is necessary in the exercise of will habits; otherwise what is being
(necessarily) willed is not a qualified good and hence not a true
object of a will habit.

The same line of reasoning which proves that habits of the will
can only be exercised when they are consciously and freely intended also proves that they are acquired only under conditions
of consciousness and freedom. We cannot acquire a modification
of our tendency to the known good of intellect without being
conscious of that object and intending it. There are no unconscious acts of intellection; modifications of rational tendency
necessarily involve volition. Since the will is free with regard to
objects known as qualified goods, the acts of the will involved in
the acquisition of will habits (which all concern qualified goods,
known as such) are also free. Thus consciousness and freedom

---

[17] Yet it is true that *man* often has the possibility of freedom where the will
is necessitated, because man can use his intellect to change the specification of
the will's object and view it as qualifiedly good. Such a qualified good the will
can choose or not choose.

This process of changing the specification of the will's object is not automatic. Many people, because of defective education and background, go
through life thinking that some things which are actually qualified goods (e.g.,
pleasure) are goods-without-qualification. To the extent that they do this, they
are not free.

are necessary both in the acquisition and in the exercise of habits of the will.

SUMMARY

The following list summarizes our conclusions concerning the relationship of consciousness and volition to the habits of man's operative powers.

Motor Skills: Both consciousness and volition are required to some minimal degree in the acquisition of motor skills. Both may be absent in the exercise of certain motor skills.

Imagination: Habits of the imagination sometimes operate independently of consciousness and volition.

Discursive Estimation: Habits of the discursive estimation sometimes operate independently of consciousness and volition.

Sensory Appetites: Perhaps not all acts of the sensory appetites are conscious, but certainly some of the habits of these appetites operate in at least partial independence of volition.

Intellect: All intellectual habits are intrinsically dependent, in both their acquisition and exercise, upon consciousness and volition. They are not all necessarily free.

Will: All will habits are intrinsically dependent in both their acquisition and exercise upon consciousness and *free* volition.

A glance at this list makes it apparent that there are at least two types of habits represented here. All the categories except the last two (intellect and will) contain habits which can at least sometimes be exercised independently of rational consciousness and/or volition. Intellectual and will habits can be acquired and exercised only in dependence upon rational consciousness and volition. Will habits are also necessarily freely exercised.

Because of the necessary presence and function of consciousness and volition in the habits of intellect and will, we can now divide the general class of habits (i.e., acquired modifications of behavior) into two groups: (1) those which have a necessary connection with consciousness and volition and (2) those which do not have a necessary connection with consciousness and volition. *Because the first group of habits is always under the control of the agent (since they necessarily involve rational volition), we*

shall call them "mastery habits."[18] *Because the habits of the second group incline toward independence and away from consciousness and volition, we shall call them "automatism habits."*[19] *When
a habit has become completely unconscious and independent of
will, we shall call it an "automatism."*

We can see at once that all habits of the intellect and will themselves will be mastery habits. Habits in the other powers will have
to be examined individually, since any of these other powers may
have habits which operate independently of rational consciousness and/or volition. If a necessary connection with consciousness
and volition is discovered, then they are mastery habits, no matter
what power they are modifications of. If no such necessary connection is discovered, then they are automatism habits or simply
automatisms. There is a difference in kind between mastery and
automatism habits. There is only a difference of degree between
automatism habits and pure automatisms. Automatism habits,
strictly speaking, have no necessary connection with consciousness
and volition; they can operate independently of either consciousness or volition or both. They are found in the imagination
(which also controls motor activities), the discursive estimation,
and the sensory appetites.[20] Normally, however, they are found
with at least a minimal volition or consciousness or both. If such
habits lose their *de facto* connection with consciousness and volition, so that they no longer *can* be made subject to volition or to
conscious awareness, they are then called automatisms or pure
automatisms.

The intrinsically *automatic* character of automatism habits is
shown neatly in the way in which we can best make use of motor
skills. More than minimal consciousness or volition is undesirable.
For example, if while dressing one pays too much attention to the
movements of the fingers in buttoning the buttons, one will find
the job almost insuperably difficult. But if a motor skill is "self-

---

[18] This is the English equivalent of St. Thomas's *habitus,* the Latin term
which he uses to describe those modifications of operative powers in man
which necessarily involve consciousness and volition.

[19] St. Thomas has no proper word for these modifications; he sometimes calls
them "habits in a secondary sense" or "dispositions." These are the habits
which are commonly studied in experimental psychology.

[20] There are also mastery habits in these same powers, of course.

controlling" to the extent that one need not pay much attention to the detailed movements, many tasks can be done quickly and easily.

In most modern studies of habit, the mastery habits have been largely ignored and attention has been concentrated upon the automatism habits and pure automatisms. That is why we often think of habituation as a process of making an activity nonconscious. Hence, we frequently read, "Habits are ruts," "Habits take over the work of choice," and similar statements. There is no harm in this concentration on automatism habits, except that it either leads people to ignore mastery habits altogether or misleads them into attributing to all habits the restricted characteristics of automatism habits.

DEFINITION OF HABIT

In the light of these experientially described differences, we can begin to construct some definitions. Looking back over our detailed discussions, we see that in every habit examined there was some indetermination which received some kind of determination. Yet we have also seen that the very meaning of "indetermination" and "determination" has to be pinned down in each case. This shows that "habit" is an analogous term, a term which has a slightly different meaning every time it is used of a different habit. Habit is not a kind of common genus, equally divided into species. Habits in different powers differ, but they do not differ according to genus and species (as man differs from brute, for instance). Even habits of the same power have extrageneric differences. Science, for example, is a genus, divided into species according to the distinctions of proper objects; but science, wisdom, prudence, art, and opinion (all habits of the intellect) are not species of one common genus. We shall try to respect the analogous nature of habit by respecting the individual differences of habits.

Before we try to formulate a definition of habit, we should reflect a moment on the process of defining. What should a definition do? It should do two things. First, it should be built up from intelligibilities that are more simple than the object to be defined.

Ideally, an absolutely complete definition is made up of elements which are themselves not further composed but rather directly understood. Second, a good definition orders its component elements in a series, beginning with the one which is common to the largest number of other similar things, and progressively adding less and less common elements, until the last element is added as the ultimate specific difference. For example, the complete definition of "man" is: a material substance which is living, sentient, and rational. In this definition, the ultimate genus (*material substance*) is common to all the beings of our experience; the next two intermediate genera are progressively less common (*living* to plants and animals as well as to men, *sentient* only to animals and men) ; and the last element (*rational*) is the ultimate specific difference. From this example, we can see that the construction of at least some definitions involves first a prior analysis and then a composition of the elements uncovered by the analysis.

First, then, we must ask what is the most general of the traditional Aristotelian categories into which we can put habit. A habit is not a substance,[21] but a modification of a substance. Neither is a habit a relation, nor a quantity, nor an action (though it may involve relations, quantitative changes, and actions) . Thus habit must belong to the category of quality; that is, it is a formal determination or modification of a substance or of a substance-modified-by-accidents which renders that substance "such-and-such." Habits *qualify*, further determine their subjects. They do not directly modify a nature, but rather modify the operative powers of a nature. Wisdom is a habit which further determines, perfects, modifies the operative power of intellect in man; a wise man has a modified human nature only to the extent that one of the operative powers of his human nature, his intellect, has acquired a new determination. Habits are thus discussed in connection with the operative powers which they modify.[22]

---

[21] When we first approached the subject of habit, considering it as an acquired modification of some kind, we excluded substantial change, since when the thing itself changes we cannot reasonably speak of *that* thing being modified.

[22] We have not considered the so-called "entitative habits," by which a substance is modified in relation to its being and form, for example, health,

On the ground of empirically described differences, we can begin with a preliminary line of demarcation. Strictly *physical* acquired modifications replace other determinations which were present earlier. A new structure, for example, can only replace another structure. Consider the case of a person in whom some member never developed, and who acquires the organ by transplantation. The surgeon must destroy the original structure in order to replace it with another. Again, we considered the modification of activity due to a broken leg; we saw in such a case, too, that one structure was replaced by another. All such acquired modifications which involve replacement of one quality by another (of the same or similar kind) we will call acquired dispositions. We also noted that such changes happen *in* the subject which changes, but not *from* the subject's activity.[23]

In contrast, the remaining acquired modifications involve a gain or addition to the power. What does a habit do to an operative power? It gives it a further determination or perfection or specification; it makes the operation of that power good; it perfects the power in the line of operation. This is what St. Thomas means when he says that a habit is a kind of quality by which the operation of an operative power is made good.[24] A habit increases the efficiency of an operative power.

If a habit is a perfection of an operative power, it follows that the power without the habit is imperfect with regard to its operations. Therefore, it must be by its very nature determinable; it must have a capacity for added perfection. When we investigated

---

beauty. These entitative habits differ widely from the operative ones, and the English term is not often used of them except in a transferred sense.

[23] It will be recalled also that we excluded "mechanical" adaptations, not only because the application of the term to machines is a forced one, but also because there is no intrinsic openness of a machine to other types of activity and because in all the modifications which it undergoes there is always a loss as well as a gain.

[24] Note a difference between the definition of a habit (or any form or act) and that of a substance. In defining a substance, we find that a genus is divided by disjunctive differences. In defining a form, the subject or recipient is like the genus; in place of a difference we put what the form does to its subject; but what the form does to its subject can be expressed as a disjunctive alternative only when the form has a contrary. Now, habit has no contrary; it is an addition, not a replacement of another form (though it may be possible that one habit be contrary to another, as virtue is to vice).

the external senses, we found that they are without acquired modifications; there are no habits of the external senses. Why is this? Are they capable of any acquired modification, any further determination? We know that the power of sight goes into act by the external stimulus of the object. The whole operation of the power is therefore accounted for by the innate structure of the power and the external stimulus. The power of sight (and all the other external senses) is a power which by its very nature is determined to one object and operation. When the adequate stimulus is given, the power goes into act and only one act is possible under those conditions. Therefore, the external senses neither have nor need any acquired perfections distinct from themselves and from their operations. Only those operative powers which are capable of varied responses to a single external situation are the proper subjects of habits.

Are there operative powers which are capable of varied responses to a single external situation, which allow diverse reactions under the same set of circumstances? The will, the power of free choice in man, is evidently able to respond to an object in various ways: it may choose or not choose the object; it may choose it in this way or that. Therefore, by its very nature the will is a proper subject of further determination and is capable of being perfected by habits. Most directly connected with the will is the intellect. This power is in potency to know all being. It can operate in an almost infinite variety of ways and attain truth (and falsehood) under countless aspects. It can even construct its own objects. Thus the intellect is also by its very nature a proper subject of further determination by habits.

A review of what we have already said about man's imagination, discursive estimation, and sensory appetites will establish the fact that each of these powers is capable of varied responses to the same situation and thus can be perfected by habits. Of course, each of these powers is a potential subject of habits in a different way. The control habits involved in motor skills such as typing and dressing insure uniformly successful behavior instead of the erratic behavior of powers not perfected by such habits. Habits of the imagination such as language skills make easy and accurate the recall of patterns of images instead of a chaotic welter of images. Habits of the discursive estimation add determinations to the largely indeterminate emotional responses of infants. Habits of the desiderative and aggressive appetites stabilize the activities of these appetites; the courageous man consistently responds to a sensible-evil-to-be-overcome in a proportioned manner. All these operative powers can and need to be perfected by habits because they are capable of diverse reactions to the same situation; they are not (like the external senses) fully determined to react in only one way in any given set of circumstances.

In summary, then, a *habit* (in general) is a quality which determines an operative power which is in some sense indeterminate, so that an ordered operation flows from that power with ease, consistency, and pleasure. A *mastery habit* is a quality which determines an operative power in dependence upon consciousness and volition, so that a consciously willed, ordered operation flows from that power with ease, consistency, and pleasure. An *automatism habit* is a quality which determines an operative power which was previously indeterminate, so that an ordered operation flows from that power with ease, consistency, and pleasure and, normally, with at least minimal consciousness and volition (although with no *intrinsic* connection with consciousness and volition) . An *automatism* or a *pure automatism* is like an automatism habit except that it has not even a *de facto* connection with consciousness and volition, so that it *cannot* operate in dependence upon volition and/or consciousness.

SOURCES FOR CHAPTER TWO

General Sources

Siwek, Paul, S.J., *Experimental Psychology* (New York, J. F. Wagner, 1959), pp. 333-342; on habits.
Woodworth, Robert S., and Schlosberg, Harold, *Experimental Psychology*, (New York, Holt, Rinehart and Winston, 1954), pp. 528-530; general indications of different types of "learning."

The Nature of "Habit"

Aquinas, St. Thomas, *Summa theologiae*, I-II, qq. 49, 50, 51, 54.
Bourke, Vernon J., "Saint Thomas and the Transfer of Intellectual Skills," *The Modern Schoolman*, vol. 18 (1941), 69-73.

Bourke, Vernon J., "The Role of Habitus in the Thomistic Metaphysics of Potency and Act," in *Essays in Thomism,* Robert E. Brennan, O.P., ed. (New York, Sheed, 1942), pp. 101-110, 370- 373.

Castiello, Jaime, S.J., *A Humane Psychology of Education* (New York, Sheed, 1936; Chicago, Loyola, 1964).

Castiello, Jaime, S.J., "The Psychology of Classical Training," *Thought,* vol. 10 (1936), 632-654.

Castiello, Jaime, S.J., "The Psychology of Habit in St. Thomas Aquinas," *The Modern Schoolman,* vol. 14 (1936), 8-12.

Lonergan, Bernard J., S.J., "St. Thomas's Thought on *Gratia Operans,* Part III. Habitual Grace as *Operans et Cooperans,*" *Theological Studies,* vol. 3 (1942), 69-88; a detailed analysis of the texts of St. Thomas on *habitus.*

Pegis, Anton C., "Man as Nature and Spirit," *Doctor Communis,* vol. 1 (1950), 52-63; an excellent presentation of some facets of human reason relevant to our treatment of "mastery habits."

Pinckaers, S., O.P., "Vue Synthétique sur l'analyse Thomiste de l'acte humain," in Saint Thomas d'Aquin, *Somme Theologique,* "Les Actes Humaines," I-II, qq. 6-17 (Paris, Desclée et Cie, 1962), pp. 405-449; a detailed and careful presentation of some of the points about the unity of human activity and the order of its parts of which use is also made in this study.

Renard, Henri, S.J., "Habits in the System of St. Thomas," *Gregorianum,* vol. 29 (1948), 88-117; another good philosophical analysis of "habits" stressing their relevance to the study of man.

Roton, Placide de, O.S.B., *Les habitus* (Paris, Labergerie, 1934); perhaps the best full-length study.

Experimental Evidence of the Difference Between Habits

Brownell, William A., and Moser, Harold E., "Meaningful *versus* Mechanical Learning: A Study in Grade III Subtraction," *Duke University Research Studies in Education,* No. 8 (1949).

Commins, W. D., and Fagin, Barry, *Principles of Educational Psychology,* 2nd ed. (New York, Ronald, 1954), pp. 615-776; on the different kinds of learning.

Cronbach, Lee J., *Educational Psychology* (New York, Harcourt, Brace & World, 1954); pp. 276-309, concepts and principles; pp. 310-354, learning of attitudes; pp. 355-378, learning of skills; pp. 521-554, emotional learning.

Duncker, K., "On Problem Solving," L. S. Lees, trans., *Psychological Monographs,* vol. 58, no. 5 (1945); by examining the solution to a mathematical problem, the author concludes that not all learning is associationistic.

Hilgard, Ernest R., *Introduction to Psychology*, 2nd ed. (New York, Harcourt, Brace & World, 1957), pp. 232-259; on the kinds of learning.

Katona, G., *Organization and Memorizing* (New York, Columbia, 1940); contrasts memory of solutions with understanding of principles.

Lefford, A., "The Influence of Emotional Subject Matter on Logical Reasoning," *Journal of General Psychology*, vol. 34 (1946), 127-151; on the influence of emotional habits on intellectual ones.

McKellar, Peter, *Imagination and Thinking* (New York, Basic Books, 1957).

Oldfield, R. C., "The Analysis of Human Skill," *New Biology*, vol. 13 (1952), 49-60; careful distinction between skills and "habits" which are purely automatic. The author uses the term "habit" in the sense of "automatism habit," a usage which is in harmony with the general usage of psychologists, but quite different from the one used in this book.

Tolman, E. C., "There Is More Than One Kind of Learning," *Psychological Review*, vol. 56 (1949), 144-155; distinguishes six types of learned connections and gives his interpretation and the scientific laws relating to them.

Woodworth, Robert S., *Dynamics of Behavior* (New York, Holt, Rinehart and Winston, 1958); pp. 48-75, motives and drives; pp. 134-160, control of muscular movement; pp. 221-255, types of learning.

Chapter Three

Complex Habits

THE INTERRELATIONSHIP OF POWERS

Though we investigate the powers of man one by one in order to find out which are the proper subjects of habits, we must always remember that in concrete human activity powers are in almost constant relationship. As we shall see, there are very few instances of powers acting in isolation. This fact is of great importance for the study of habits, since habits too, as acquired modifications of operative powers, are very often related to other powers or even other habits in some sort of relationship leading to composite activity. Some people seem to feel that we ought to be able to examine the entire nature of every habit simply by examining one power at a time. However, man's powers are not intended to work one at a time but in composition with other powers in complex and unified operations. As a result we must investigate not only the habits which are simply modifications of a single power, but also those complex habits which, taken adequately, are modifications of two or more powers, as well as those habit groups which involve complete habits of different powers unified in one complex operation.

As a preliminary point, we may emphasize the complex nature of most human activity by examining an ordinary act of perception. When we look out of the window at the busy street scene below, we perform a single operation and do so with great ease. Even a little reflection, however, reveals that this single operation is highly complex. Notice that reflection does not discover that what appears to be a single operation is in fact a series of discrete operations. Rather reflection reports that one apparently simple operation of perception is actually a highly complex (though still admirably unified) operation involving a number of man's operative powers. Our perception of the street scene below us obviously includes several different types of external sensation (the noise of automobiles and the newsboy's cry, the smell of exhausts and the popcorn machine, the glare of windshields and the flash of ladies' hats, the waves of heat rising from the pavement), all of which are unified into one complex sensation. It also includes such elements as images of distance and duration, as well as intellectual awareness of the beings below us and ourselves perceiving them. Most such perceptions would also involve sensory estimations of the objects perceived and sensory and rational appetitive reactions. And yet we experience only a single, highly unified operation: we perceive the street scene below us. All the operative powers involved in this perception are unobtrusive components of a single complex operation. This is the norm rather than the exception in human activity: our operative powers are intended to work in relationship with other powers.

Probably most people would agree that we do not exercise only one power at a time; many operations are going on simultaneously. This is true enough, but it is a minor point to insist on the temporal and spatial unity of a man's actions. It is much more important to realize that these simultaneous and successive activities influence and modify each other. And we need to insist, in addition, that there are various kinds of influence—as Aristotle put it, there are four *kinds* of causes. So, some activities of a man are related to each other as efficient cause and effect, but others are related as means to goal or agent to purpose, and still others are intrinsic components which specify and limit each other.

The fact that there are different kinds of unification in human activities is a basic consideration which is presupposed for any accurate understanding of complex activity. Consequently, though we have often presupposed background knowledge in other cases, it is practically necessary here to digress briefly on the different sorts of roles played by various kinds of human activity.

The most important of these differences can be seen from a consideration of the relationship between cognition and appetition in man, as well as the influence of cognition and appetition on man's motor powers. Habits are involved in the sequences of activities which we discover on this level; yet although they are involved in complex operations, they are not necessarily complex habits. For instance, we see something in front of us and by means of the proper kinesthetic sensations we guide the movements of our arm and hand to reach out and grasp it. Here we have a case of cognition leading to appetition and motor activity. For simplicity's sake, let us abstract for the moment from the intellectual awareness and rational volition involved in this series of operations. What powers and habits are operating here? First of all, there is external sensation unified by the unifying sense and reinforced with spatial images and memory associations from the imagination and with an estimation (habitual or spontaneous) from the estimative power. Second, there is an appetitive reaction to the perception, either of the desiderative appetite (if the object perceived is estimated as a pleasurable good) or perhaps of the aggressive appetite (if the object perceived is estimated as a threatening evil to be overcome or fled from). Third, there is in this case a motor activity elicited and controlled by the kinesthetic images of the imagination. Since these kinesthetic images are habitual, we have here a case of a habit involved in an operation which serves as a stimulus for another operation (of the executive powers); but we do not have an instance of a complex habit, since the only *habitual* modification present is a modification of the imagination.

We can use the analysis of St. Thomas to give further clarification of the relationship between cognition and appetition and between cognition and motor activity. Cognition, St. Thomas says, is on the side of form or specification. Things that have no knowledge at all have their activities determined entirely by their natural, physical forms (substantial forms and natural forms like structure). Thus, the activities of a plant or a mineral are determined ultimately by their substantial forms, and proximately by the accidental forms that flow from the substantial forms as their properties. In a machine, all activities are determined by a physical accidental form, its structure. A machine, however, needs in addition to its formal structure a source of energy.

A thing which has knowledge has as the basis of its activity a substantial form and the formal physical accidents that are its properties. But it has in addition other forms which are not the natural physical forms of the knower, but precisely cognitional forms. These forms "act" inasmuch as by their actual presence in the knower they modify the total structure of the agent. A dog seeing a chop in front of him is formally different from a dog who does not see it, and so his activity will be different.[1] In addition to the knowing powers, a knowing being also has appetites, which are on the side of movement, of efficiency (similar to the energy source in a machine).[2] The executive motor powers are likewise on the side of efficiency. Thus, in a dog, guidance by knowledge is a real causality (formal causality), although it is not efficient causality. The knowledge does not act upon the sensory appetite and the executive powers efficiently, any more than the structure of a machine acts upon the energy input and output.[3] Yet no one would say that the structure has no influence upon the output. In the dog, all the efficiency is at the level of sensory appetite and executive motor powers; but this efficiency is specified, determined by the dog's cognition, his awareness of the chop in front of him.

In human beings, this situation is immensely complicated by the presence of intellect and will. Intellect, as knowing power, specifies and guides activity; will, as appetite, efficiently controls activity but does so *through intellect*. Will and intellect working together (will as drive and intellect as direction of drive) can modify, in various ways, sensory awareness and thus control motor activity and sensory appetition. We know from experience that our rational powers work in close cooperation with our sensory powers, but the precise nature of their union is seldom clear and always complicated. This much can be said. Will does not act

[1] We might imagine a machine controlled by a punched card. The different patterns of holes on various cards do not *do* anything; they perform no action, yet they certainly make a real difference in the activity of the machine. The various punched cards might be likened to the cognitional forms of the knower.

[2] Sensory appetites do not produce activity in the executive motor powers directly, but only by focusing the proper kinesthetic image in sensory awareness.

[3] To say that knowledge does not act upon appetite is not to say that knowledge itself is not an activity. Indeed, knowledge itself is an operation, but its mode of operation is immanent. Knowing is not transient activity, though it may well guide (formally, not efficiently) the transient activity of the knower as well as some of his other immanent activities (such as desiring and willing).

directly upon the motor powers or the sensory appetites. It acts through and with intellect. Intellect, too, acts upon the sensory powers (in conjunction with will) only by modifying the contents of sensory awareness. The proper kinesthetic image present in sensory awareness will stimulate the motor powers to their determinate activity; the proper image-and-estimation will elicit the natural response of the sensory appetites. Sometimes the control of will-and-intellect over the sensory powers is what Aristotle called "despotic control." We exercise this kind of control over voluntary motor activities; will-and-intellect despotically (though still indirectly, i.e., through the proper kinesthetic images) controls the executive powers. At other times the control of will-and-intellect over the sensory powers is what Aristotle called "political control." We do not simply command, like a despot, and watch our command being carried out. Rather, we find that our sensory powers (here our sensory appetites) act like free men in a democracy; they can be "persuaded" but not commanded. Here will-and-intellect controls the sensory appetites only very indirectly, by gradually altering the judgment of the discursive estimation and thus modifying the complex image which is eliciting the response of the sensory appetites. In a case of despotic control, we will-and-know to move our finger; the proper kinesthetic image is recalled; the finger moves. In a case of political control, we will-and-know to feel a certain way about an object and still our feelings do not automatically obey; we modify them only by gradually changing the estimation of the discursive power and thus the image which is eliciting the appetitive reaction, the undesired feelings. When external sensation is involved in the appetitive reaction, we can of course easily modify the reaction by interfering with the external sensation which is causing it.

We may conclude from this preliminary analysis of the relationships between man's cognitive, appetitive, and executive powers, both on the sensory and on the intellectual level, that these relationships are (1) extensive, (2) complicated (i.e., multiple), and (3) often indirect. We have seen that man's powers seldom act in isolation from other powers, but many of the activities we have examined are not truly complex operations but rather stand in some sequence-relationship. For example, we have already noted that all appetites act in dependence upon cognitive powers, since the object of appetite is a known good. On the other hand, a number of the activities just described in which rational activity modifies sensory awareness are truly complex operations. Thus, the operation by which will-and-intellect carries out our rational choices is a complex operation, as is the activity in which the intellect modifies the judgment of the discursive estimation or the imagination. This extensive composition of human operations should lead us to expect that habitual modification of the operative powers involved in such complex behavior is equally complex.[4]

TYPES OF COMPOSITE HABITS

An analysis of the various types of composition present in human operations reveals three basic types which involve more than one operative power:[5]

1. Form-matter relationship in which the intellect stands in relation to some other power as substantial form is related to primary matter: e.g., intellect and imagination in the science of geometry.
2. Accident-substance relationship in which the intellect stands in relation to some other power as an accidental form is related to substance: e.g., intellect and sensory awareness in daydreaming.
3. *a.* Principal-instrumental relationship in the line of efficient causality: e.g., the intellect in the order of "creative art" efficiently moves the imagination to construct an image.
   b. Principal-instrumental relationship in the line of telic causality: e.g., the habit of intending an end makes a habit concerning some means also able to move the will.[6]

We shall now try to describe various types of complex habits prominent in human activity in terms of one or another of these three types of composite operations. We are not speaking here of

[4] It is important, of course, not to hypostatize man's operative powers into independent entities; analysis is necessary but should not distort our original experience of marvelously unified activity.

[5] Cf. G. P. Klubertanz, S.J., *The Philosophy of Human Nature* (New York, Appleton-Century-Crofts, 1953), for a more detailed discussion of composite human activity.

[6] Also see p. 198.

a simple habit (i.e., modification of a single power) which serves as a stimulus for the operation of another power (e.g., habitual kinesthetic images involved in motor activities) or which depends upon another power to present its object (e.g., love of friendship depending upon the intellect). Neither are we describing habit groups at this point; such groups involve a habitual modification in one power united in operation with a habitual modification in another power. Here we want simply to discuss complex habits, i.e., a composite modification of activity which, taken adequately, is located in two or more powers. A *simple habit* involves one habit and one power (though it may depend upon another power to present its object or may serve as a stimulus for another power); a *complex habit* involves one habit but two or more powers; a *habit group* involves two or more powers and two or more habits. All three produce habitual activity which is unified no matter how complex it is.

FORM-MATTER RELATIONSHIP

Have we seen any examples of habits which, taken adequately, are located in two or more powers related as substantial form is related to primary matter? Any habit of science answers to this description. Suppose we take the habit of mathematical reasoning. No reasoning can occur without something about which to reason (facts, data, information; at the very least, symbols and their meaning). This material must be supplied from memory; in man the power of retaining and recalling facts is a sensory power, the imagination. Thus the mathematician must use his intellect (to understand relationships, etc.) *and* his imagination (to supply the right symbols, etc.) when he is reasoning mathematically. Moreover, the images used in scientific reasoning must be supplied in a certain order. Thus a good mathematician must have certain symbols and formulae at his finger tips, and must be able to recall them in the right order; he cannot be continually looking them up and putting them in sequence. But *order* is a work of intellect. When we say that a mathematician needs an ordered series of images readily available when he reasons mathematically, we are pointing out the composite nature of the habit of mathematics. There are not two habits involved in mathematics, one in the imagination and the other in the intellect. There is only one habit, located partly in the imagination (which supplies the symbols and other images which the intellect requires) and partly in the intellect (which uses the symbols supplied by the imagination in a meaningful way to express abstract relationships). The unified activity of mathematical reasoning, under analysis, turns out to be a composite activity of intellect and imagination, flowing from a composite habit of intellect and imagination. Both powers must be modified if the operation of mathematical reasoning is to take place. Understanding of formal relationships cannot occur without symbols to express such relationships, and understanding will be impeded unless these symbols are apt and readily available, standardized and distinct from one another. Neither can mathematical understanding take place unless the intellect grasps the relationships involved and gives "meaning" to the symbols supplied by the imagination. An example of the absence of the intellectual component of such a complex habit occurs when a student who has all the necessary information for a scientific demonstration still does not comprehend the order involved. Thus, a student of geometry may understand each individual word of a proposition but not grasp the import of the proposition, or he may understand each step of a proof but still "not see it." This need for "meaningful symbols, meaningfully ordered" highlights the composite nature of the habit of mathematics.

How are the two powers involved in such a composite habit related? The intellect's role is a determining one: intellect orders the images; intellect gives *formal* structure and meaning to the *materials* supplied by the imagination. These materials are of themselves almost structureless, highly determinable. They require the ordering influence of intellect. Thus ability to handle mathematical relationships and their implications is formally an intellectual ability, materially an imaginative ability. The habit of science which we call mathematics is a composite habit, located formally in the intellect and materially in the imagination. The analogy here, of course, is the relationship of substantial form to primary matter in material substances. Form makes a material substance what-it-is; it specifies and determines it to be this kind of thing. Matter is the determinable element in a material substance, that which is specified and structured by form. Mathematics and other habits of science are composed of a formal element (a modification of the intellect) and a material element (a modification of the imagination). They are not material substances; they are *habits*. But the manner of their composition somewhat resembles the composition of material substances. Therefore, the relationship between their component elements is one of form-to-matter in an analogous sense of those terms.

It is easy to see that other habits of science besides mathematics are complex habits of the intellect and the imagination related as substantial form to primary matter. The physical sciences need sense data (supplied by the imagination, the sensory memory of man) upon which they impose organization (the work of intellect). Normally this organization is in terms of mathematical or representational structures called "constructs." Without this organization the flow of images is structureless and useless for science. Scientific symbolism involves both intellect and imagination. Philosophy and related disciplines try to explain the evidence of reality according to basic insights and first principles leading to an organized body of philosophical conclusions. To do this they require the proper images of reality supplied in a suitable order by the imagination and the understanding of these images by the intellect. The habit of philosophy thus involves a habitual modification of the intellect and a habitual modification of the imagination.

The intellectual habits of opinion also illustrate the form-to-matter relationship of intellect and imagination, although not to the same degree as habits of science. Primary matter in material substances is purely determinable; it has no structure of its own apart from substantial form. The symbols supplied by the imagination in scientific reasoning are more like primary matter than the symbols supplied in operations of opinion. Scientific symbols are almost entirely structureless apart from the ordering influence of intellect; the imaginative components of habits of opinion are much less under the ordering influence of intellect. Most habits of opinion, however, seem to be basically intellectual, at least in a minimal sense, and therefore are instances of form-to-matter

composition. A few types of opinion (such as prejudice and superstition) are perhaps better classified as accident-to-substance com-
posites. We shall take up this type of composition in complex
habits immediately after we discuss the kind of composition involved in habitual discursive estimations.

We have seen that the very nature of the *discursive* estimation
in man is to make concrete sensory judgments of good or evil
under the guidance and control of intellect. Whenever this power
acquires a habitual modification, therefore (except in abnormal
behavior connected with unconscious activities of the imagination or panic reactions), that modification will be the material
part of a complex habit, the formal part of which is a modification
of the intellect. When we come habitually to *like* praying or
studying or dealing with small and noisy children, we have acquired a complex habit in which intellect and discursive estimation are related as form-to-matter.

ACCIDENT-SUBSTANCE RELATIONSHIP

We have examined habits in which the intellect is related to
the imagination or discursive power as substantial form is related
to primary matter. Such habits are *essentially* intellectual (just as
substantial form makes a material substance essentially what-it-
is). We shall now inquire whether man possesses any complex
habits which involve an intellectual element but which are not
essentially intellectual. Since intellect is always present as a formal, determining power, such habits are analogous to the composite of accident and substance. Just as the accidental determination of shape or size further qualifies the substance which it
modifies without changing it essentially, so the intellectual element in a composite habit can further determine a modification
in another power without changing it essentially. A rubber ball
can change in shape without ceasing to be rubber. Intellect can
be a component of a complex habit without making that habit
essentially intellectual. For instance, we have all experienced habitual daydreaming, both in ourselves and others. Let us examine
this habit. The daydreamer is not a brute; his intellect is active;
he understands while he is daydreaming. But if there is a habitual

pattern of daydreaming, it is not a logical one, but is governed
by the laws of imagination: continuity and sensible similarity.
This is an example of a complex habit which is not essentially
intellectual even though intellect is one of its components. Daydreaming is essentially imaginative. Intellect is present and present (as always) as determining form, not determinable matter.
But the intellect's formal determination here is not substantial
but accidental. Intellect is here related to imagination as accidental form is related to substance. Other instances of complex
habits which are accidentally (but formally) intellectual and substantially imaginative are certain opinion-habits like prejudice
and superstition.

PRINCIPAL-INSTRUMENTAL EFFICIENT CAUSE RELATIONSHIP

Sometimes the relationship of the intellect to the imagination
or the discursive estimation is more like an efficient cause using an
instrument than an intrinsic formal cause determining matter or
substance. This is particularly true of the creative activity of the
intellect. The creative mathematician or poet or physicist *makes*
symbols of the imagination to express his new concepts. After he
has created these symbols, his intellect "informs" and orders them
in a form-to-matter relationship, but the work of creation itself is
a work of efficiency. Such efficiency, of course, depends upon the
will and intellect working in composition; but what is produced
is a new image in the imagination, a new formal structure on the
sensory level. Similarly, the intellect (working under the impetus
of the will and in close composition with the will) *effects* a modified judgment of the discursive power; it works with this power
to produce an intellectually determined sensory judgment. A person learns to *like* to study or pray, because his intellect and discursive power (and imagination, normally) work together as
principal and instrumental causes to produce a modified habitual
sensory judgment. Once the habit is acquired, it operates as a
complex habit of intellect and discursive power related as substantial form is related to primary matter.

HABIT GROUPS

A *complex habit* involves two or more powers but only one habit. A *habit group* involves two or more powers and two or more habits (which may themselves be complex). It is a sign of the intricate nature of human habitual activity that most such activity involves not only complex habits but also habit groups. These habit groups are of two kinds. *Necessary* habit groups are such that none of their component habits work properly unless they all work together. *Contingent* habit groups are such that their component habits can exist in isolation or in different groupings. To have a group and not merely a collection of habits, a definite order is necessary among the component habits. This normally produces a complex form-to-matter relationship: one element of the habit group is purely determinable, others are both determinable and determining, and one is purely determining. There can be no habit group without order, i.e., internal relationships. Otherwise there is a mere collection, a hodgepodge. In a *necessary* habit group, in which the component habits cannot exist in their perfection apart from the rest, the order or relationships are intrinsic to the habits concerned. In a *contingent* habit group, in which the component habits can exist in isolation or in different groupings, the order or relationships are extrinsic to the habits concerned, are rationally imposed upon them.

The most important instance of a habit group in man involves the habits of the sensory appetites. When we analyzed the habitual modifications of the sensory appetites, we found that they were consistent modes of tendency. For example, a person can acquire a habit of consistently overreacting, underreacting, or properly reacting to pleasurable or difficult goods. The passions of desire (aversion), daring (fear), and anger are involved here. "Proper" reaction of the sensory appetites means that they respond to a particular object in a manner proportioned or suitable to that object. Now, what is this "proportioned" or "suitable" response? It involves a relationship of object to subject. It is not a single object which is determinate but must be determined in each instance. Temperance does not consist in eating only so many ounces of food daily but in eating a "suitable" amount of food. How much is suitable? One has to consider the individual, the circumstances, and the object (e.g., hungry, sick, working hard, holiday, unappetizing food, etc.). But how is the standard of suitability determined? Such a relationship can only be determined by the intellect. Where a standard can be embodied in a fixed way, as in a foot measure, meter stick, clock, scale, etc., then it is set once and for all by reason; it is "standardized" in a concrete fashion. But the standard of suitability in sensory appetition cannot be "standardized," cannot be fixed once and for all. It must be determined in each instance; a formal measure is required, and formal measures do not exist in the real order. Thus intellect must step in and determine the standard each time. Intellect is involved in any determination of formal measure. Even where the standard determined upon is not suitable (objectively speaking) but rather excessive or deficient, intellect is required. So we see that habits of consistent modes of tendency in the sensory appetites involve both appetite and the formal determination of intellect.

Yet a little reflection will make it clear that something else is needed. Sensory appetite responds to the sensorily known good. Intellect cannot impose a "suitable response" on the sensory appetite directly; the "measure" must reach the sensory appetite through the concrete sensory judgment of the discursive power, judging under the guidance of intellect. Thus a habit of the sensory appetite which produces a proportioned, "suitable" response to the individual objects of appetition involves a habit group. This is, first of all, a real acquired modification in the sensory appetite itself, a consistent mode of tendency. A temperate person actually *feels* the suitable appetitive response to an object of the desiderative appetite. Thus the virtue of temperance is *substantially* a habit of the desiderative appetite. Besides this habit in the desiderative appetite, there is another *complex* habit of the intellect and discursive estimation, in which intellect is related to discursive power as substantial form to primary matter. This is the habit of determining the suitable response to a particular object of the desiderative appetite in a concrete sensory judgment which can directly affect sensory appetition. Yet neither the habitual modification of the desiderative appetite nor the habitual modification of the intellect-and-discursive-power are independent habits. They are joined together to form a habit group in which the habit of the intellect-and-discursive-power is related to the habit of the desiderative appetite as accidental form is related to substance. Thus the virtue of temperance is substantially in the desiderative appetite, accidentally (but formally) in the intellect-and-discursive-power. Since the order by which the two habits are related to one another is in this instance an intrinsic one (i.e., the consistent mode of tendency in the desiderative appetite could not exist apart from the concrete sensory judgment of "measure"), this particular habit group is a *necessary* habit group. Since our example deals with the desiderative appetite, the substantial habit in this habit group is the virtue of *temperance*. The corresponding modification of the aggressive appetite is called *fortitude*. The complex habit of determining what is the suitable reaction in a particular case is located formally in the intellect, materially in the discursive power; it is called the virtue of *prudence*. As we shall see later in our discussion of the cardinal virtues, this complex virtue of prudence can also be related to the virtue of *justice* in the will (as accidental form to substance, again) in another necessary habit group.

Still other habit groups which are prominent in human activity are the practical and the fine arts. If art is considered as a kind of knowledge (and this is the only way St. Thomas and his contemporaries considered it), it can be defined by the traditional phrase *"recta ratio factibilium,"* which might be translated into modern American idiom by the term "know-how." This is certainly an element of art. Yet the knowledge factor of art, taken in abstraction from all the other factors involved, is not sufficient to make a man an artist. After all, if he lost his arms, he would retain the knowledge factor but could no longer produce works of art. Therefore art is not adequately expressed in terms of the knowledge factor. Material movements, skillfully directed, are also involved in art. Of course, such movements do not themselves constitute an art. One could build a machine to turn out reproductions of some picture by the thousands. But the art product

here is a *reproduction* of the "Mona Lisa"; it is an example of
some engraver's art, not of the art of da Vinci. Hence we can conclude that both a knowledge factor and the skillful execution of
material movements are elements of any habit of art.[7] Moreover,
the knowledge factor itself is highly complex, as even a surface
analysis reveals. Mere intellectual knowledge is insufficient for
art. Knowledge of a particular sensible thing is required; the imagination (and often the external senses) are active, as well as the
discursive estimation. There is often, especially in the fine arts,
strong appetitive reaction to the objects of sensory awareness. Art
is both "rational" and "emotional." It is certainly not purely intellectual.

Thus we see that habits of art are actually habit groups. The relationships among the various habits involved are sometimes necessary, sometimes contingent. They vary a great deal from art to
art, and even more from the practical arts to the fine arts. For instance, intellect can be related to imagination as form-to-matter,
as it is in engineering or applied science. In the fine arts, on the
other hand, it is normally related to imagination as accident-to-
substance.[8] Some types of art have little emotional content; others
emphasize the emotional aspect of an art object. Creative art
would seem to require a vivid imagination, or at least one that is

[7] It is obvious that there is a vast difference between a motor skill and an
art. A motor skill is a habitual modification of the imagination which organ-
izes perception and controls kinesthetic images and thus stimulates the executive powers to smooth and successful motor activity. Motor skills are normally automatism habits; they operate with a minimum of conscious volition
but can be brought under fuller control. Art involves a great deal of intellectual activity and cannot operate "automatically." For example, some typists
type voluntarily, in that their typing is not a pure automatism, but is started
and continued under the command of reason. But typists who have only this
much control are the mechanically perfect typists who type what is in front of
them according to some mechanical rule but who are not good secretaries.
Another sort of typist controls the typing itself by a rational control: she can
set up a good looking page, correct misspelling and bad grammar, reorder
sentences. Such a typist can be left to her own judgment; she has not merely
the skill but the art of typing.

[8] Some artists have tried to produce an entirely nonrational art; for example, some modern finger-painters seem to be striving for purely sensory activity,
for a product *without meaning*. But then, some advocates of the meaningless
think that the world is really without meaning—so the meaninglessness itself
has meaning!

not merely reproductive;[9] in the composite activity, the imagination must play a "substantial" role, not merely a "material" one. Copyists, in contrast, need great manual skill but require little creative imagination.

An explanation of all the powers and habits involved in the production of a work of art is very difficult. Any *single* detailed explanation to fit all types of art activity is impossible; even a preliminary analysis must be both quite complex and certainly quite tentative. We must beware here of both the authority of Aristotle (who seems to have been something of a rationalist in his theory of art) and of the pronouncements of certain contemporary artists (who are, by their own confession, anti-intellectuals). This much can certainly be said: Intellect has a place in art, but (at least in the case of the fine arts) imagination has a more prominent place. Both are important. A knowledge of optics will not make a man a great artist, but until the basic laws of perspective were discovered, painters were limited in what they could do. Just as materials and motor skills have an important but not exclusive role in the production of an art work, so do intellect and imagination.

The role of the intellect in the production of an art work seems to be twofold: it provides a knowledge of how to achieve the product and a knowledge of its rational meaning. Both of these will differ greatly in the different kinds of art. In aesthetic experience, on the other hand, the knowing-how is often of no importance.

Along with meaning, most theories of aesthetics investigate the area of the imagination. The imaginative construction of the art object (or its reconstruction in the case of the spectator) is perhaps the most important part of art. Again, the precise role of the imagination varies in the different kinds of arts. In some it seems to be largely concerned with the production of the exemplar itself (as in sculpture, painting, music), but in others (as in poetry) its role is more concerned with concrete meanings.

The importance of appetition and thus of the discursive estima-

---

[9] Galton's study showed that several artists did not have good visual imagery. It would seem to be almost impossible that one could be a successful artist if he could not concretize in some sensible way what he wanted to express.

tion also varies widely. A totally unemotional nonevaluative art
can be only useful art. But the precise role of appetitive response
is very hard to determine. Surely, extrinsic appetitive response is
artificial, false, and to be rejected, as real artists always reject sen-
timental art. But even in the most extreme rejection, in the most
astringent sort of unemotional art, powerful emotions are gen-
erated. It seems, therefore, that one cannot deny the element of
emotion.

The importance of rational meaning and of the consequent
volitional response is a controversial point. Artistic products like
the tragedies of Sophocles and Shakespeare clearly demand that
the role of the intellect in art not be limited merely to supplying
the "know-how" required to express the artistic image (in verse,
color and form, sound, marble, etc.). The artistic image itself is
full of *meaning*, and this is the work of the intellect, distinct from
its "know-how."[10] This meaning is accompanied by an appetitive
reaction of the will, which "enjoys" the beautiful image as an
object the very knowledge of which gives pleasure. This meaning-
factor and its appetitive response are present even in extremely
nonrepresentational art (e.g., the abstract paintings of Mon-
drian), where at least the spatial relationships portrayed have
meaning. But the extent of such "meaning" varies greatly from
work to work and from genre to genre. This explains, in part, the
need for *interpretation* in reciting poetry or performing a musical
score.

Somewhat related to the habits of art and of aesthetic appreciation are those complex habit groups that have been singled out
by some investigators as being common to many kinds of art, or to
many cultures, and the like. The fact seems to be well established.
Some metaphors, symbols, and even rather extensive stories, such
as "myths," are found in widely separated cultures, and are effective in the same way for many different people.[11] Thus, also, the

[10] The work of Ernst Cassirer and Susanne Langer on symbolism emphasizes
the role of meaning in connection with the artistic image.

[11] C. G. Jung and his followers have published the results of extensive investigations into literature, legend, art, religion, and the like. The theory of
"archetypes" is an attempt to explain the nature and genesis of these clusters.
It is not clear that this is the only explanation, and it seems that perhaps there
is no single explanation for all the elements.

effective speaker does not merely know how to apply the rules of rhetoric to his matter, he has, as we say, a "feeling" for just the emotion-laden symbols, images, and so on, that will move his audience the way he wants them to go. A good term for these various objects is "image clusters."

Because image clusters are connected with emotion, and because simple images by themselves do not directly lead to emotion, we can be sure that estimations are included in them. Consequently also, they cannot be merely simple retained images giving back simple experiences, but rather patterned groups of images and estimations. Hence, it is correct to think of them as instances of complex habits.

At the center of the image cluster there seems to be a set of experiences that is rather simple and direct, for example, those concerned with food, warmth, safety, family relationships, and the like. These may be culturally and historically determined, but it seems that they cannot be purely artificial. These experiences are emotionally toned, and so tend to gather around them other experiences of a similar emotional tone according to the general rule of association. At the same time, the image cluster can become elaborated by absorbing similar, contemporaneous, or otherwise related objects.

It seems that such image clusters are developed without much reflection or planning. Perhaps in some cases they are never brought to full awareness. But a great artist may be just the kind of person who is able to notice such image clusters in himself and to advert to the possibility that others have had the same experiences. Once he brings such an image cluster to attention, it can well become a consciously held symbol or myth for a whole group. Of course, once such an image cluster has entered into the culture of a group, its formation in the younger members of the group is made much more likely.

Finally, we will conclude our examination of habit groups by looking at the habit group of friendship, which is a *contingent*[12]

---

[12] To say that friendship is a contingent habit group is not to say that it is unimportant. Even if we prescind from the role of friendship with Christ in the life of grace, friendships are one of man's greatest goods and exercise great influence in the lives of most men.

habit group, one in which the component parts can exist in isolation or in different groupings. What we ordinarily mean by
friendship is a variable and complex affair involving many elements. Descriptively, friendship involves an act of the will, the
so-called "love of friendship,"[13] and also the knowledge that the
friendship is reciprocated by the friend. In addition, friendship
usually involves sensory affection, especially if the friendship is at
all intense. Often, too, memories of shared experiences enter into
friendship. Thus, friendship normally involves not only intellect
and will, but also habits of the imagination, discursive estimation,
and sensory appetites.

However, it is also clear that these factors are variable. Evidently, at the beginning of a friendship the memories of shared
experiences will be less inclusive than they are later on, and in
some cases the sharing of common experiences will have been
rather indirect. It is possible that a friendship arise between
people who have never met face to face. Then, too, the factor of
sensory affection can vary a great deal, so much so that in some
cases it is barely discoverable. On the contrary, there can be memories of shared experiences by people who are not, or at least are
no longer, friends. There can also be affection where there is no
love of friendship at all. Therefore, the habits involved in friendship can and sometimes do exist separately or in other combinations; their union and order in a given friendship constitutes a
contingent habit group.

KINDS OF COMPLEX HABITS AND HABIT GROUPS

As a final question in this chapter on complex habits, we may
ask which of the habits and habit groups we have examined involve mastery habits and which involve automatism habits or
pure automatisms. Complex habits or habit groups in which the
intellect enters as a necessary formal (either accidental or substantial) element are obviously mastery habits, habits which can operate only under conscious volition. This includes most of the
habits or habit groups discussed in this chapter: science, opinion,
prudence, the appetitive habits related to prudence as substance

13 We will deal with this act in detail later.

is related to its accident (i.e., temperance, fortitude, and justice),
friendship, even daydreaming; all are mastery habits.[14] The only
automatism habits we have discussed in this chapter are those involved in motor skills, where the imagination usually operates
with a minimum of conscious volition and sometimes acquires a
pure automatism (i.e., a habit which can no longer be brought
under the influence of conscious volition, at least not without
some training). However, most of the complex habits and habit
groups we examined had as material or substantial components
habitual modifications of the imagination or the discursive estimation or both. There is always the possibility that these elements
may "get away" from the control of reason. When this happens,
they cease to be material or substantial parts of mastery habits
and become automatism habits.

This situation becomes clear when we examine an experience
we have discussed before. When a person with the vice of intemperance (a mastery habit in which an excessive response to
pleasurable goods by the desiderative appetite is consciously
willed in union with the discursive estimation) is "converted" or
"reformed," he rationally determines that he will never again act
in excess with regard to pleasurable goods. He is sincere; his acts
of intellect and will are intense. Yet he still experiences great difficulty. He discovers that he still sensibly *desires* pleasurable goods
in an excessive manner. What is the cause of this excessive desire?
The substantial part of his previous mastery habit of intemperance is still present in the desiderative appetite, but it is now
functioning as an automatism habit. The "convert" finds he must
rationally control this automatism habit; he must fight for mastery. It is true that he gradually develops a new habitual modification in his desiderative appetite which serves as the substantial
component of his new mastery habit of temperance, but until this
occurs (and it never occurs in some "converts," since it must be
consciously willed), he has to struggle with an automatism habit
which leads him to desire excessively. Sometimes (e.g., in drug ad-

---

[14] Daydreaming is not simply a stream of structureless images; the images
have some "meaning" even when they are not ordered by intellect. Yet daydreaming is an example of a mastery habit (not a particularly good one,
either) which can easily break up into an automatism habit in the imagination
and structureless thought in the intellect.

diction) the remnants of a previous vice include not only automatism habits (which can, with effort, be controlled by conscious
volition) but also physical dispositions and pure automatisms
(which cannot be controlled except by physical means and special
training, respectively).

A similar phenomenon is observed when complex habits of the
intellect and the imagination or the intellect and the discursive
estimation are changed. The material components of the previous
mastery habits remain as automatism habits until new material
components (habitual modifications) of the new mastery habits
are acquired in the imagination or the discursive estimation. A
person who once had an erroneous opinion has to work to bring
his images and estimation into line with this new (and correct)
opinion. The man who all his life has felt and rationally approved
of aversion for children does not grow to *like* children overnight,
even when he consciously wills to do so.

It is worth noting that people find themselves fighting undesirable automatism habits even when they never had the corresponding mastery habits. Such automatisms cannot be the substantial components of previous mastery habits. How are they
acquired? If men always acted fully rationally, automatism habits
in the sensory appetites, the imagination, and the discursive estimation which should be under the control of reason would only
be acquired as the substantial or material components of mastery
habits. The fact is, however, that men often do not act fully rationally. Children act and have to act before they have the use of
reason. Young people and people not so young often act irrationally. When they do this habitually, automatism habits or even
pure automatisms are acquired without rational control. Furthermore, even people who are seriously endeavoring to acquire virtue
make many mistakes in the process. If they develop habits that
are not under the control of reason, they are faced with the problem of breaking them, even though they developed such automatisms with the best of intentions. People with the wrong notion of premarital chastity sometimes acquire a repugnance to
any use of their sex organs. Now, to feel repugnance to sex as
such is an automatism habit, not a virtue. St. Thomas says that to
feel even shame is a sign of imperfect virtue. To live the married

life, people with such an automatism must try to destroy it and substitute the virtue of chastity which subjects the tendencies of the desiderative appetite to the control of right reason. The problems and methods involved in acquiring and destroying both automatism and mastery habits will be discussed in the following chapter.

SUMMARY

In this chapter we have discussed complex habits and habit groups. We began by noting the composite activity which is characteristic of human operations. We saw that a *simple habit* involves one habit and one power (although it may depend upon another power to present its proper object). A *complex habit* involves one habit but two or more powers, each of which possesses a habitual modification which is a component element of the complex habit. The component elements of complex habits may be related as form-to-matter, as accident-to-substance, or as principal-efficient-cause-to-instrumental-efficient-cause. If intellect is one of the component elements, it is always related to the other elements as form (either substantial or accidental). If will or sensory appetite is one of the component elements, it is always related to intellect as substance-to-accident. The principal-instrumental-efficient-cause or final-cause relationship is found in the use of the other powers by intellect or will in creative activity or in activity which has a multiple ordering. A *habit group* involves not only two or more powers but also two or more habits (which may be complex themselves). Necessary habit groups (like the cardinal virtues and some arts) are such that none of their component habits work properly unless they all work together. Contingent habit groups (like friendship) are such that their component habits can exist in isolation or in different groupings. Most complex habits and habit groups involve the intellect and hence are properly mastery habits. Pure automatisms or automatism habits exist not only in the motor skills of the imagination but also as remnants (material or substantial components) of old mastery habits or as habits acquired without the direction of reason.

SOURCES FOR CHAPTER THREE

Note: Very rarely have authors elaborated on the unity-in-complexity of human activity. We can note that almost all contemporary psychologists strongly reject "psychological atomism," that Gestalt and field theories of perception insist on the mutual influence of acts and objects, that recent work on perception has emphasized the influence of attitudes and emotions on what we perceive, and so on. But there has been very little work done on the *kinds* of influence that take place. For an analysis of St. Thomas Aquinas's views on this unity, see the following articles: "The Unity of Human Activity," *The Modern Schoolman,* vol. 27 (1950), 75-103; and "St. Thomas and the Knowledge of the Singular," *The New Scholasticism,* vol. 26 (1952), 135-166.

Chapter Four

Importance,
Growth and Destruction,
and Generalization of Habits

In this chapter we shall consider three questions: (1) Why is it important for man to acquire and perfect habits? (2) How do the habitual modifications of the various operative powers of man grow, and how are they destroyed? (3) How are specific habits generalized but not overgeneralized? The first question will show that man needs a complicated structure of habits to live a full human life. The second will reveal the role of intensity and repetition in the acquisition or breaking of habits in the various powers. The third will handle the important problem of transfer of training in man.

MAN'S NEED FOR HABITS

Granted that such things as habits are possible, why should man bother with them? A common attitude could be expressed this way: in order to live a life that is, morally speaking, perfect, one need only follow his conscience accurately in every act; and for this all that is necessary is sincerity and good will, or love. With one qualification, this is a good description, and the qualification is this: provided that his conscience is judging correctly. One judges correctly if his rational judgment is enlightened and strengthened by prudence (and grace), otherwise in the complexity of concrete circumstances human judgment falters. A lax or blinded or ignorant conscience does not bring about a good act; ignorance may indeed excuse a person from responsibility altogether, but this is not the same thing as performing a good act.[1] If, then, a person acts according to a well-informed and delicate conscience, all he needs is a "sincere" (that is, unencumbered) "good will" (or, rightly ordered will). In order to have this situation, all other powers except the will must be rightly ordered by their proper habits and the will itself ordered by its own intrinsic habits. So the alleged simplification of allowing pure love to follow conscience, when examined carefully, does not eliminate the need for habits.[2]

There are other and quite different questions about the need for habits. Thus, the objection is sometimes given that this whole view implies a very low opinion of man. Does not the indetermination of a power which can be modified by a habit bespeak imperfection? Yes, indetermination implies imperfection in one order, but it may at the same time imply that the order is a very high one, ultimately capable of great perfection. For example, a mineral has no indetermination, no imperfection of operation. It is perfect in its line of operation from the very beginning. But then, this is a very imperfect line. A human baby is much more helpless than a baby animal, and for a much longer time. But the human baby has possibilities that the baby animal does not have. The indetermination of the baby's powers of activity implies that the baby is very imperfect in the order of rational behavior, but precisely because it does have the power of reason it is capable of much greater perfection than the more fully determined animal can ever attain.[3]

Further, it is necessary that the animal powers in man be indeterminate. Man has intellect and will; he is free. But if his animal powers were completely determined by nature, man's freedom would extend only to the external world; it would not bear upon himself. Man would then be capable of reworking matter, but not of achieving a character. The scope of his responsibility would

[1] See p. 186, n. 12.

[2] The meaning and nature of love are examined in greater detail, pp. 226-230.

[3] See St. Thomas Aquinas, *On the Virtues*, q. 1, art. 8 ad 10; and *In I Ep. ad Corinth.*, cap. 11, lect. 3.

extend to lesser things, but would not include the greatest responsibility of all, himself.

But why must the powers of man be further determined by relatively permanent habitual modifications? Would it not be better to work out the necessary determination each time? It is of course possible in any given case to elaborate deliberately the order and determination which an act must have to be successful; otherwise habits could never get started. But what is possible in a single case, and in all cases taken distributively, is not possible in all cases taken cumulatively. And man so lives in time that his life is cumulative. What is a slight burden the first time is more difficult the second time and becomes irritating and finally impossible as it is repeated again and again.

Moreover, cases are not simple. It is true that one can get himself into the disposition required for any given action, *if* he has the time and there are no interferences. But in fact we do not always have the time to deliberate; often action must proceed promptly. What is still worse, often there are pulls and counterpulls. The work of deliberation in a welter of passion does not go easily. The problems of living a fully human life are too involved to be resolved all over again each time they come up.

What human life would be if we tried to make our way on what we can think up on each particular occasion in the light of our own personal experience is vividly brought out by several well-authenticated cases of human beings who grew up away from all human contacts.[4] The so-called "wolf-children," who were abandoned by their parents in infancy and were "adopted" by animals show the great need man has not only for habits, but for habits developed in dependence on others. The behavior of these children was animal-like; when they were found by kindhearted neighbors, they were unable to acquire more than a very limited amount of what we think of as normal human accomplishments. Most of them were able to learn to talk, but acquired only a limited vocabulary which they were able to use only inade-

[4] Accounts of more than thirty cases have been published; of these, several are careful, detailed firsthand accounts. For a recent summary and evaluation of the literature, see J. Timothy Sprehe, S.J., "Feral Man and Social Animal," *American Catholic Sociological Review*, vol. 22 (1961), 161-167.

quately. Science and art, as well as the refinements of gesture and carriage, seemed to be beyond their concrete possibilities. Nevertheless, where their benefactors' patience and skill were up to the task, they were able to show basic human traits.

As a result, there is no single case in which habit can be said to be absolutely necessary: any action can proceed without habit. But over the long haul and under all sorts of adverse conditions, habits are necessary whenever there are many actions to be performed by a power which is not itself fully determinate. This necessity extends not only to isolated habits but includes whole habit groups and even groups of habit groups (such as the four cardinal virtues, each of which is a habit group composed in turn of several complex habits).

Finally, habits make for the perfection of an act. This can easily be seen in some motor skills: the trained athlete acts not only more consistently and rapidly than the unskilled person, but also his actions are usually smooth. The ballerina executes her intricate steps not only flawlessly but also gracefully. So, too, the trained thinker not only reaches correct conclusions easily, but he does this with a sureness of touch and a competence which the student laboriously working out a single conclusion can desire but not attain. Similarly, the just man not only does what is just voluntarily but with pleasure. It is for him not a difficult choice, but a harmonious expression of an integrated character. Even an evil man, when he is an accomplished rogue, shows a certain attractiveness and harmony of behavior. The skill and perfection of act which accompanies a habit enable the person who possesses the habit to achieve difficult tasks which are possible but unachieved velleities for others. The performers at a track and field meet do not merely do better what most of the spectators could do after a fashion; they do what most of the spectators simply could not accomplish. Similarly, the advanced thinker can formulate and solve problems which the beginner cannot even understand. Habits make for the perfection of an act, true; but for this reason they also make possible acts which the indeterminate power practically cannot perform without the habit.

GROWTH OF HABITS

We have already had occasion to comment in passing on the way in which habits are acquired and lost in the various operative powers of man. It is obvious that different powers are further determined by habits in different ways. We have pointed out that it is a serious mistake to attempt to "make or break" all habits in the same manner in which motor skills are acquired or destroyed. We must respect the nature of the particular power which is being modified by a habitual modification. Furthermore, since the process by which habits are destroyed is similar to but not identical with the process by which they are acquired, we shall have to treat first the acquisition of habits and then discuss the destruction of habits.

How is it possible for a habit to increase? It would seem that the action either is ordered or not; in the first case, the habit is present, in the second, it is totally absent. This is obviously not a practical difficulty but a theoretical one; it was discovered by the Stoics, who held that a virtue is either present or not, and that a habit cannot increase if this would mean an essential change. Thus we can also say that a habit is not formally changed when it grows or increases. Thus, if a person knows mathematics, it is the same mathematics he knows whether he knows it as a beginner or as a proficient mathematician. But his relation to his habit is different; as a beginner, he hardly possesses the habit at all, as an accomplished expert, he has made it entirely his own, has deeply impressed it in his intellect. St. Thomas says this metaphorically: a habit grows "by getting deeper roots in the power."

Habits in different powers are acquired in different ways, and mastery habits will be developed in a different manner than automatism habits or pure automatisms. But all habits have one thing in common: *the activity by which a habit is acquired and grows is of the same sort as the activity which is the act of that habit.* With this fact in mind, we shall examine the habitual modifications of the various determinable powers of man to see how such modifications are acquired. We shall ask two questions in each case: (1)

Is intensity a factor in the acquisition of the habit? (2) Is repetition required for the acquisition of the habit?

Motor Habits

We have already seen that all that is necessary for the acquisition of a motor skill is that we go through the proper motions with a minimum of conscious volition. Freedom is not required; neither is understanding. We may perform the motor activity reluctantly, passionately, or phlegmatically; it makes little difference. Intensity is not a factor in the acquisition of motor skills. We can acquire them by simply repeating the motions of a demonstrator. Of course, we can have the principles involved in the skill explained to us as we go through the motions and thus combine understanding and repetition of the proper act. But this is not necessary. In some types of training (e.g., learning to dress oneself as a child), it is even more efficient not to reflect on what one is doing; one need only be awake and follow the pattern. Other types of training (especially if the subjects are adults) proceed most efficiently if some explanation is added along with repetition of the proper act of motor activity. This is always true if we are interested not so much in developing a highly specific skill and no more, but rather in developing a specific skill which can later be generalized or transferred to other (similar) objects. Here instruction in the basic principles involved is desirable, even if it slightly prolongs the period of training. One technique which does *not* work well is to begin training by sheer repetition of a demonstrated pattern and then in the middle of the training period switch to a combination of instruction and repetition of the proper act. This causes interference and results in inaccurate and impaired learning of the motor skill.

Since intensity counts for so little and repetition counts for so much in the acquisition of a motor skill, can we not say that such learning is purely mechanical? Freedom and understanding are unnecessary and sometimes undesirable. All that is required is that a person be awake and repeat the proper activity often enough. Why is not this acquisition explained by a purely mechanical or physical modification? For example, why can we not say that acquiring a motor habit is like creasing a paper or running a chisel in a groove? Obviously, there are some similarities, and this is to be expected, since men and animals are material organisms. But there are also differences. In the first place, motor skills are at least partly guided by cognition, at least at the sensory level. Secondly, many researchers have pointed out that motivation (which involves an appetitive response) cannot be totally neglected in accounting for the acquisition of motor skills. Thirdly, there is evidence to show that both discrimination and organization of perception must be admitted. Finally, we mentioned in our first discussion of motor skills that the essential elements are (1) the organization of perfection and (2) proper kinesthetic imagery, both of which are modifications of the imagination. These modifications aid in the control of the executive or motor powers of man. If a person's motor activity is habitually modified, we must conclude that he possesses habitually modified imaginative impulses to which his motor powers respond. Motor activity of this sort, therefore, always involves sensory cognition (though this may be subconscious or even in rare cases unconscious).

There is another type of motor activity which does not involve the imagination, namely, reflex activity (to which can be added the activity of the smooth muscles controlled by the autonomic nervous system). Men and animals possess many natural reflex responses (often called "unconditional" or "unconditioned" reflexes), such as the iris reflex; these bring about accurate and successful responses to their proper stimuli without sensory cognition being involved, at least not as an intervening cause. Since natural reflexes are not learned, they are not pertinent to our discussion of acquired habitual modifications of activity.

However, there are also acquired reflexes, often called "conditioned" or "conditional" reflexes. Since the classical cases are so well known, they will be presented very briefly. A response (for example, secreting saliva) will follow upon a conditional stimulus (the sound of a buzzer), if the conditional stimulus is presented slightly prior to the presentation of the natural, or innate, stimulus (sight of food). When these facts were first presented, it was thought that they were capable of an entirely mechanical explanation, and the case was taken as the paradigm of all learning. But further study has cast doubt on the possibility of interpreting all learning as conditioning. Moreover, psychologists have stressed the function of an attitude of expectancy in the working of conditioning (some call this a "set"). Moreover, the "extinction" of a conditioning in the absence of reinforcement (e.g., if food is no longer presented at all, the animal may become bored), provides strong evidence that cognition and motivation are also present here.[5]

The notion of an expectancy or "set" is also useful for understanding how some types of pure automatisms work. For example, a good driver responds to the situation of an imminent accident so rapidly that we cannot say that he deliberately planned his movements, and he will not be aware of any images controlling these movements. Similarly, a third baseman who stabs at a line drive in a split-second response or an outfielder who is off at the crack of the bat seem to be acting unconsciously, and such actions are popularly called "reflex." In the same way, sports writers say of an aging or tiring athlete that "his reflexes are slowing down." The highly skilled actions that are referred to by this term are not simple reflexes, but usually complex habits involving organized perception and refined control of movement. But they have become largely automatic: there is no longer any "voluntary" or deliberate connecting up of the parts of the action, no conscious selection of sensory cues, and so on. They remain "voluntary" only in the sense that the agent voluntarily attends to, and "sets" (prepares himself) for, a certain sort of skill suited to the situation.

As a final point in connection with the acquisition of motor skills and reflexes, we may mention that these automatisms and automatism habits are acquired more easily by a person who once possessed them and subsequently lost them than by a person who never possessed them. Gross motion, in particular, is retained. Perhaps this is due to the fact that coordinations of gross motions are also exercised in other activities and so kept active. Because motor

[5] We are purposely making our discussion of conditioned reflexes in man very brief. Such habits usually play a quite obscure role in normal human life. Some of them are quite particularized; other seem to accompany rather than determine more conscious activity. It is possible, however, that in some individuals they affect a much larger area of activity.

skills and reflexes are material and therefore indefinitely divisible, probably there is always some residue of previously possessed motor habits in man.

Imagination

We have stressed the fact that repetition of the proper act is the key factor in the acquisition of motor skills and reflexes. The degree of intensity with which the act is performed makes very little difference. For the imagination, however, though repetition is important and required, intensity is a highly significant factor. Those areas of the imagination concerned with guiding motor activities seem to be able to acquire modifications with little or no regard for concentration, attention, etc. This is not true of the other habits of the imagination. Intensity manifests itself in various ways, depending on the circumstances; but it is primarily a matter of attention, concentrated attention. For instance, if a child is learning a language, a strong emotional factor will fix his attention on the task and enable him to learn rapidly. If the child is disinterested and studies with only minimal awareness, not much is retained. What the emotional factor which fixes attention consists of makes little difference. A child will learn if he finds the work fascinating or repulsive; he will not learn if he finds the work dull, boring. Other things being equal, of course, interest or attraction is a better means of securing attention than repulsion or fear, especially where the habit involved demands quiet judgment and fine discrimination or where favorable estimations should be associated with the habits; but the fact remains that any strong emotion is an effective means of concentrating attention and thus producing the intensity required to acquire a habit of the imagination. The schoolmaster's rod has a place in habit formation. As is the case with all habits, habits of the imagination are only acquired if the proper act of the habit is performed (and, with the imagination, performed repeatedly). But this does not seem a difficult thing to do with most habits of the imagination and so does not require special treatment here. Here we wish to emphasize the role of intensity in the acquisition of habits of the imagination: *Habits of the imagination are formed or strengthened by acts of the desired habit repeated with greater intensity*

*than the power or the habit-already-possessed spontaneously elic-
its in its activities.*

What is attention? How does it make an act "intense"? As we
have previously noted, attention is of two kinds: object-directed
attention and subject-directed attention. The first kind of attention is forced upon us: a sudden, sharp stimulus (noise, bright
light, slap) will at least momentarily demand our attention, unless we are entirely wrapped up in what we are doing. Production
of object-directed attention is part of the teacher's job where
habits of the imagination are concerned. The second kind of at-
tion is subject-directed attention. This can be obtained in various
ways, all of which somehow involve appetite. Will-and-intellect
working together can keep certain images in the center of awareness and relegate others to the peripheries of awareness. But it is
often difficult to impose such control from above. Often it is much
easier to keep certain images in or out of the center of awareness
by means of appetitive reactions on the sensory level. Thus, emotion is one of the surest ways to control attention and thus develop the desired habits of the imagination. Emotion (or sensory
appetition) focuses attention by keeping an emotional stimulant
in the "bright center" of imaginative awareness.

Some people claim that they have acquired a habit of the imagination in the area of language skill by listening to a language record playing softly as they slept. How do such claims affect what
we have been saying about the acquisition of habits of the imagination? First, we should note that what is being claimed here is not
only that sensation (i.e., hearing) took place during sleep but
that a habit of the imagination (i.e., patterned recall of language
images) was acquired during sleep. Second, we should point out
that the fact of *patterned recall* has not been established beyond
all doubt; it may well be that only familiarity with language
images (not patterns of such images) is acquired. Such familiarity
with language images can be a large part of learning a new language, and therefore can be quite useful. However, it can be explained merely by the imagination's retention of external sensations, without any habitual modification. And even if patterned
recall of language images were conclusively established, this evidence would not contradict our conclusion that intensity is an

important factor in the acquisition of habitual modifications of the imagination. We would then conclude that sensory activities (external sensation and imagination) have been going on in sleep without sensory awareness or with an absolute minimum of sensory awareness and that habits of the imagination have been formed as a result of this activity. The imagination did not merely record such activity (as a tape recorder might); it developed a habitual modification by which it can now arrange and recombine in a patterned sequence the sensations experienced during sleep. But such modifications during sleep are *slow to form* and *very limited in extent*. Precisely because sensory activities during sleep are not intense, the habit forms slowly and extends only to a limited area. Furthermore, it is much more likely that inaccuracies occur in habits formed during sleep than in habits formed under intense sensory awareness. Intensity is a factor of awareness, just as velocity is a factor of locomotion. If one walks, he must walk with some velocity. Similarly, if one is aware, he must be aware with some intensity. Our point is that the degree of intensity in awareness is an important factor in the acquisition of habits of the imagination. Other things being equal, the more intense the act of the imagination is, the more that act will contribute to the formation of a corresponding habit in the imagination. Mere repetition of the proper act is not enough (as it is in the acquisition of motor skills); what is needed is repetition of the proper act at a greater level of intensity than is normal. This is the way habits of the imagination are acquired and strengthened.

Discursive Estimation

Habits of the discursive power present a special problem because intellect is normally involved in their acquisition and operation. Still, we know that man's discursive estimation is habitually modified and modified by proper acts corresponding to the habits produced by them. Hence we can ask the question, "How are such acts modified so that they produce a habitual modification of the discursive power?" St. Thomas speaks here of a "gathering up" of reason (*collatio rationis*). By this term he is referring to an ability which we all possess and have often exercised. Under the guidance of reason, elements and aspects of a particular situation can be ignored or brought to the center of awareness: we can stress to ourselves the snub as an insult to our personal dignity or as forgetfulness and absorption on the part of the party who snubbed us. By concentrating on one or the other aspect, the relatively significant good or evil of the snub will be increased or decreased, and the concrete sensory judgment of the discursive power will be modified accordingly. Such modifications can be habitual if selective concentration is repeated often enough and intensely enough.

Moreover, there is no doubt that people can learn to estimate as good or evil concrete objects (persons, things, situations) which at first they did not consider to have any relevancy to them at all or which they considered in an estimation contrary to the one they eventually learn. Such learning can take place under the guidance of reason (just as intellect-and-will can impose their control on the imagination), but it is often achieved much more easily if a favorable (or unfavorable) emotional reaction accompanies the judgment of the discursive estimation. It is especially difficult to judge *in the face of* contrary sensory appetition, though intellect-and-sense working together can accomplish even this with enough time and effort. Often they must associate pleasant or unpleasant experiences with the object they wish to estimate differently, and thus they modify the emotional reaction; sometimes they can modify the estimation merely by concentrating on certain elements in their present experience of the object and do not need to bring in new experiences of that object.

Thus we see that habits of the discursive estimation are acquired (under the guidance of reason *and* with the help of sensory appetition, if possible) by frequent repetition of the proper act of the habit at a level of intensity greater than normal. Such habits, once acquired, are increased and strengthened in the same way. However, two qualifications must be added: (1) Though repetition is always required in the acquisition of habits of the discursive power under the guidance of reason, it is possible to form an automatism habit in the discursive power from a single extremely intense experience. Such habits always concern some very specific object and generally are short-term acquisitions unless reinforced by subsequent experiences. (2) Intensity is an important factor in forming habits of the discursive estimation, but intensity is not the same thing as overcoming great difficulties. It is true that only very intense acts can overcome such difficulties, yet there can also be very intense acts where there are no difficulties at all. The intensity of an act refers to its own intrinsic perfection, which is reflected by its relative prominence in sensory awareness. It does not necessarily imply strain or great effort: the "intensity" of a shot-putter is only one type of intensity.

Sensory Appetites

As is true of all habits, habits of the sensory appetites arise only from the proper acts of such habits. People differ, of course, a great deal in their native endowment in the matter of emotions. We already know from experience that some persons have violent appetitive responses and that others barely respond at all. But we have also seen that no matter what the native reactions of the sensory appetites may be, they are still capable of modification. People can acquire consistent modes of tendency in their sensory appetites, and these modes of tendency can be excessive, moderate, or deficient. But such habits can be acquired only in one way: by the performance of the proper act of the desired habit. We do not become temperate by thinking about temperance but by practicing acts of temperance; the same thing is true of daring, fear, and anger.

Granted that merely *thinking* about actions is not enough to bring about habits of the appetites, is it possible to imagine a situation and thus have a sensory response from which habits could be formed? To some extent this is possible. But the image has a certain unreality about it; as Aristotle remarked long ago, no one fears an imaginary fire. However, it is possible to imagine a very concrete situation and to make it personally relevant, and to such an imagined situation there will often be a weak sensory response.[6] Reading great literature appreciatively is often an extremely important way of enlarging our experience, but it is not

---

[6] On the other hand, the imagination of some objects almost necessarily brings with it some sensory responses, and so involves morally good or evil acts.

a substitute for the basic experiences themselves. Similarly, one of the intended results of meditation is to make possible acts of the will concerning the objects a person has been praying about. This is sometimes the only way that particular actions can be actually performed, that is, in imagination, intention, and desire. So it is good and necessary, but not sufficient.[7]

From this one might conclude that the acquisition of habit (and especially of virtue) depends on the presence of temptation, but this is not so. For what is necessary is that a person *act*. Suppose a person wants to acquire the virtue of abstinence (a subdivision of the virtue of temperance), that is, the inclination toward the proper, reasonable use of food. That man must first grasp the goodness of this act, and then actually so desire. Now, it may happen that the urgency for acquiring a particular virtue comes from a temptation, for it is reasonable to concentrate on acquiring a virtue which is very necessary. But in this way the presence of temptation or difficulty is an occasion or a reason, but not a cause bringing about the virtue. It is true that we often do not work hard at things which come easily for us, so that if there were no difficulties we might not rise above mediocrity. Yet even then, the difficulty is a challenge, not a cause.

In addition to the performance of the proper act of the desired habit, two other factors enter into the acquisition of habits of the sensory appetites. (1) Repetition is always necessary except in the case of traumatic experiences such as we discussed in connection with the discursive estimation. Traumatic experiences can develop an automatism habit with a very specific object (e.g., excessive fear of a particular person, place, or situation), but such automatisms fade away unless the original experience is periodically reinforced. Repetition is necessary not only because a material power is involved but because no single act of sensory appetancy normally contains the whole perfection of the corresponding habit. Hence a series of acts concerned with objects which are specifically the same but differ in particulars must normally be performed before the perfection of the habit is acquired. One cannot learn how to tend moderately to a pleasurable good of sense

---

[7] St. Thomas remarks that a poor man cannot fully acquire the virtue of liberality.

from a single act, because no single act contains all the elements which are involved in a consistent mode of tendency toward such an object. One can learn to react excessively to a difficult good, however, if the good is sufficiently specific and if the traumatic experience is sufficiently intense. A single act can form a habit of this sort because the limited perfection of the habit can be contained in a single act of the sensory appetite involved. (2) Intensity is a second condition for the acquisition of habits of the sensory appetites. The acts which develop the habit must be more intense than normal acts of the sense appetites which do not modify habits. Here again, *intensity refers to the intrinsic perfection of the act, which is reflected by its relative prominence in sensory awareness.*[8] The notion of intensity differs from power to power and from habit to habit. The intensity of habits of the sensory appetites can be compared to the velocity of locomotion. The velocity of a body in motion is by no means identical with its direction, but depends on the force with which it is moved. In appetite, we find not only the object of appetite (which is similar to the direction of locomotion) but also an element which we call "intensity," which is similar to velocity of locomotion.

We must be careful not to confuse intensity with violence or excess. A moderate act can simultaneously be very intense. We can think of a mother's love for her child which is violent, uncontrolled, disordered, excessive. We can think of a grief that is a paroxysm, an anger that is violent rage, and so on. But we can also think of a mother's love which is quiet, well ordered, balanced, and yet extremely intense. Similarly, there is intense but controlled grief, as in the Pietà, and intense but controlled anger, as in Christ's cleansing of the Temple. We could not imagine anyone who had a more intense ("greater") love of God than the Blessed Virgin, and yet there was nothing violent or excessive about that love.

St. Thomas, in trying to explain this kind of intensity, speaks of an act as being "more deeply rooted in the power." Another way

---

[8] The material, extended nature of the unifying sense permits only a limited prominence to individual acts in sensory awareness. The more perfect activities (i.e., those performed with most intensity) thus tend to occupy the bright center of awareness and crowd out the less perfect, less intense activity which may be going on simultaneously in sensory cognition or appetition.

of expressing this would be to say that a more intense act is one which is performed more wholeheartedly, which concerns an object to which one is more deeply committed, etc. Generosity is often another name for intensity. Spiritual writers often speak of being generous in our acts of virtue. In contrast, they speak of an ungenerous, selfish person, one who does not wholly give himself to anything. It is obvious that an excessive act can be intense, but so can a moderate act. Indeed, some acts are even intensely apathetic: the entire personality is committed to such a deficient response.

In summary, habits of the sensory appetites are developed only by the proper acts of such habits, repeated (normally) at an intensity level greater than equal to the power (or power-plus-habit) which is being modified. Repetition is necessary because we are dealing with a material power, and because the perfection of the act of the desired habit normally cannot be contained in a single act of the sensory appetite involved. Intensity refers to the perfection of the act of appetition, not to violent or excessive appetition. It is important to stress the fact that habits are developed only by their *proper* acts because of the propensity men have to substitute other, easier acts for the proper acts of the habit they are trying to develop. A person does not acquire temperance or fortitude or prudence or justice by simply telling himself often enough, "I will be temperate (brave, prudent, just)." Such acts are velleities, unless they lead to the performance of acts of temperance (bravery, prudence, justice). There is all the difference in the world between the will-and-intellect *approving* virtue or *desiring* virtue and the will-and-intellect *practicing* virtue. Only by this last activity will virtue actually be developed. Without practice, good resolutions are more or less predictably false propositions about future activity.

Intellect

The most important thing about habits of the intellect is that they are acquired and developed only by performing the acts proper to them. We cannot merely go through the motions or perform the external or material part of the act proper to an intellectual habit. For instance, to acquire a habit of science, one must understand *the movement of thought* of a scientist, not just consider each statement separately. One must understand why this statement follows that other one, and why and how they effect the conclusion (though of course they need not explicitly be called premises and conclusions). Reasoning is not just understanding each of a series of terms separately, nor even a series of propositions. They must be understood as belonging in a certain order. It is the movement of reason *as such* which is to be understood, not merely the individual propositions formulated as a result of that movement of reason. Thus, intellectual habits are acquired only by the acts proper to those habits.

Is repetition always required in the acquisition of intellectual habits? Once it is established that a person is actually performing the act proper to the habit he wishes to acquire (e.g., actually reasoning and not just accidentally following a series of understandings), there is a certain type of simple reasoning where there is no contingence, where the perfection of the habit can be contained in a single act proper to that habit. In such a situation it is possible for a person to acquire an intellectual habit without repetition, by a single act proper to that habit. If a person completely understands the necessity of the relation of premises to conclusion in a simple science in a single act of that science, he can acquire the habit of reasoning proper to that science in a single act. This is not merely an insight into the truth of a judgment, an isolated proposition, but involves a habitual knowledge of a movement of reasoning.

An example of the acquisition of a simple science (intellectual habit) by a single act which contains the perfection proper to the habit is the learning of a simple mathematical science like geometry. Some young people do seem to learn geometry or arithmetic or even algebra in this way. If they do not see all the conclusions immediately, at least they see them as soon as the particular premises for those conclusions are proposed to them. Of course, most people do not learn mathematical sciences in this fashion. They have to go over the proofs more than once. Yet the fact is that mathematical sciences are strictly causal, proceeding with a priori necessity from basic postulates and insights. If repetition is needed for an individual to learn mathematics, this is because the individual has not grasped the reasoning involved clearly enough. It is not that the reasoning cannot be adequately contained in its perfection in a single act of the science.[9]

Can a person learn philosophy in a single act? He cannot. Philosophy is not an a priori science like mathematics. The perfection of reasoning involved in the reasoning proper to a philosophical discipline cannot be contained in any single act of philosophical reasoning. The same thing is true of the physical sciences. Total necessity is present in the reasoning only of a strict causal, a priori science. Once the mathematical science of geometry is mastered, for example, a person can demonstrate how many conclusions can be drawn from it. There are finite logics, too, and the number of conclusions possible in such logics can be demonstrated a priori.[10] But no philosopher or physicist knows his science so well that someone else cannot know it better or that he himself cannot improve his knowledge of that science. Habits of opinion, the habit of prudence, and habits of art are all obviously contingent habits whose perfection could never be contained in a single act proper to the habit. Such habits can only be acquired by *repeated* acts proper to the habit.

Furthermore, since all intellectual habits have a material component in the imagination, to this extent they all require repetition (and intensity) in their acquisition and growth. The imaginative components of intellectual habits follow the laws of the imagination in their development.

[9] There are many sciences of mathematics, not a single science of mathematics. Euclidean and the various non-Euclidean geometries are distinct sciences, as are algebra and trigonometry. The reason is that principles (axioms, postulates) help to specify a science, and so different principles determine different sciences. This is not to deny the many generic similarities nor to suggest that the "way of discovery" is specifically different.

While the habit of a specific science of mathematics can be acquired in a single act which contains the perfection of the habit of reasoning proper to that specific science, a *generic* habit of mathematics cannot be so acquired; because, without comparison (and so more than a single act), there is no way of knowing what is specific and what is generic in a mathematical science like geometry or trigonometry. Even if a generic habit of mathematical reasoning is acquired from repeated acts, of course, such a habit must be further specified before it can operate in any specific area of mathematics.

[10] Some logics are purely a priori and hence mathematical. Thomistic logic is not a priori but intentional; it is a logic of being, and nonmathematical.

Finally, we may ask whether intensity is required for the acquisition and growth of intellectual habits. Intensity in a spiritual power like the intellect means something quite different from intensity in acts of the imagination, the discursive estimation, or the sensory appetites. It refers simply to the perfection of the act proper to the habit. In this sense, it is correct to say that intellectual habits are acquired and grow by acts proper to these habits performed with a greater intensity of perfection than the intellect (or the intellect-plus-imperfect-habit) spontaneously elicits. In the case of a habit whose perfection can be contained in a single act, the intellectual component (but not the imaginative component) of the habit can be acquired in a single act; all other intellectual habits require repeated acts proper to the habit which is being acquired or increased.

Will

As with habits of the intellect, habits of the will are acquired and grow by the performance of the will-acts proper to those habits, and only in this way. *One does not become humble by wishing to become humble or by approving the practice of humility but by practicing acts of humility.* The same thing holds true for justice and friendship and the supernatural virtue of charity. Repetition is necessary in the acquisition of any habit of the will because no finite will-act exhausts the perfection of the will's tendency to the "good as such." The will always tends to particular goods, and the habits of the will have as their objects complex and in some sense limited goods. Intensity is also required in the acquisition of habits of the will. As is the case in the intellect, intensity in the will refers to the perfection of the will-act proper to the habit. It is not a case of grunting and groaning, but of *more perfectly* ("more intensely") willing the good-of-another in friendship, the good-due-to-another in justice, or the good-due-to-oneself in humility. It is particularly clear in the case of habits of the will that intensity involves a change from the "normal" activity of the power or power-plus-imperfect-habit involved. One does not become more or less just or humble by performing will-acts at the intensity level which the will-plus-its-previously-acquired-habits spontaneously elicits. More intense or perfect will-acts are required to change the will-plus-its-habits, to pass from virtue to vice or from vice to virtue. Experience certainly bears this out.

DESTRUCTION OF HABITS

The process of destroying or weakening habits is in some ways more complicated than the process by which they are acquired or strengthened. First of all, we may note that some habits (in fact, most habits) have contraries. Such habits can be destroyed or weakened by the practice of their contraries. A person can get rid of the habit of typing badly by typing correctly. The new habit thus acquired replaces the old habit which is its contrary. But this method cannot always be employed. Some habits have no contraries. Others have contraries which cannot be practiced, at least in certain circumstances. For instance, an unmarried person who habitually misuses his sexual powers cannot break such a habit by using those powers correctly; at least he cannot do this as long as he remains unmarried.[11]

Habits which are habits of a material power or have a material component can be weakened or destroyed without the practice of their contrary. Here one can make use of the fact that the body is in constant change: the matter of the organ involved is constantly being replaced. Mere nonuse of the undesirable habit will in time eliminate it or at least so weaken it that for all practical purposes it is gone and no longer has any effect on activity. There is a continual replacement of body tissue through metabolism. For example, if a muscle is built up through body training, it will deteriorate by itself if it is not constantly used. Similarly, a person immobilized in bed for three months finds it difficult to walk afterwards: he has neither the required strength nor the required control of movement. Metabolism necessarily goes on as long as one is alive. Thus, a motor skill can be lost simply by failing to practice it.

A habitual appetitive reaction can be lost by never letting it take

[11] N.B. This is not at all the same as saying that a person with such a habit should marry in order to overcome his bad habit! Ordinarily the habit should be corrected *before* marriage, and ordinarily the obligation to do this would be very serious. All that the text above intends to point out is that there is no *usable* contrary, in the situation mentioned.

place. This statement is true enough and often provides an important principle of guidance, but it conceals a problem. For habits of cognitive and executive powers do not by themselves incline to action, but only to a kind or mode of action. But appetites are by their nature strivings toward an object, and so habits of appetitive powers incline a person to the act itself. Hence, once an appetitive habit has been acquired, its future nonactivity cannot be ensured by a merely negative position of the agent. The person who has such a habit must take positive steps to prevent the action from occurring. There are several ways of doing this, and the choice of the appropriate one will depend largely on the kind of habit and its object. For example, a person has an appetitive habit about a particular kind of sensible object, and that object can be avoided by the choice of external action. We could think of an intemperate person, whose intemperance occurs in a certain place or with certain people, and these places or persons can be avoided. If he is serious about ridding himself of the habit, he will avoid such situations. But at other times the object is not avoidable, or it is within the person himself. When this is the case, omission of the act of the appetitive habit will consist almost entirely in the control of the imagination and the estimative power. This control is a positive activity, but it often will not be properly the practice of a contrary habit of the same kind as the one to be removed. Consider the case of a person who worries about certain things, and whose worry is of a sort as to be a serious drawback. Suppose he were to try to overcome his bad habit by letting his imagination present the situations, actions, and so on, about which he habitually worries, yet not yielding to them, or trying to practice confidence in their regard. Simply saying to himself, "This is nothing to worry about, this I can do," will be utterly ineffective; the imaginative presentation of the object immediately arouses the sensory appetitive response, and his contrary volition only serves to fix the image more firmly in his consciousness, thereby causing the habitual sensory reaction to be stronger. Thus, the deliberate attempt to practice the contrary habit only serves to exercise the habit he is trying to overcome. There is the same sort of unwanted effect in cases of scrupulosity, temptations against faith, anxiety, and temptations against chastity.[12] The only solution lies in the control of the imagination, and often there are reasons why this control of the imagination is very difficult. In very severe cases, professional help may be necessary in order to discover why certain images keep coming back.[13]

The imagination is likewise a power with a material organ, so it can gradually lose its acquired modifications. Many people find that they lose their command of a language which they do not read or speak at least occasionally; this shows the loss of a patterned habit of images, the material component of a complex habit.[14]

Thus we see that nonuse of a habit involving a material organ is a rather slow, though sure, way of losing or at least weakening that habit.[15] The process is speeded up somewhat if we can also use the same power for some other activity and thus develop a new habit, even though this new habit is merely different from, and not contrary to, the habit which we wish to lose.

If a particular habit has no contrary and is not material, it cannot be destroyed. That is why ideas in the state of habit cannot be destroyed, although their material counterparts in the imagination may be destroyed. Ideas in the state of habit, however, are isolated units and therefore not habits in the usual sense of the

[12] This is why ascetical writers quite correctly say that such temptations should be fled from rather than fought directly. Note that what is being approved is the *practical* advice (not necessarily the reason alleged by the writers, which at times sounds Manichaean).

[13] Sometimes the common-sense direction of an experienced person may be sufficient; sometimes nondirective counseling will be effective; in some cases recourse will have to be had to a skilled psychotherapist.

[14] In a complex habit which has both intellectual and material components, the intellectual component aids one to recover the material component(s) after they have been lost. For instance, a brain injury may destroy the imaginative component of a language habit and result in aphasia. In this event, the person can relearn the language much more rapidly than he originally acquired the skill because of the intellectual component of the original habit which is still present. He has all the ideas; all he needs are words.

[15] It is often said that every experience leaves an ineradicable impression, so that in principle a man could recall every experience he ever had. This statement seems to be exaggerated. On the other hand, total and complete forgetting probably does not take place either, except perhaps through a physical destruction of the organ.

term. All habits intellectual in the full sense have contraries and so can be destroyed (i.e., turned into false science, false opinion, bad art, etc.), with one exception. The habit of first (practical and speculative) principles has no contrary[16] and so cannot be destroyed.

GENERIC AND SPECIFIC HABITS

We have already seen something of the importance of habits in human life. This section will deal with the problem of generalizing specific habits and of generalizing such habits in the proper way. The possibility of doing this seems to be a basic supposition of all liberal education and even of most vocational schooling. School (even vocational school) seldom teaches the exact habits and skills which are required in later life. Some specific skills are taught, of course, along with a certain amount of purely factual information; but a great deal of time is also spent developing general attitudes, methods, and ideals. For example, mathematics is studied in liberal education not only to develop the skills needed in making a budget, computing income tax, or working as an accountant; it also enables one to understand, appreciate, and practice a habit of orderly thinking, of accuracy, and of the ability to abstract from irrelevant traits even when the problem is abstract or difficult. Similarly, Shakespeare's *The Merchant of Venice* is studied not merely to learn the artful use of words in contracts and certainly not to develop hatred for the money-lender, but rather to learn to appreciate the humanity of all men, the value of having devoted friends, and so on. Even a vocational course for a machinist does not merely familiarize the apprentice with certain machines; it also tries to give him general habits involving the care and use of machines. Therefore, unless it is possible somehow to transfer school habits to various life-situations,

16 It has no contrary because it is inchoatively innate, as we have seen; and because, in order that a contrary habit could be acquired, it would be necessary to make judgments clearly and consciously opposed to the habit. But though people can become confused about first principles, they cannot give a really intellectual assent to a proposition contrary to those principles—this is physically impossible.

to make the adaptations necessary in such situations, and to specifically further the generic methods learned in school, the whole
institution of formal schooling seems pointless.

Philosophically, there seems to be a problem with generalizing
specific habits because every habit is specified by its own proper
object. It would seem, then, that habits can be "transferred" only
in so far as other objects are reduced in some way to their proper
objects.

The problem of transfer of habits has also been a perennial
problem for experimental psychology. Early in this century, reacting against the excessive claims of a certain school of educators,
a number of experimental psychologists worked to prove that
there is no such thing as automatic transfer of habitual skills
("transfer of training"). They formulated the results of their investigations in the doctrine of "identical elements": the only
transfer which takes place is really no transfer at all; identical
skills are applied without modification in situations which contain identical elements; there is no significant modification to
cover life situations which contain few elements identical with the
learning situation in school. E. L. Thorndike, the leader of this
group, reduces habit formation to the association of neural bonds
in terms of stimulus-response or situation-reaction units; identical
elements are, from the point of view of the subject reacting to two
identical situations, "mental processes which have the same cell
action in the brain as their physical correlate."[17]

Subsequent research (some of which was carried on by Thorndike himself) revealed the inadequacies of the doctrine of identical elements. While the theory could handle simple mechanical
skills (e.g., cross education of members), maze running, and rote
memorization, it could not explain the adaptation characteristic
of more intellectual habits, the influence of attitudes on learning,
and "learning how to learn," all of which are prominent objectives of formal schooling. Thorndike could not handle this sort of
evidence merely by changing "identical elements" to "similar elements" or by speaking of "similar reaction patterns" or of "a
generalized mode of response." Such evidence points to specific

[17] Cf. E. L. Thorndike, *Educational Psychology, Briefer Course* (New York,
Columbia, 1922), p. 269.

habits acquired by the subject, then generalized, and finally applied to specifically different situations.[18]

Because of the divergent interpretations which have been given to the large body of evidence that has accumulated on the problem of transfer of training and the related problem of generic and specific habit formation, perhaps the best approach is to review a representative series of experiments and then evaluate the results of the investigation in terms of the doctrine on habit developed earlier in this book. We shall examine the research of Jaime Castiello, S.J., whose work is one of many which study "learning how to learn" and the acquisition of ideals.[19] We choose Castiello not because his findings are unusual, or even very original, but because his analysis of the evidence is superior.

Castiello was interested in two questions: (1) Does transfer of training occur and in what sense? (2) What are its conditions? Two general areas of investigation were selected: insight and ideals. The subjects for the experiment were students, ranging from the equivalent of sixth grade to first year high school. In the experiment on understanding, the students were divided into three groups. To one group, Castiello taught the law of optics that light rays are bent in passing from a thin to a denser medium. This group was instructed in the law in an abstract, general formulation and was given the example of glass and air as media. To another group the law was given in the same formulation, but it was illustrated in a series of instances. To a third group Castiello taught the law in a series of instances and then made the individual students apply it for themselves by having them put sticks in water, making them see and learn the law in its concrete applications. Castiello was also careful to point out to this third

[18] For a good summary of the evidence on transfer of training, cf. Robert S. Woodworth and Harold Schlosberg, *Experimental Psychology*, rev. ed. (New York, Holt, Rinehart and Winston, 1954), pp. 733-778, 825-830.

[19] Jaime Castiello, S.J., *Geitesformung* (Berlin, Dümmlers Verlag, 1934). For a significant series of recent experiments on "learning how to learn," see the work of H. F. Harlow of the University of Wisconsin.

The experiment used by Father Castiello was first devised by Charles H. Judd and reported in his article, "The relation of special training to general intelligence," *Educational Review*, vol. 36 (1908), 28-42; he also pointed out the significance of his results for education. Father Castiello's version is used because he explicitly correlated it with a philosophical conception of habit.

group that the law held in many other instances, wherever the conditions of the law were fulfilled. When he was satisfied that each group was well taught, he took all the students on a picnic. Among other games and contests, he had the young people throw stones at a rock under water. The first two groups went at this by trial and error, and many of them never got very far. Only the third group made use of the general law they had learned in school—and this was done only after their first efforts were unsuccessful.

In the experiment on ideals, another group of students was similarly divided. This time the intention was to imbue them with the ideal of cleanliness. In the first group, Castiello explained the general idea of cleanliness but did not illustrate it. In the second group, he explained what cleanliness was and illustrated it with references to the students' clothes, hands, and nails. In the third group, he explained cleanliness and showed them that it was an ideal in many areas with which they came into daily contact. The first and second groups responded well in the classroom situation, and the third did also. But when a check was made a week later at the homes of the students, only the mothers of the third group had noticed any improvement in the way in which the students took care of their rooms and clothes at home.

On the basis of these experiments (which were repeated a number of times, with the same results) the following analysis can be made: (1) There are both generic and specific habits, with corresponding proper objects. (2) Desirable transfer implies the possession of both a specific habit and a generic habit. (3) Even if a generic habit is present, it will not be applied to specifically new situations unless it is possessed consciously *as generic,* that is, as applicable to various situations and activities. (4) Specific or even generic habits, if transferred to areas which do not fall under their proper objects, will lead to undesirable and unsuccessful activities. We need now to examine each of these conclusions in detail.

First of all, there are both generic and specific habits, with corresponding proper objects, but there are some important differences between them as habits. As an example, we may think of the generic habit of "science" and of the specific habits of science (physics, biology, psychology, and so on). Now, we know from metaphysics that in the real order genus and species are not really distinct things. There is no existing genus of animal which is not really identical with the various species of animals. But in the order of knowledge (habits are perfections of beings that have knowledge) there can be a genus which is distinct from its species. There can be a concept of animal which is distinct from all the species of animals, such as horses and flies. Of course, the idea of animal as a genus is indeterminate as compared to the ideas of the species.

Since the "formal objects" which specify habits are intelligibilities ("ideas"), there can be generic habits if there are formal objects which are related to other formal objects in the way that genus is related to species. Such a generic habit will be somewhat indeterminate and potential (as the genus is indeterminate and potential in contrast to the species) ; in addition, the generic habit is often only the formal part of a habit adequately taken. Thus, the specific habits of science, such as physics and biology, taken adequately, consist of a formal substantial part in the intellect and a material part in the imagination. The generic habit of science-in-general does not have a corresponding material part— there are no facts-in-general with which it could work, and so it can be exercised only together with some specific habit of science. When, however, the specific habits are composed of a formal (accidental) part and a substantial part, the corresponding generic habit includes not only the formal (accidental) part generalized, but also either the knowledge of the substantial part of the habit[20] (as is the case when the habit is substantially in the sensory powers) or a generalized variation of the substantial part itself (if the habit is substantially in the will) .

Now, with regard to the use of habits once gained, there are two senses in which we can talk of transfer.[21] In the first instance, a habit is acquired in some relatively concrete situation. In Father

[20] Thus, the form of the moral virtues is prudence; the generic virtue of temperance is not simply prudence, but prudence seen to be applied to tendency toward rightly ordered use of sensible things.

[21] Most discussions of "transfer" have failed to distinguish these two senses, and so there has been a basic confusion. In addition, some authors speak of transfer where there is simply failure to discriminate—we "transfer" in the sense that we fail to perceive any differences between two cases which are different.

Castiello's experiments, one and the same habit had to be applied to different situations. Many of the students did not apply it in the new situation, evidently because the habit had been concretized by accidental circumstances (the classroom situation) so that it was not for them applicable even to specifically the same objects. The mere possession of what is in fact applicable to many objects is no guarantee that a person will apply it. Only the exceptional student generalizes spontaneously, and even such a student will often generalize erroneously if he does not have good direction. The difficulty of generalization of a habit in regard to objects which are essentially the same and differ only accidentally is only the psychological difficulty of abstracting from accidentals. At the first level of learning, this is a great problem and one that takes explicit effort.

Transfer in a stricter sense of the term means the application of what has been learned in one specific field to another particular field which is essentially different. In this case, desirable transfer implies the possession of both a specific habit and a generic habit. There is no possibility of transfer unless (1) some specific habit is learned and (2) a generic habit is acquired subsequent to the learning of the specific habit. It is impossible (and would be undesirable even if it were possible) to acquire a generic habit without previously learning one of the specific habits which fall under that generic habit. Furthermore, the acquiring of the specific habit by no means involves the gaining of the more inclusive generic habit. If it is true that people find it difficult to abstract from the accidental changing circumstances, it is even more certain that they will find it difficult to abstract from essential differences to reach the level of generic community. Yet such a level must be reached if education is to be fully effective. Without generic habits, the learner can possess only specific ones. If he realizes that a particular habit is specific, no transfer can possibly occur. For example, if a person has learned the method of physics and thinks that this method is relevant only within that field, he will not attempt any transfer and none will take place. On the other hand, the learner may mistakenly think that the specific habit he has is a generic one, universally applicable without change; in this case transfer may well occur, but it will be illegitimate and will lead to undesirable and unsuccessful activity. This second possibility requires a more explicit discussion later.

The third general conclusion is that transfer even of a generic habit is not effected automatically. This is evident, not only from ordinary experience, but from some of Father Castiello's experiments, where it was shown that possession of generic habits does not ensure application of them. Even when the learner is explicitly told that a given habit is generic and can be applied to other kinds of situations, he rarely transfers. Most students need to have the specific applications pointed out to them repeatedly, and then need to make some applications themselves under the direction of the teacher, until they learn the proper way to specify generic habits so that they can be exercised in various situations.

Fourthly, specific or even generic habits, if transferred to areas which do not fall under their proper objects, will lead to undesirable activities. In the area of intellectual knowledge such erroneous transfer leads to one-sided attitudes like rationalism or scientism. These attitudes begin with a habit which is properly and effectively used in some area; subsequently they are mistaken for a habit of larger applicability. In either case, misapplications of the originally good and successful habit will be made. Thus physics (species) is sometimes thought to be the generic habit of science: "dogmatic behaviorism"[22] in psychology is the result of trying to treat psychological problems as though they were properly physical problems. Similarly, a person who scorns all humanistic or spontaneous knowledge as worthless is actually mistaking the generic habit of science for a general habit of intellectual knowledge. In the order of appetite, if a person responds to a situation with a specific response which he thinks is generically valid, the response is generally inappropriate. For example, some people with a passion for orderliness even try to organize their picnics or their love life. Others manifest sexual responses to all kinds of love situations, including passing friendships, or even to sensibly desirable inanimate objects. This occurs when sexual

[22] "Dogmatic behaviorism" denies that conscious activity exists, usually on grounds of a materialistic philosophy of man. "Methodological behaviorism," or "behavioristic method," studies man only from external, objective observation. It is a completely legitimate method, provided that its restrictions are understood to be methodological.

love, a specific response, is substituted generically for all love responses. In the order of emotional responses, the substitution of a specific emotional response for a generic one is normally the sign either of emotional immaturity or of a mental breakdown. Very young children manifest such behavior before they learn to discriminate objects of sensory appetition. A child for a time tries to put everything into his mouth, even moth balls and razor blades, or tries to bite everything he comes into contact with, even his mother and baby sister. But what is normal in infants is undesirable and even disastrous in adults.

As a fifth and final conclusion from Castiello's experiments, we should note that even after generic habits are acquired and recognized as such, specific habits are still needed. People sometimes think that once they have acquired a generic habit of temperance or justice or fortitude they need no longer worry about specific habits of these virtues, or even about the original specific habits from which they generalized. This attitude does not account for the fact that generic habits, like generic ideas, are indeterminate and need to be specified and further determined when they are applied to specific situations. One cannot be temperate in general: he must be sober or chaste or temperate in some specific way. Similarly, if a person practices fortitude, he must practice it in a specific way: he must be brave or he must be zealously angry. The whole secret of learning how to *apply* generic habits to new situations consists in learning how to develop the new specific habit which is suited to the particular situation. Such a habit can be developed apart from the generic habit, of course; before the generic habit is possessed it must be so developed. But human experience shows that such absolute beginnings are difficult and, in practice, seldom made. It is much easier to apply a previously acquired generic habit to specific situations as they arise. This, we repeat, is the basic supposition of all formal education.[23] It constitutes *the* major means by which most men acquire and

[23] Notice how inadequate the doctrine of identical elements is to explain the habitual modifications which men acquire through education. The knowing-and-willing subject is modified in education, and in successful education he is modified in such a way that he can adapt to situations specifically different from his school situation, precisely because he has acquired *generic* as well as specific habits.

strengthen the habits which are so necessary for a fully human life.

CONCLUDING REMARKS

In this chapter we have discussed man's need for habits, the ways in which man's various powers are perfected by habits ("the growth and destruction of habits"), and finally how specific habits can be generalized and even wrongly extended beyond their suitable limits. Several points here are of very great importance both for education and for asceticism.

First, habits can be acquired only by performing individual acts - of the sort that pertain to the habit. Thus, a science can be learned only if the student actually engages in some instances of scientific reasoning. In the case of experimental science, this will mean that the student must himself perform some experiments, must himself elaborate laws, must frame a few hypotheses and test their validity. If acts of this sort are not performed, talk about scientific proof, experimentation, and method is mostly empty. Of course, economy will dictate to the teacher that once several acts have been performed and the habit is underway many similar propositions and conclusions can be presented after the manner of sheer information. But it remains true that a science cannot be learned by passively listening to information about science. Similarly, in a literature or text course, a particular piece of literature or a particular text must be actively read and analyzed by the student. There is no use in talking *in vacuo* about beauty— the most students can learn from this is what statements the teacher wants them to make. It is necessary that they first concretely learn how to look for beauty, or how to find the meaning of a particular phrase in a given text.

In ascetical training, likewise, a habit of virtue cannot be acquired except by the practice of a relevant act. Books on ascetical theory are insufficient by themselves, as are ever so personalized instructions about virtue.[24] But, as we have seen, in the case of

---

[24] A fortiori, virtue cannot be implanted by requiring a person to perform the *external* act which pertains to a virtue. In St. Ignatius Loyola's terms, this would be the first degree of obedience which is simply insufficient by itself.

appetitive habits a mistake can be made also by the would-be
practitioner: he thinks that "making an act" of virtue consists in
wishing that he had the virtue, or in making a statement to himself about the act—"I humble myself," "I restrain myself." Admittedly, it is difficult so to describe an act of appetite that the
hearer knows at once what is to be done; we are here dealing with
a case of *practical* knowledge, and practical knowledge is not complete until it reaches the knowledge of the singular act. But the
singular act cannot be *entirely* individualized and concretized
until it is performed. So a person cannot realize entirely what an
act of humility is until he performs one. By and large, this means
that virtue is acquired through the mutual influence of knowledge and action. We begin by trying to understand as much as
we can, then perform an act, then reflect on the act just performed to improve our knowledge; from this improved knowledge
we perform a second and better action, and so on. This is not
easy; it involves both effort and reflection; yet it is the only way.

The second important point is this: abstraction and generalization must be deliberately attended to and sought for. In education, almost from the beginning, the teacher must explicitly point
out what is being done and explicitly point to future applicability. In the experiment, the student must come to see a *kind* of
experiment, in the proof, a kind of reasoning. In the course of
the repeated acts, this intelligibility must be isolated from its concrete instances, and the scope and limits of its applicability must
be shown. Further generalizations—for example, the nature of the
scientific method itself—can be brought out through the instances
of several different kinds of experiments, preferably within different sciences. In literature, the experience of beauty must be dis-
engaged from the particular instance, and the student shown how
to find beauty in any good poem, novel, and so on.

In ascetical practice, the person must be brought to attend to
the intelligibility of his action and to discover its truly universal
goodness. Explicit reference must be made to future situations,
and care must be taken to point out differences as well as similarities, limits as well as scope. Mechanical routine can easily substitute itself for personalized action, and such routine destroys the
individual prudential judgment that is the very life (because it is

the *form*) of the virtue striven for. Mastery habits, it will be recalled, are always conscious and voluntary; that is why a constant alertness is required. Additional problems concerning the practice of virtue will be discussed in detail later.

Several important questions concerning the acquisition of habits still remain to be answered: What habits should man develop? In what order should he develop these habits? How can man unify the habits he acquires? These and similar questions will be answered later. Here we wish merely to make two remarks.

First of all, how does one know when a habit should be acquired? We have already seen that habits are necessary over the long haul. Individual acts can be performed without habits; a consistent mode of behavior demands a habitual modification. If something comes up only occasionally, we normally do our best to handle it but do not bother to form a specific habit to do the job. Sometimes, when a number of habits are really needed, we find that we must concentrate on one or two and let the others go, at least for the time being. Our study of the virtues and their interrelations (in Chapter Five) will help us decide which habits are most important and which are secondary. Individual temperaments, particular situations, and personal goals all are added factors which complicate our problem of deciding which habits to acquire and in what order to acquire them. These factors will be discussed in Chapter Six.

Our second remark concerns the problem of unifying the habits we acquire. This is primarily a problem of our vocational-ideal, the personal goal we set for ourselves in the light of our nature, our particular temperament and situation, and our ambitions. We must guard against oversimplification. We must always remember that we need specific habits, not only generic habits, and that we need proper habits, proportioned to the object in its concrete circumstances, not just any habit. Both substituting generic for specific habits and substituting improper for proper habits have disastrous results in character formation. The drunkard will not stay sober for long if he tries to "make do" with the generic virtue of temperance. Similarly, those who substitute charity for social justice seldom are successful in restoring the social order, as Pope Pius XII often pointed out. It is a hard fact of experience

that there is no adequate substitute for specific habits, specifically
understood and specifically developed. One grand, general habit
will not do.

SOURCES FOR CHAPTER FOUR

Barlow, M. C., "Transfer of Training in Reasoning," *Journal of Educational Psychology*, vol. 28 (1937), 122-129.

Bourke, Vernon J., "Saint Thomas and the Transfer of Intellectual
Skills," *The Modern Schoolman*, vol. 18 (1941), 69-73.

Castiello, Jaime, S.J., *A Humane Psychology of Education* (New York,
Sheed, 1936), pp. 170-174.

Castiello, Jaime, S.J., "The Psychology of Classical Training," *Thought*,
vol. 10 (1936), 632-654.

Chambers, E. G., "Transfer of Training: A Practical Problem," *Occupa-
tional Psychology*, vol. 30 (1956), 165-168; has a number of references
on the practical aspects of the problem.

Commins, W. D., and Fagin, Barry, *Principles of Educational Psychology*. 2nd ed. (New York, Ronald, 1954); pp. 588-614, transfer of training; pp. 480-486, conditioning, explained as a sequence of need-sign-
expectancy.

Cronbach, Lee J., *Educational Psychology* (New York, Harcourt, Brace
& World, 1954); pp. 245-275, transfer of learning; pp. 355-378, learning
of skills.

Harlow, H. F., "The Formation of Learning Sets," *Psychological Review*, vol. 56 (1949), 51-65.

Hendrickson, G., and Schroeder, W. H., "Transfer of Training in
Learning to Hit a Submerged Target," *Journal of Educational Psychology*, vol. 32 (1941), 205-213.

Hilgard, Ernest R., *Introduction to Psychology*, 2nd ed. (New York,
Harcourt, Brace & World, 1957); pp. 265-268, transfer of training;
pp. 260-280, management of learning; pp. 237-244, conditioned response.

Katona, G., *Organizing and Memorizing: Studies in the Psychology of
Learning and Teaching* (New York, Columbia, 1940).

Kolesnik, Walter J., *Mental Discipline in Modern Education* (Madison,
University of Wisconsin Press, 1958); good summary of literature on
transfer; upholds the value of mental discipline, but does not seem to
have any good explanation of why worthwhile transfer occurs.

Lewis, A. Dexter, "On Teaching the Systematic Transfer of Training,"
Harvard Educational Review, vol. 19 (1949), 127-141.

GROWTH AND DESTRUCTION OF HABITS 161

Sutherland, Robert L., Woodward, Julian L., and Maxwell, Milton A., *Introductory Sociology* (New York, Lippincott, 1961); this book summarizes most of the material on children who grew up in extreme social isolation.

Wertheimer, M., *Productive Thinking* (New York, Harper & Row, 1945); produces evidence showing the difference between general and specific habits, and between understanding the nature of a problem and its solution in contrast to memorizing a concrete procedure to be followed.

Woodrow, H., "The Effect of Type of Training Upon Transference," *Journal of Educational Psychology*, vol. 18 (1927), 159-172; transfer through principles can be likened to "learning to learn."

Woodworth, Robert S., *Dynamics of Behavior* (New York, Holt, Rinehart and Winston, 1958) pp. 228-256; conditioning as sequence learning based on expectancy, curiosity, or "exploratory drive."

Woodworth, Robert S., and Schlosberg, Harold, *Experimental Psychology* (New York, Holt, Rinehart and Winston, 1954); pp. 192-207, 733-778, transfer of training; pp. 541-581, conditioning.

Chapter Five

Virtue and Vice

WHAT IS VIRTUE?

We often speak of virtuous or vicious behavior, of virtuous habits or vicious habits. How do virtue and vice relate to what we have said about habits? We can answer this question by asking another question: In what senses can a habit be said to be "good"? What do we mean when we call a habitual modification of behavior "good" or "bad"?

First, there is one sense in which every habit is good, since every habit is a perfection, a further determination of the power in which it inheres. In every case, habit perfects potency; as act, it is good. Even the habit of consistently typing "adn" for "and" is good in the sense that it is a further determination of the imagination which, through the executive powers, gives rise to consistent, accurate, easy performance. A person with such a habit types "adn" consistently, accurately (i.e., he never slips and types "and" or 'nad"), and easily. However, such a habit is called good merely in the sense that it is an act, and thus better than the absence of act (potency) or the loss of suitable act (privation).

Second, some habits are called good or bad in the sense that they aid or impede the successful operation of the power in which they inhere. Some habits make the operation better in the sense of getting it done better; others hinder the proper performance of the operation. A twitch in external movement is a bad habit in this sense; stuttering is obviously a bad habit also; a smooth habit of typing (which always types "and" instead of "adn") is a good habit in this sense. A habit of erroneous opinion in the intellect is a bad habit because it hinders the intellect in its work of acquiring knowledge; right opinion is a good habit because it helps the intellect reach truth, as we shall see more in detail below.

162

However, as further determinations or perfections of the power, both erroneous and right opinions are good.

Third, we can consider not only the sort of power being perfected and further determined by habit, but also the sort of nature which possesses such a power. The nature can be considered either generically or specifically. *As animal,* man can possess habitual modifications of his operative powers which are bad for his animal nature, and others which are good for it. For example, habitual worry leading to ulcers is a bad habit for man as having a sensitive nature. Such habits are generically good or bad for man. *As rational animal,* man can also possess habitual modifications of his operative powers which are bad for his human nature, and others which are good for it. Such habits are specifically good or bad, not for the proper operation of a power but for the nature which possesses the power; they have as their proper objects properly human goods, or properly human evils.

Properly human goods or evils are *moral* goods or evils. Habits which have such goods or evils as their proper object are called virtues or vices. A *virtue* is a further determination (a perfection of one of man's operative powers), which has as its proper object a properly human good; it not only makes the power or the operation of the power good, it makes the man good. Similarly, a *vice* is a further determination (an ontological perfection of one of man's operative powers), which has as its proper object a properly human evil; it still makes the power good (i.e., as act is better than potency or privation), it may make the operation of the power good (i.e., if considered in isolation from the nature), but it makes the man bad.

ABSTRACT GOODNESS, EXISTENTIAL GOODNESS, AND MERIT

Much confusion surrounds the notion of virtue and good action, partly because people fail to make necessary distinctions. On the one hand, Christians know that without faith and charity, it is impossible to please God and save one's soul. On the other hand, pagans have spoken clearly about moral good and evil, and Christian thinkers have been able to assimilate all of this teaching into an entirely Christian teaching; moreover, it seems obvious to those who deal with people who do not have the faith that at least some of them are truly good men. How can an action which does not lead to eternal salvation be called truly good? On the other hand, how can an act of justice performed for justice's sake, even though performed by a person who does not have the virtue of divine charity, be called evil? Or is it even merely morally indifferent, like walking? To clarify this matter, let us look at the many meanings of the term "good."

$good_1$ = any act or perfection or even its possibility—transcendental good

$good_2$ = a proper good, that is, in relation to some kind of nature

$good_{2-a}$ = the proper good of an action itself: success

$good_{2-b}$ = the proper good of an operative power: success in relation to the goal of the power

$good_{2-c}$ = the proper good of a nature: success in relation to the goal of a nature

$good_{2-c-1}$ = the proper good of a nature considered somewhat indeterminately, for example, man as animal

$good_{2-c-2}$ = the proper good of a nature considered in its full specific reality: the proper good of man as man. This is the moral good with which the philosopher (ethician) is concerned.

$good_3$ = the good of man in the concrete order, inasmuch as he is called to participate in the divine life

In relation to this scheme, a few remarks must be made. First, all Catholic theologians hold that grace (and charity) does not destroy nature, but perfects it. Secondly, it is theologically sound, and philosophically certain, that charity is the form of the virtues, according to the way in which an accident is the form of a substance. Because charity is the form of a good act ($good_3$) whose matter may be already morally good ($good_{2-c-2}$) independently of its information by charity, or may be indifferent in the way in which some objects have goodness only through the intention of the agent, it is perfectly legitimate for the philosopher to abstract from the information by charity.[1] For to include the information

[1] For an analysis of St. Thomas Aquinas's view of the moral virtues, see the article, "Une théorie sur les vertus morales 'naturelles' et 'surnaturelles,'" Revue Thomiste, vol. 59 (1959), 565-575.

St. Thomas explicitly makes these distinctions in In Ep. ad Romanos, cap. 8,

by charity is to consider man not merely as a nature with specified powers and relations, but as such a nature is found in a concrete order of reality. Hence, there is a perfectly correct way in which a philosopher distinguishes between the transcendental good ($good_1$) and proper goods inadequately considered ($good_{2-a}$, $good_{2-b}$, and $good_{2-c-1}$) on the one hand, and the proper good of man as man ($good_{2-c-2}$) on the other. Only the latter is the moral good.

To say that human goodness can be legitimately spoken of only by a theologian who alone knows what "real goodness" ($=$ $good_3$) is, results—not necessarily perhaps in theory, but in practice—in reducing all objects of choice to the status of morally indifferent ones, and thereby depriving man of objective grounds for any choice of particular, intermediate goals except to the extent that these particular objects have been revealed to be good. It seems that this cripples thinking on moral matters.

On the contrary, it seems that with St. Thomas we can distinguish between "perfect" and "imperfect" virtue (in one of the many meanings of this pair of terms) :[2] "perfect" virtue is that which relates to man's goodness in the existential order ($good_3$), whereas "imperfect" virtue concerns the goodness which is directly proportioned to the nature of man ($good_{2-c-2}$). Any philosophical account of virtue will thus be a study of "imperfect" virtue. But a virtue which is imperfect in the sense just specified may still be a perfect virtue from other points of view and so be entitled to the name "virtue" without further qualification. For example, a moral virtue is a perfect virtue; whereas a virtue of the speculative intellect is only an imperfect virtue, namely, in relation to the proper good of man ($good_{2-c-2}$).[3]

Finally, goodness is sometimes discussed in terms of "merit." Merit may be considered to be the worth or value of a human life in relation to the attaining of the goal of human life viewed as re-

---

lect. 1, and especially cap. 14, lect. 3 ad finem; see also, *Summa Theologiae*, I-II, q. 78, art. 2, and I, q. 94, art. 1.

[2] See St. Thomas Aquinas, *Summa Theologiae*, I-II, q. 65, art. 2 and ad 1; and II-II, q. 23, art. 7 (in the latter text imperfect virtue is said to be true virtue and to be quite different from a "fallacious appearance of virtue" which arises from a wrong ultimate end).

[3] See also "Vertus morales 'naturelles' et 'surnaturelles,'" *op. cit.*, 565-575.

ward (or punishment). Taken concretely, merit relates to the concrete, existential good of man (good₃) ; and in this sense is a purely theological term. The notion of "merit" obviously is derived by analogy from that of a worker's just claim to a proportionate wage. Now, we can view the worker's just claim as the product of two qualities: the value of the work itself and the length of time the worker puts into doing that work. The former represents the qualitative worth of the work (in relation to other sorts of activity, as bookkeeping in relation to sweeping) and the excellence with which the particular worker does his task; the latter represents the duration. Now, these two functions can also be considered in relation to any activity. So, in a transferred sense, we can speak of the "merit" of a humanly virtuous act (good₂₋c₋₂). For, the duration of a virtuous activity itself has a moral quality which is not reducible to either the qualitative worth of the act or the intensity with which it is performed.

VIRTUE AND PLEASURE

Before we get any further into our consideration of virtue, we ought to consider a difficulty which bothers many, even though they may never formulate it explicitly for themselves. Virtue, as a habit whose object is a moral good (a good proper to man), has as one of its characteristics that it makes its operation *pleasant,* as well as consistently successful. How can this be? Is not the life of virtue opposed to the life of pleasure? Is not the life of pleasure precisely a life of vice?

Obviously there is an ambiguity here.[4] Often, pleasure means sense pleasure, the delectation found uniquely in the exercise of the sense of touch, sense gratification. Sometimes it means appetitive preference, the active attitude toward an object, an act consequent upon a known goodness. Thirdly, pleasure is a general term denoting the special suitability of an activity to an agent. It is in this third sense that we speak of the pleasure to be found in a habitual operation.[5]

[4] See pp. 14-15.
[5] This term *pleasure* does not have a single equivalent in Latin. In the sense first mentioned above, it translates *delectatio sensibilis.* In the second

Pleasure is a sign that a power or a nature is functioning well. Pain or sorrow or distress, on the other hand, is a sign that something is wrong with the power or the nature. A man who "controls himself" with a great effort, who barely manages to practice continence, does not enjoy himself. A person who has one or many vices enjoys his vicious practices in the sense that his morally bad habits lead to operations which are "easy and pleasant" to perform, as well as consistent and accurate. If his vices are located in the area of desiderative appetite, he also "enjoys" his excessive reaction to pleasurable goods of sense. But other than this, he does not enjoy himself. His vices make him a bad man, create a disorder in his nature which is painful, and prevent the harmonious development of his character in terms of moral goodness which is man's highest pleasure. The virtuous man, on the other hand, leads a life of pleasure precisely in so far as he is virtuous. His morally good habits lead to operations which are "easy and pleasant" to perform as well as consistent and accurate. They make him a good man, create an order in his nature which is pleasant, and develop a harmonious moral goodness which is the source of great pleasure. The person who is temperate and enjoys it because he thinks it is the rational thing to do takes great pleasure in an external activity (responding moderately to pleasurable goods) which would cause a merely continent man great hardship and which an intemperate man could only perform at the cost of great violence to his established patterns of behavior. Yet the temperate person's act is no less temperate because it gives him pleasure; rather the degree of pleasure it yields is a sign of the degree of virtue he possesses. Difficulty is not necessarily a sign of virtuous conduct, and pleasure is not necessarily a sign of vicious conduct. It is literally true that virtuous activity (in so far as it flows from previously acquired virtues) is not difficult but pleasurable.

However, once this much has been said about conduct which flows from previously acquired virtue, it must also be emphasized that the acquirement of virtue is usually a difficult task; and indirectly the degree of difficulty experienced may well correspond to

sense, it is *gaudium,* either sensible or intellectual. In the third sense, there is no single term; it might be *beatitudo* or *delectatio* or *voluptas* (as in St. Augustine's *voluptas cordis, animi;* see *In Joannis Evangelium,* tract. 26, par. 6).

the degree of intensity present in our striving after virtues. The in‚ temperate man who is content to remain intemperate experiences little struggle with regard to pleasurable goods; he enjoys responding to them excessively (though, accidentally, he may have to suffer the consequences of such excessive response—"hangovers," obesity, etc.) . The reformed drug addict or alcoholic suffers torments in his efforts to act temperately. Unless he makes great effort and performs extremely intense acts (i.e., perfect acts) , he is not able to overcome the previous habit of intemperance and acquire the desired virtue of temperance. Here the difficulty he experiences is a sign of the intensity of his effort. In a similar fashion, anyone who is trying to *increase* in virtue must struggle to do so, must make acts proper to the desired virtue which are more intense than those he spontaneously elicits in his present state of imperfect virtue. Such intensity costs him much effort and is often painful. It is necessary because he is still in the state of imperfect virtue; were his state of virtue perfect he would experience pleasure, not pain, in practicing the virtue. Difficulty is not a cause of virtue, it does not produce it. But often it is a sign that virtue is being acquired, that imperfections are being eliminated, and that effort at improvement is being made. Furthermore, since no man is in a state of absolutely perfect virtue and since any virtue is capable of indefinite increase, a person who experiences no pain or difficulty in life can be sure that he is neglecting some things which he ought to be doing, even if he is not actually practicing vice. Few of us have grounds to suspect that we are confirmed in grace.

What does an eminent authority in Christian asceticism like St. Ignatius mean when he says that people striving for perfection should choose what is most repugnant to nature? Certainly he does not mean that to be perfect one must always be experiencing repugnance in what one is doing. St. Ignatius is here referring to the fact of experience that gains in virtue cost effort. If we are striving for perfection, we must go against imperfect nature, nature which has not yet acquired the various habitual perfections which we call virtue. Other things being equal (and they seldom are) , the more we act against our imperfect nature, the sooner we shall perfect it. Thus, we do better to choose to preach to the unwashed rather than to the perfumed, but there is still no reason why we should

not try to *like* preaching to the unwashed. Difficulty is not a cause
of virtue; at best, it is only a sign of intense effort to acquire virtue.

Of course, it is often true that obstacles and suffering are the
occasions for acquiring virtue, inasmuch as they challenge us, put
great demands upon us to elicit intense acts which do, in fact, develop virtuous habits. Temptation to morally evil activity has been
the occasion for many persons to acquire valuable virtues. People
often (but by no means always) rise to such occasions and sometimes perform heroically intense (i.e., perfect) acts of virtue which
they would never have performed in a different, less difficult situation. Yet it is not the difficulty of the situation but rather what we
do in such a situation that counts. Suffering is a blessing for one
who uses it correctly to grow in virtue, it is an occasion of sin for
one who collapses or rebels against God's Providence as a result of
it. Some go to heaven because of suffering, others to hell. It is good
to have one's virtue tried, because then one has an opportunity to
make the extra effort, the more intense or perfect act of virtue
which permanently increases virtue. But there is nothing automatic about this response; there is no guarantee except God's own
unmerited gifts and one's own generosity that the challenge will
be met and virtue made perfect.

Once we realize that an act of virtue is not intrinsically modified
because of the difficulty or lack of difficulty which accompanies it,
we can save ourselves many misunderstandings and much mis-
guided asceticism. Difficulty is often a *sign* of increasing virtue;
suffering is often an *occasion* of developing virtue; neither is ever a
direct *cause* of virtue. Intensity of an action is the key factor in developing habits of virtue, and intensity refers to the intrinsic perfection of the proper act of a virtue, not the external circumstances
in which the virtue is practiced.

But when all this has been said, a very delicate point remains.
The great saints are characterized by a "love of suffering"; lovers
want to give costly gifts or do difficult things to show their love;
and our Lord Jesus Christ, as St. Paul says, "emptied himself, taking the nature of a slave and . . . humbled himself, becoming
obedient unto death, even to death on a cross" (Phil. ii, 6-8, Con-
fraternity version). How is this, and how does it fit in with what
has just been said about virtue and pleasure?

Love is a very subtle emotion. Love brings great pleasure, but love-for-pleasure's sake is not love of benevolence (pure love); it is self-love. A person who is deeply in love is very happy, and, if he is a sensitive person, can be disturbed lest his love become mixed with and replaced by self-love—love of the pleasure of being in love. Hence, to prove *to himself* in the first instance (and sometimes to the beloved) that his love is pure, a man wants to show his love by acts that are to his disadvantage in being for the good of the beloved. Hence, a lover's gift should have cost something—money, time, danger, or effort to get it, and so on.

But when the beloved is God and the good, what can the "gift" be? Yet there remains the necessity of showing that love is pure. Hence, the glad acceptance of suffering, the seeking out of difficulty and suffering, and even the inflicting of pain on one's self; all are ways of purifying and intensifying love, for then one is clearly not merely "enjoying the thrill of loving." Why does it have to be physical pain? Why cannot God be loved with an absolutely pure love even in the midst of comfort? After all, what is involved is the will, a spiritual power. This question leaves out of account the fact that man is an incarnate nature, not a spirit, no matter what some philosophers wish to hold. Man is truly an animal, and the "thrill of being in love" is largely due to a sensory component of affection and feeling, which is accepted as an object by the will in place of the person beloved. So the proof of the "purity" of love is to suffer physical, sensible pain.

A sign that the love of suffering is a rightly ordered one in the context of the love of God is that it is joyous, lightsome, fresh, and wholesome as the air of a spring morning. We will consider this attitude toward sensible things later in connection with temperance.

It is necessary clearly to distinguish this attitude from masochism. Psychologists know that there are such attitudes as self-hate, self-contempt, aggression against one's self, self-destructiveness, and that these attitudes lead to self-punishment. There is even a perverse pleasure in inflicting pain on one's self. How can pain be pleasurable? There seem to be two aspects: a more indirect one, in that the person takes pleasure in being "justly" punished by himself; and a more direct one in that pain, especially self-inflicted pain, is a stimulation of the sense of touch and so is closely connected with sexuality.

It is also necessary to distinguish these two attitudes from a third, namely, penance. In penance, a person truly realizes that he has done wrong, and reasonably desires to punish himself. But the practice of penance does not have the emotional involvement characteristic of masochism. The pain inflicted is simply painful, and the satisfaction found in the suffering is the purely rational one of atonement. The attitude of penance would be classified under justice.

HOW IS VIRTUE ACQUIRED?

A virtue is a habit. Like all habits it is acquired only in one way: *by the performance of acts proper to that virtue.* We do not learn to love our friend merely by observing the external rituals of friendship; we must will his good selflessly.[6] We do not acquire temperance merely by being put on a starvation diet, or learn sobriety by being too poor to buy liquor. Rather, we learn to be temperate about our food by responding to the pleasurable goods of the table in a moderate way; we learn sobriety by responding to bottled goods in a moderate, proportioned manner.

People often practice acts which are quite other than the proper act of the virtue they wish to acquire, especially when they perform acts of understanding or intention rather than acts of choice or acts of the sensory appetites. For instance, a person may feel a sensory repugnance to people with red hair. To overcome this repugnance, he forms a habit of repeating a little formula to himself every time he meets a person with red hair: "I *do* like people with red hair!" What habit does he acquire as a result of this practice? Probably the only habitual perfection acquired is the habit of responding to the sight of a person with red hair by reciting the pat formula. It is most unlikely that the sensory response will be modified at all. The individual will continue to dislike persons with red hair until such time as he educates his sensory appetites

6 See the more extensive treatment pp. 226-231.

to like them. To do this, he must not only resolve to like them: he must actually like them, that is, perform acts of the sensory appetites which will bring about the desired habitual response.

It is clear that when a person is engaged in the business of acquiring a particular virtue, he must consciously advert to what he is doing. Virtues have as their objects properly human goods, goods that involve intellect and will. Therefore they cannot be acquired "by accident" or "automatically." Furthermore, a person must also advert to what he is doing if he wishes to practice a virtue once he has acquired it. He must be consciously and willingly just if he is to be (formally) just at all. Such advertence need not involve a distinct act, but it must be present.

Ascetical writers employ certain technical terms to describe various types of *intention* in moral acts, including acts of virtue. An *actual intention* is a tendency of the will to an intellectually known good which enters into the moral act, directs it, and is adverted to at the time the moral act takes place. It is explicit if attention is focused upon it, implicit if it is on the periphery of consciousness. A *virtual intention* is a tendency of the will to an intellectually known good which enters into the moral act and directs it but is not adverted to at the time the act is being carried on and completed. A virtual intention receives all the efficacy it possesses from a prior actual intention; it is really nothing other than the continuance of the causal efficacy of a previous actual intention.[7] Particular virtual intentions continue throughout a continuing action, but they are interrupted by being forgotten or by any cessation of actual consciousness. On the contrary, the determining intentions a man has in his life may remain effective for a long time. Thus, a man's intention to keep his job because it is the way he supports his family may be effective for many years without ever being explicitly stated to himself. How can this be? It is not so hard to see if we remember several things. First, the human intellect, once it has an actual understanding, is never again reduced to simple potency concerning that object. Secondly, our consciousness always contains more than we are able to verbalize; this is especially true of the context which is adverted to but

[7] One of the classical discussions is that of distractions during prayer; see St. Thomas Aquinas, *In I. Ep. ad Corinthios*, cap. 14, lect. 3.

never expressed and perhaps never expressible.[8] Thirdly, given that an object continues to be intellectually known even in a highly implicit form, it can continue to be a good adhered to by our will. Consequently, basic attitudes, long-range choices, and the like, can continue to exist and be influential perhaps for years without being explicitly and distinctly willed during that time. However, what is possible is not thereby ideal. Though a merely implicit orientation is sufficient, no growth in it is possible as long as it remains implicit, and it can be replaced by another almost without being noticed.

There is, in addition, the so-called *"habitual intention."* This is an act of the will which was once actually made and has never been revoked, but which has no influence upon a present moral act (except in rare cases when an act of the will is needed only as a condition—for example, in the reception of baptism by an adult who is unconscious). It is easy to see from these definitions that an actual intention must be involved somewhere (in the past or in the present) in every moral act. Furthermore, this actual intention must be proper to the act which is intended. One does not practice chastity by intending to be good-in-general, but by some type of efficacious intention to practice chastity. And this is the minimum requirement. When there is a question of acquiring or increasing virtue, an explicit actual intention is required, the more explicit the better. It is not the ideal to make habits of intellect and will minimally conscious; *they are supposed to be conscious.* More intense or perfect acts of these habits (the kind by which such habits are acquired and strengthened) are more fully conscious than less intense or perfect acts of these same habits.

Now that we have seen that virtues are only acquired by the performance of their proper acts and that such acts must be actually intended even after the virtue is acquired, we can turn our attention to the problem of intermediate ends in human activity and the virtues which regulate such activity. We shall discuss the interrelationships of virtues later in this chapter, but we already know of the existence of *some* order and subordination among

[8] This point has been made emphatically by Michael Polanyi, "Tacit Knowing," *Philosophy Today*, vol. 6 (Winter, 1962), 239-262.

man's virtuous habits. We wish here to apply to this area of sub-ordinated virtues what we have said of the need for exercising and actually intending the proper act of a virtue. Some people try to aim only at generic goodness and relegate specific goods to the status of pure means. In other words, they try to bypass the proper objects of specific virtues and get along with generic virtues or even some extrageneric goals like "generosity" or "selflessness." These are the people who read poetry because their teacher orders them to read poetry, not because they want to enjoy great literature. This process reduces intermediate ends (which have their own intrinsic goodness as well as serving as means to a more ultimate end) to the status of pure means. The specific goodness of the intermediate end is not intended; consequently the proper act of a habit or virtue ordered to that intermediate end is never performed, and the habit or virtue is never acquired. People who read poetry out of obedience may develop their virtue of obedience, but they will not develop their intellectual appreciation of literature. A doctor who practices *only* to make a living will not become a great physician; he must also *aim at* being a great physician *as an end,* an object with its own intrinsic goodness which is to be obtained through proper activities and proper habits and virtues; otherwise he will neither be a great physician nor achieve his more ultimate end, making a living.

The following diagrams illustrate various ways in which the will can tend to objects. The first diagram involves only one end, the second involves an ultimate and an intermediate end, and the third involves an end and a pure means.

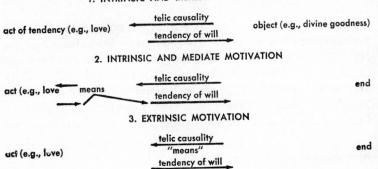

1. INTRINSIC AND IMMEDIATE MOTIVATION

act of tendency (e.g., love) ← telic causality / tendency of will → object (e.g., divine goodness)

2. INTRINSIC AND MEDIATE MOTIVATION

act (e.g., love ← means ← telic causality / tendency of will → end

3. EXTRINSIC MOTIVATION

act (e.g., love) ← telic causality / "means" / tendency of will → end

The third diagram shows a habit of the will which tries to wash out the intrinsic secondary goodness of an intermediate end. This can involve single acts or habits. From a metaphysical point of view, such a procedure of bypassing the intrinsic goodness of intermediate ends is the equivalent in the line of tendency to the equally unsuccessful attempt in the line of efficiency to ignore the distinct natures of creatures as secondary efficient causes. From a psychological point of view, trying to perform an individual act of the will only from the love of the ultimate end is possible; but trying to do this *habitually* is to do violence to one's nature and ultimately to fail. *Violenta non durant.*

Another difficulty plagues a person who attempts to act from ultimate, external motives alone and to ignore intermediate ends. Where all but the ultimate end is treated as a means, how is one to decide which means to use? Unless one recognizes the intrinsic goodness (good$_{2-c-2}$) of intermediate ends, by what criterion does one choose one "means" rather than another, or choose any "means" at all? Thus, to act only from ultimate motives means either that a person does nothing at all or that he acts from masked motives—and such motives are usually low ones.[9]

[9] It should hardly be necessary to point out that only morally good or morally indifferent actions can serve as true means to good ends. Some of the intermediate ends we have been discussing are morally indifferent; the habits which have these ends as their objects are thus not virtues, because they are not ordered to properly human goods, though they are true habits and may be very important in a man's life. Most of the intermediate ends we have been discussing are themselves morally good; the habits which have these ends as their objects are true virtues which make the man who possesses them good. Morally evil actions, which (if habitual) flow from vicious habits, cannot function as true means to a good end, though they can function as true means to a bad end. Thus, when the psychologist Knight Dunlap devised a method which enabled him to cure stuttering by making the stutterer stutter in public, this method was both successful and morally good. The technique used an indifferent activity (stuttering, a motor activity flowing from habits of the imagination) to accomplish a good objective (curing the stutter). But when Dunlap tried to apply this same technique to break a person of the habit of masturbation, the technique became morally evil. It used a morally evil activity (masturbation) to accomplish a good objective (breaking the person of his habit of masturbation).

Along the same line, we should also remember that a morally good or indifferent means is vitiated by a morally evil end. Yoga asceticism aims for temperance in order to bolster pride, it is sometimes alleged. If this is true, this is a case of a morally good means being vitiated by a morally evil end. Of course, if the morally good means is willed both for itself and for the sake

For these reasons, it is important to remember that man needs to act with an activity proportioned to the intrinsic goodness of intermediate ends as well as to the goodness of the ultimate end. Since such goal orientation is a permanent situation, man also needs habits and virtues which have as their proper objects the intrinsic goodness of intermediate end. Charity, love of the ultimate end, is not enough to guide human activity, though it is needed to give ultimate direction. This conclusion will become very significant when we begin to discuss the interrelationships and subordination which are characteristic of human goal orientation and the corresponding interrelationships and subordination of the virtues (and vices) by which a man habitually regulates his tendencies toward properly human goods. The object of most human acts of tendency will then be revealed as having many goodnesses, properly subordinated of course, but still multiple. A man studies poetry to learn to appreciate literature and thus obey his teacher's orders. The object of the will act, the intention, involving such activity is a *complex* object composed of *multiple goodnesses subordinated to one another*. The intrinsic goodness of intermediate ends is recognized and willed in an act proportioned to that goodness (as well as to the goodness of the ultimate end).

As a final point in our discussion of the acquisition of virtues, we should again point out that virtues, once acquired, are capable of indefinite increase. The Stoic view that a man either has a virtue wholly or does not have it at all does not agree with our experience of possessing the essentials of a particular virtue but growing steadily in that virtue over the years. The acts flowing from a virtue (or a vice) can become more or less consistent, accurate, and easy, even though the proper object of that virtue never changes. St. Thomas is referring to this experience when

---

of the morally evil end, there are really two human acts involved, one of which is morally good, the other morally evil. The philanthropist who donates lavishly but conspicuously practices no virtue if he gives *only* to inflate his ego; if he gives both to help the poor and thereby inflate his ego, however, he is intending an intermediate end which is not completely vitiated by the morally evil ultimate end, and thus practices at least some virtue. The question is more than an academic one if one considers the prevalence of mixed motives in human activities.

he speaks of a virtue getting deeper roots in the power which it modifies.

ST. AUGUSTINE'S CRITERION OF VIRTUE

We have already described a virtue as a habit which is ordered to a proper good of man (good$_{2-c-2}$), a habit which makes good not only the power (good$_{2-b}$) or the operation (good$_{2-a}$) of the power, but also the man. St. Augustine has another criterion for virtue which examines man's habitual activity from a slightly different point of view. He defines a virtue as *a habit which cannot be misused*. Conversely, a vice is a habit which cannot be properly used for the good of man.

Virtue, thus, is an intermediate end. On the one hand, inasmuch as it is truly an end, it has an intrinsic goodness of its own by reason of which its possession makes a man good. On the other hand, it is intrinsically ordered to other ends and to man's last end. Therefore it must always of its nature be ordered to that end. At the very least, it cannot be explicitly deprived of this relationship or explicitly ordered to another end. Virtue, thus, is a means, but not a *mere* means.

Back of this requirement is the realistic view that things have their relations to each other prior to and independent of our arbitrary desires. If all relations were the product of man's intention, then we could indeed use anything for any purpose, and the things would derive their goodness or evil from such use alone. But if some things are intrinsically related to man's nature, then the goodness of our use depends on these prior relations, not on our arbitrary choice. That is why a sinful act *cannot* be ordered to a morally good end, much as in a particular case some one might wish to order it. Conversely, a morally good act (such as an act of virtue) *cannot,* while remaining unchanged, be subordinated to a morally evil purpose.

It will deepen our understanding of our original statement— that virtue involves moral goods which make the man good—to apply St. Augustine's criterion of virtue to the various habits and levels of habit in man. We shall examine each power of man which can be further modified by habit.

MOTOR SKILLS

Motor skills involve habits of the imagination which organize perception and provide the proper kinesthetic images to stimulate and control man's motor powers. Thus, motor skills are not only good because they are acts (good$_1$) and not potencies or privations, but they are also good (or bad) because they perfect (or impede) the proper operation of the imagination and the executive power (goods$_{2-a}$ and $_b$). Habits of typing or dressing are good or bad in this sense. But do habits of typing or dressing make the man good or bad? Do they involve properly human goods, moral goods? In St. Augustine's terms, can a good habit of typing be misused? Obviously it can. A man may use his good habit of typing to write pornographic literature; a woman may use her good habit of dressing to dress for an assignation. Of themselves, motor skills are neutral to the proper goods of man; they have no intrinsic moral perfection. They may be used for the good of man, they may instrumentally make the man good, but they need not do so. There are no virtues or vices among man's motor skills.

IMAGINATION AND DISCURSIVE ESTIMATION

Like the imagination habits involved in motor skills, other habits of the imagination and habits of the discursive estimation can be good or bad in the sense that they perfect or impede the proper operation of the power. In addition, some habits of the imagination are directly good for man as a sensing organism (good$_{2-c-1}$). A person who habitually uses double negatives in English has a bad habit of the imagination; a person who uses negatives properly has a good habit of the imagination. But does bad English make a man morally evil or does good English make him morally good? It does not, at least not necessarily. Similarly, a person who can readily imagine actions he has not yet performed has a good imagination (good$_{2-c-1}$); a person whose activities are interfered with by annoying recollections or fixed images has a bad imagination (bad$_{2-c-1}$). Habits of the imagination, like motor skills, are morally neutral: they may instrumentally make a man good, but they need not do so. They can be misused and thus are not virtues (or vices) according to St. Augustine's criterion.

Habits of the discursive power are more closely connected with properly human goods, since the discursive estimation operates under the guidance of reason to form concrete sensory judgments of good or evil, suitability or unsuitability. In so far as habitual modifications of the discursive estimation are material components of complex habits whose substantial, formal components are habitual modifications of the intellect, they may well be ordered to properly human goods and make the man good, not simply the operation of the power good. We will later consider such complex habits from the viewpoint of their substantial, formal components, not their material components. When the discursive estimation operates independently of the guidance of the intellect (and thus independently of the virtue of prudence), it operates according to automatism habits. Such activity and the habits which control it are not necessarily ordered to the good (good $_{2-c-2}$) of man. Automatism habits in the discursive estimation may be misused: sensory good (good$_{2-c-1}$) and evil (object of automatism habits of the discursive estimation) are not of themselves identifiable with moral good and evil, with properly human goods and evils.

DESIDERATIVE AND AGGRESSIVE SENSORY APPETITES

We have seen that there are two types of habitual modifications of man's sensory appetites. Mastery habits (temperance and fortitude) in the sensory appetites are consistent modes of tending to the proper object of the sensory appetites in an excessive, proportioned, or deficient manner, under the direction of reason (conscious volition, prudence). Automatism habits or even pure automatism are consistent modes of tendency which can operate independently of reason. A person who irrationally fears the dark or has habitual stage fright has an automatism habit of the sensory appetite. A moment's reflection will show that mastery habits of the sensory appetites are true virtues (or vices), ordered to properly human goods (good$_{2-c-2}$). A good mastery habit of the sensory appetites cannot be misused. Good habits in these powers regulate man's reaction according to right reason, the virtue of prudence. Because of such habits (substantially in the sensory appetites, accidentally but formally in the intellect), man responds to concrete sensory goods in a proper, proportioned, reasonable way. Such a response is a proper good of man, a moral good. Similarly, bad habits in the sensory appetites which are true mastery habits cannot be properly used. Because of such habits, man responds to concrete sensory goods in an improper, disproportioned, unreasonable way. Such a response is a moral evil, a true vice. A person, of course, can misuse sensory goods and pretend to be acting out of temperance or fortitude; but he cannot actually be exercising a good mastery habit of the sensory appetites and still perform morally evil acts. Thus, all mastery habits in both sensory appetites are either virtuous or vicious. There are no neutral, morally indifferent mastery habits in these powers.[10]

There are also automatism habits in the sensory appetites. These elicit responses to sensory goods which are not under the control of reason (e.g., a person feels afraid of the dark whether he wants to or not; an inexperienced speaker feels stage fright no matter what he does). Are such habits true virtues (or vices)? Obviously they are not. These habits are not ordered toward properly human goods or evils; they are not intrinsically moral habits; they function independently of reason; they do not make a man morally good or evil. Unlike mastery habits, therefore, automatism habits in the sensory appetites are not true virtues (or vices).

INTELLECT

Are intellectual habits ordered to properly human goods (good$_{2-c-2}$)? Do they make a man good or evil as man, or do they

---

[10] It must be remembered that these mastery habits are habitual modifications of the sensory appetites themselves, even though they are part of complex habit groups which include prudence (itself a complex habit located formally in the intellect and materially in the discursive estimation) as an accidental but formal component. A change in the judgment of right reason, prudence, is not extrinsic to the sensory appetites; *it results in a change in the response of the sensory appetites themselves.*

merely make the operation of the intellect good or bad? In other words, are intellectual habits virtuous and vicious; or are they morally neutral, like motor skills or automatism habits in the imagination, discursive estimation, and sensory appetites?

We are immediately aware that the intellect is different from the powers we have so far considered, for the intellect is already by itself a properly human power, it pertains to the specific perfection of man as man. In speaking of the intellect, therefore, we necessarily refer to the nature of man adequately considered. Now, the object of the intellect is what is intelligible, and when it is able to work perfectly as an intellect, it reaches the truth of the intelligible. Hence, we can say that the object or goal of the intellect is truth. Because intellectual knowledge is a properly human function, truth is a properly human good. But the intellect is a knowing power; and so, though what it attains is a good for man as man, it does not attain it *as good*. Consequently, the truth as known is a properly human good $(good_{2-c-2})$, but imperfectly such, since it is not related to the intellect precisely as good.

By way of contrast, ignorance and error are evils for man. Some ignorance is merely an absence of perfection, and so is not strictly an evil. But other kinds of ignorance are really evils; namely, when ignorance is strictly a privation, an absence of a truth which a man ought to know. For example, every man necessarily has to act; and to act rightly he must have at least some knowledge of himself, of the goal of his whole life, and of the objects with which he has to deal. If he acts in such ignorance that he has no reasonable grounds for choice, his action is not merely defective in a broad sense (that is, deprived of some $good_1$), but deprived of a properly human good. Error, inasmuch as it is a positive reality (namely, an act of the intellect), is even more of an evil. In every case, error is an evil of the intellect (opposed to $good_{2-b}$). When error affects action, it could be harmless or advantageous only accidentally;[11] usually it brings about harm and sometimes

[11] As logicians point out, accidentally two false premises can lead to a true conclusion, but not *as* true, as in the example: "All fish have short legs; all short-legged animals live in the water; therefore all fish live in the water.". But two errors do not ordinarily cancel each other out so neatly; usually they accumulate.

very widespread evil. Moreover, if it affects the acts and objects which in some way or other are necessary for man, it interferes with, and, if it is culpable, destroys the properly human good $(good_{2-c-2})$.

Next, we must consider the relation of the intellectual habits to this imperfect good of man. We cannot make a general statement about *all* intellectual habits at once. As we have already seen, there are several different types of intellectual habits, each of which can have many species. We will therefore have to examine each one of these types and see how it is related to the intellect's attaining of its good.

First, let us consider habits of opinion, which are the most imperfect and which control such an extensive portion of human intellectual activity. What is the function of an opinionative habit? We can understand it by examining the nature of an act of opinion. An opinion is a judgment or assent which is not entirely determined by the object as known or by an extrinsic motive. When the evidence of the object as known determines our assent and it is seen in itself, we speak of a *per se* known proposition, and such knowledge is a simple insight, not an opinion. When the evidence of an object is known through some intelligible medium, we speak of a demonstrated proposition. When we judge something to be true on extrinsic grounds, we call the act an act of faith; and, if the grounds are sufficient, our judgment attains truth. Now, this leaves room for opinion where the evidence as known or the grounds for faith are insufficient. In either case, a judgment might possibly attain truth; it might just as possibly be mistaken. There is nothing about opinion itself, intrinsically, that guarantees that we reach the truth. We can well grant that an opinion in itself may be right or wrong, but the person who holds it as an opinion is not sure on that score that his opinion is right.

Habits of opinion bring about consistent acts of opinion easily and firmly. For example, we can consider the average man's acceptance of scientific conclusions, his political allegiance, his knowledge of Chinese history. Though he has some reasons for holding the opinions he does hold, his reasons are not such as necessarily to bring about the truth of those opinions. His political allegiance, for example, may be determined by his family tradition or by promises of personal or group advantage. Now, a habit which as such does not ensure the proper operation of a power cannot be called a virtue in any sense.

Scientific knowledge is another kind of human intellectual knowledge. A habit of science certainly perfects the operation of the intellect, because it orders it to truth, demonstratively attained. We have already insisted that a habit of science does not exist unless the knower is reflectively aware that his reasoning processes arise from true premises and lead to their conclusions with the appropriate logical necessity. Therefore, the habit of science intrinsically leads to truth; and as a consequence it is a true, but imperfect virtue, as we have seen earlier in considering the sense in which truth is a good of man. If we offer a strict disjunction "Is a science a perfect virtue or not?" then we must say that science is not a virtue. St. Thomas Aquinas compromises by calling science a virtue "in a secondary, or imperfect, sense," for it is not ordered to a properly human good in an adequate sense of that phrase unless it is also connected with a good act (or habit) of the will.

What about habits of art? We have seen in a previous analysis that an artistic habit group is quite complicated; its unity comes from the fact that all the activities involved are ordered to the production (and appreciation) of the art work. Art in this meaning of the term is an intellectual habit but is not a virtue. It is not ordered to a properly human good, a moral good, and it can be misused. A good artist is not necessarily a good man. However, contemporary usage often confines the meaning of "art" to "fine art" and excludes the so-called "practical" or "mechanical" arts. Fine art does involve a virtuous habit as one component of the art habit group, and that is the virtue of veracity. The creative or fine artist must be true, must "tell the truth" in his expression of his artistic experience. Fine art is necessarily a communication, and as such is either true or false. So veracity, a virtue which is a species of justice, is required in the fine artist. Bad creative art which lacks this virtue is meretricious; it prostitutes the original artistic experience and expresses the meaningful artistic image falsely. It points to a vice in the artist, a habit which makes him a bad man and not simply a bad artist. Similarly, good creative art which involves this virtue points to an artist who is not only a good artist but also a good man.

Wisdom is the special intellectual habit which concerns the knowledge of ends and orders other intellectual knowledge (including habits of the intellect) in subordination to these ends. Is this habit of the intellect a virtue? Before we can answer this question we must note that there are different types of wisdom and briefly examine the role of these various wisdoms in human life. Only then can we decide whether wisdom is ordered to a properly human good (i.e., moral goodness) and whether wisdom can be misused.

Wisdom has been highly extolled by many different thinkers, but it has not always been clear just what is referred to by this honorable name. For our purposes we will follow the various analyses of St. Thomas Aquinas. According to him, a habit is called a "wisdom" if it is certain and in some way inclusive and ultimate. In the order of natural speculative knowledge, first philosophy or metaphysics is a wisdom, for its object is being as being; it is therefore all inclusive at this level; it is ultimate, since the causes of being are simply the ultimate causes—the more common the effect, the more ultimate the cause; and it is certain, since it is a scientific knowledge. In the order of supernatural speculative knowledge, theology is a wisdom, for its object is God as revealed and all things as referred to God; it is ultimate, since God is the unique cause of all things; and it is certain, since it is also a scientific knowledge. In the order of supernatural practical knowledge, there is an infused wisdom based on divine charity; this wisdom is ultimate and all inclusive, since it rests on the love of God who is the first cause, and it has the certitude of an ordered love. Finally, it seems that there ought to be admitted a wisdom of experience, based on ordered knowledge and right order toward reality as a whole; this also is ultimate and all inclusive, and it too has the certitude of a right appetite toward being.

In every perfect scientific knowledge (and also in every perfect moral attitude), we find that the one who knows completely judges all the particular conclusions of his science. Now, when a science is in some way all inclusive, it is able to that same extent to judge all things. A wisdom such as metaphysics does not know the details which are known by the particular sciences; and as metaphysics does not know what to do with them, it does not know whether they are true or false, and so on. But it does know their relevance for the whole of life. It judges them in that it knows why there is truth at all and what the significance of particular truths is in relation to the inclusive truths about reality as a whole. Wisdom's judgment, therefore, is in the first instance a judgment about itself and other types of knowledge; and it orders all of these—that is, it sets the right value on them. In the second instance, because wisdom is a knowledge of reality as a whole and of its major classifications, it is able to judge their relative importance for the living of human life as a whole.

Because the judgment of wisdom is not so much a judgment about truth as it is a judgment of good (and in various senses, depending on the kind of wisdom of which we are speaking), it is more closely related to good than any other speculative habit of intellect. It is still as such an imperfect virtue (though both the infused wisdom and the wisdom of experience presuppose perfect virtue), even though of all such virtues it is the closest to perfect virtue.

The two speculative wisdoms, metaphysics and theology, seem to be possessed occasionally by someone who is not a morally good man. Both of these habits are also from another point of view scientific disciplines. As scientific, they certainly can be acquired by someone without involving the goodness of his will. But it seems doubtful that an evil man can exercise the full scope of the judgments of wisdom as long as he remains evil. For in judging the value of objects in relation to human life he must come to realize that his own actions proceed from a different evaluation. The easiest way for him would be to restrict the application of this speculative knowledge to the purely speculative order. Thus, *for him,* what is a wisdom in itself would not work as a wisdom, but would remain in an imperfect, unfulfilled condition.

We will close our discussion of intellectual habits from the point of view of virtuous or vicious behavior by examining the habits of prudence, imprudence, and astuteness. These habits all are habitual modifications of the intellect's last practical judgment, which forms part of the composite act of choice. This last practical judgment is related to will in the act of choice as accidental form is related to substance: the intention (or tendency of the will to an end-to-be-attained) is the substantial drive which is formally directed by the conclusion of the intellect's deliberation about the means to this end or about the end viewed concretely; the composition of drive-plus-direction results in the composite act of choice, which is formally in the intellect but substantially in the will. The last practical judgment does not concern ends formally taken; it directs a choice of means to an end previously intended or to a concrete end. We know from experience that the intellect can acquire habits in connection with the last practical judgment (or the conclusion-judgment, as we shall call it hereafter). The intellectual habit of judging properly about concretely good means to a good end is called *prudence*. The intellectual habit of judging improperly about means to a good end is called *imprudence*. The intellectual habit of judging properly about means to a bad end is called *astuteness*. The intellectual habit of judging inappropriately about means to a bad end has no standard name; we might call it bungling. Conclusion-judgments which direct choice need not flow from any habit at all: only if they reveal a consistent, accurate, and pleasurable (i.e., easy) pattern of such judgments do they imply an intellectual habit as their source.[12]

[12] Moralists speak frequently of the *judgment of conscience* involved in human acts. This judgment does not consist of general moral principles or laws; it is a concrete, particular judgment which takes the following form: "Here and now, under these circumstances, this is the morally good (or one of the morally good) thing(s) to do."

The judgment of conscience (1) can be about past or future actions, not only about acts to be performed here and now; (2) is present in a sinful act, though there it is disregarded, as well as in a morally good act; (3) can be made by a sinner, by a man who has not yet acquired virtue, and by a virtuous man; (4) may be about several courses of action, provided only that they are all morally good.

The conclusion-judgment of prudence (1) is only about acts to be performed here and now; (2) is present only in a morally good act; (3) can be performed easily, consistently, and pleasurably only by a man who has the virtue of prudence; (4) is about only one act (even when other alternatives are morally good).

Thus, in many good acts of a prudent man, the judgment of conscience is also the judgment of prudence (except in those cases where a conscience-judg-

We shall have to discuss prudence and the other habits of the conclusion-judgment at length when we examine the cardinal virtues in man. At this point we merely want to ask whether such habits involve virtue and vice. We shall use prudence as our example, but what we say can also be applied (with the proper modifications) to the habits of imprudence, astuteness, and bungling. Now, is prudence a virtue? Is the habit of prudence ordered to a proper good of man? Can prudence ever be misused? We can see that prudence is indeed a virtue in the full sense of that term if we recall that prudence not only involves the good operation of the intellect (i.e., the proper selection of means) but also presupposes a will ordered to good ends. Thus a prudent act will always be good *in the moral sense:* prudence directs a will ordered to moral goods, ends, in the selection of suitable means to those ends. Prudence is ordered to properly human goods; it cannot be misused. A habit which directs a man in his selection of good means to a morally good end cannot make a man morally evil: it can only make a man, as well as the operation of his intellect, good. Thus, prudence is an intellectual virtue in the full sense of the term; imprudence, astuteness, and bungling are intellectual vices.

We have already seen that prudence is a complex habit—formally in the intellect, materially in the discursive estimation—which is also part of habit groups like temperance, fortitude, and justice, to which it is related as accidental form is related to substance. When we speak of the measure of reason involved in such mastery habits of the sensory appetites and the will, we are referring to conclusion-judgments. "Reason" in this sense refers not only to intellect but also to intellect-directing-will-in-its-drive-towards-morally-good- (or evil) -ends. A habitually good or bad measure of reason (excessive, moderate, deficient) involves an intellectual habit (prudence, imprudence, etc.) which is virtuous or vicious. Thus, prudence and all virtues directed by prudence are *morally* good because they are all related through prudence to man's tendency towards morally good ends.

---

ment might approve several alternatives, but prudence will select one). Nonetheless, conscience and prudence are formally two different aspects of moral action; so they should not be confused, even when they concretely coincide.

WILL

Are the various habits we have discovered in the will virtuous and vicious habits, or are there morally neutral habits of the will? Do habits of the will merely make the operation of the will good or bad, or do they also make the man good or bad? Do they involve moral goodness or moral evil, do they tend towards properly human goods or evils? Can a good habit of the will be misused, or can a bad habit of the will be properly used?

All these questions can be answered rather easily if we recall that the will is by its very nature a moral power, concerned with the intention of ends suitable to human nature and the selection of means which lead to such morally good ends. Once the will is oriented towards its final end, all its activities are concretely morally good or morally evil. Therefore, all habits of the will which regulate such activity are either virtues or vices. This shows why such habits must be both acquired and exercised with intellectual awareness and with freedom. Included among these virtues are justice, friendship, humility, and the supernatural virtue of charity.

MATTER AND FORM IN THE VIRTUES: NECESSARY HABIT GROUPS

We have already seen that habits can stand in various relationships in which they mutually affect each other. Are there any special instances of such interrelatedness among the virtues?

We have already in passing adverted to the fact that prudence is the (accidental) form of the moral virtues. This relationship deserves fuller analysis. On the one hand, prudence cannot exist alone: there must be other virtues to set the ends. For prudence, as we have seen, is practical reasoning about the ways of attaining good ends. The notion of *means and ends* as used in this particular context needs elaboration. What is the "end" with which prudential reasoning begins? It may be, for example, the intention of using food moderately. And what precisely remains for deliberation, given this intention? The discovery of *what is mod-*

eration in this particular case. Actually to have a moderate desire for a sensible good requires a knowledge of what is moderate. On the other hand, a person would never examine what is moderation in this contingent instance unless he desired moderation.

Prudence therefore does not establish the object of another virtue; it must presume that to desire sensible things moderately according to the measure of reason is good and is in fact desired. Prudence does not say, "It is good to pay your debts"; this is either synderesis or moral science. Nor does it say, "I want to pay my debts"; this is merely the knowledge that I have an inclination. Precisely, it says, "Seeing that to pay my debts is good, and that I want to pay them, what are they concretely here and now, and how do I go about it?"

Another way of stating the function of prudence is to say that it applies general principles to particular cases. This application must be correctly understood. The relation of singulars to general principles in the practical order is not like the inclusion of singulars in universals in the speculative order. In the order of speculative knowledge, we correctly abstract from individual differences, and this quite legitimately; therefore the application of general laws to singular cases is easy and can even be reduced to a set of mechanical rules. But in the practical order, far from abstracting from the singularities, we must include them formally in our judgment. Now, the complete description and understanding of a singular as such includes strictly contingent elements whose factual copresence in the individual object or act cannot be reduced to any a priori rule, but must be found from sense experience. Hence, the "application" of a general principle (e.g., "Debts must be paid," "Moderate use is good") is never mechanical and cannot be brought about by adding the pronoun "this" or even the possessive adjective "my" to the proposition. This is not to say that "general principles" or "universal laws" are not necessary in the practical order—far from it; as we have seen, prudential reasoning is impossible without an "end" which when stated in a proposition is a general principle. But it is to say that general principles (or ends) are insufficient. An example from temperance will easily illustrate this insufficiency. Suppose a person intends to use food moderately, according to the measure of reason. Within certain limits he can find out what is generally reasonable. For example, a good dietitian could establish the minimum subsistence level as well as the point of obvious overindulgence. But the two points cannot be brought closely together. A certain amount of trial-and-error is necessary. Often, one must tend toward one or the other extreme to find the limits. And since one does not begin from the beginning, but already has habits (most likely not well proportioned), the practice of leaning toward the lesser point is a sound practical norm.[13] But the purpose of this cutting back is ultimately to find the ideal norm in the middle. From this example we can see that the measure of reason is not a fixed mathematical point which could be established by scientific reasoning, but rather is a constantly reevaluated norm between fixed extremes.

A third way of stating the function of prudence is to say that it takes into account the circumstances and conditions of time, place, and person. This is also a correct formulation, *provided that* one does not think that the moral virtues already have a fixed object which is entirely definite and concrete and that the consideration of circumstances is entirely secondary and accidental. The circumstances in question are precisely what determine the object in the concrete. For, what is temperate for me may be too much or too little for the next person.

From these considerations, it will be seen that prudence cannot be exercised without the moral virtues, because that with which the prudential judgment deals is the acts of the moral virtues.[14]

On the other hand, the moral virtues require prudence. Temperance, fortitude, and justice are perfecting modes of appetites, or perfected tendencies, to the good in a measure determined by

[13] Often this advice is given on a faulty theoretical basis, for example, the Manichaean view that sensible things are bad. Or, deliberate insufficiency is suggested to overcome sensuality. This is the substitution of one vice for another.

[14] Prudence has no relation to the objects of the other virtues such as wisdom, or love of God, or science. It concerns them only indirectly, inasmuch as a person might too eagerly desire to practice them, or might be too apathetic, and so on. But in these cases it still directly concerns the object of a moral virtue, for example, the moderation of the *desire to exercise* other virtues. On this point, see St. Thomas Aquinas, *In Epistolam ad Romanos,* cap. 12, lect. 1.

reason. To exercise these virtues, it is necessary each time to determine what the good is here and now. "The good as determined
by reason" is not a concrete object like eight ounces of food or a
wage of two dollars an hour. Thus, prudence is not necessary
merely to practice moral virtue well—it is constitutive of the
moral virtue *as virtue*. Without the specifying function of the
prudential judgment, there is only a blind inclination, which may
be an automatism habit, but no more. Therefore, the moral virtues are substantially in the appetites, but formally in reason; this
form of the moral virtues is prudence.

Is there any direct connection or relationship of justice, fortitude, and temperance? In the way in which we are taking these
virtues, they deal with three different matters, which as such (that
is, abstractly) neither include nor exclude each other.[15] That is
why, in principle, a man can be just without being temperate.
But concretely a particular act may simultaneously have several
relationships to the agent; for an act may affect a third party, and
at the same time the agent can be variously disposed toward that
act. For example, a proposed action may be an act of justice, such
as returning borrowed property, and at the same time may involve parting with a desirable object. In such a situation, the act
of justice will not be placed easily and therefore will sometimes
fail, unless the person has the disposition of temperance. That is
why it is said that all the moral virtues are connected, at least if
they are to be practiced always and perfectly.

For the sake of completeness, we can indicate in a paragraph
what a theologian would add. For, as we have already noted, in
the existential sense of virtue, no moral virtue is existentially a
virtue without charity.[16] According to St. Thomas, charity has

[15] Because all three of these virtues have the same form (that is, prudence),
a person could not deliberately plan to be explicitly vicious in one area of
activity and virtuous in another. He would be intending to be prudent at some
time and imprudent or astute at another. But there is no prudence for fixed
times only. This shows a "negative" connection between fortitude, justice, and
temperance—that is, one or two of them cannot be explicitly combined with
a vice.

[16] This is not the same as saying that without charity all acts are sins; see
the explanation by St. Thomas, *In Epistolam ad Romanos*, cap. 14, lect. 3 ad
finem.

three functions. (1) It is a complement to the very nature of the
will, giving it a new orientation to the supernatural good of man.
As such, it is related to action somewhat as a potency is and gives
to the will the proximate principle of acting in the supernatural
order. In this relationship, according to many theologians,[17] it is
not explicitly attended to nor is its object—God as man's supernatural end—distinctly willed. (2) Charity is also the end or goal
of all other virtues. In this order, one of the reasons that a man
performs any good act at all is to increase in charity. (3) Charity
can also be explicitly attended to and distinctly willed in combination with any other virtue; and in this relation it is a form of
the other virtues somewhat like prudence, that is, an accidental
form.[18] In addition, many theologians also think that there are infused moral virtues, which would then stand to the natural moral
virtues as form to matter.[19]

MATTER AND FORM IN THE VIRTUES: CONTINGENT HABIT GROUPS

We have already seen that in addition to necessary combinations of habits there are also habit groups which make up complex combinations. Are there any special considerations about
virtue?

Let us first look at activities. Can one (complex) activity come
from two virtues? From what we have seen in considering habits
in general, we can conclude that two virtues cannot be the sources
of one and the same act on the same basis. A man cannot formally
be doing mathematics and metaphysics at the same time, and such

17 Among them, St. Thomas Aquinas, *In II Sent.*, d. 38, q. 1, art. 1 ad 4.
18 These three relationships do not have the same equivalents in the natural
order. The first function corresponds to the very nature (*ratio*) of the will itself. The second, as such, has no parallel at all. Corresponding to the third
relationship, acts of the love of God could inform all other good acts, though
there would not be a habit or virtue to serve as a formal principle, because
this love of God would be natural (in this case, corresponding to the nature of
the will as ordered to God). St. Thomas is explicit on this; see *Summa Theologiae*, I-II, q. 63, art. 3 and ad 1; and *In II Sent.*, d. 38, q. 1, art. 1 ad 4; *In
III Sent.*, d. 23, q. 1, art. 4, qa. 3 ad 3.
19 On this, see "Une théorie sur les vertus morales 'naturelles' et 'surnaturelles,'" *Revue Thomiste*, vol. 59 (1959), 565-575.

mutual exclusiveness is found wherever two virtues divide some field of action on an equal basis, as species divide a genus.

With regard to evil acts, there can be two bad motives for one act; for example, a person might illegally give away public funds to an individual in order that he might later illegally receive special treatment. In this action there is first of all a malice in the act considered materially: that is, the giving away of money he does not own and is not empowered to give away. This malice is subjected to an ulterior motive, namely to obtain an illegal benefit. This action is an offence against legal justice and also against distributive justice. In an action where two evils are related in this way, one is for the sake of another.

Similarly, in the case of a good action, a person can intend one end for the sake of another. For example, if someone gives away some of his money to a needy person, this is specifically an act of almsgiving. This end may be intended simply in itself. The same generous donor might also realize that he is personally a sinner, and so might intend to perform this action of almsgiving to atone for his past sins. His action of almsgiving is included in a further end, the intention of satisfaction for wrong done, which is an aspect of justice.

When one end is related to another as to a more ulterior end, we can speak of a "matter-form relationship," since the act of almsgiving *could* also be ordered to other ends (for example, to win someone to a more favorable attitude to religion). Thus, the more immediate end is in some way determin*able* to more ultimate ends and so can be called "matter" with respect to an ulterior end. Conversely, the ulterior end gives a further determination and so is called "form." In analyzing such complex relationships, the act is said to be *materially* the one specified by the proximate end, and *formally* the one specified by the ulterior end. On both grounds, it would be virtuous. The action of almsgiving is not of itself indifferent but already good, but it has in addition an ulterior end imposed on it by the person's own choice.

How do we determine which virtue is matter and which form? In the example we have been using, it depends entirely on the way in which they are actually willed. They could be willed in the opposite relationship. This kind of thing can easily be illustrated from the various possibilities offered by temperance and justice. We may suppose that a certain person desires strongly to use sensible goods moderately; there is an occasion to practice justice, and he sees the good of giving something which is due to another as a way to further his overall intention of moderation. But on the other hand, there is no reason why another person might not strongly desire to be just; on an occasion for being temperate, he may wish to exercise temperance in order that he may have the money to pay his debts promptly when they fall due.

Is there an unlimited possibility of subordination of any virtue to any other virtue? Some subordinations would not seem to be even physically possible, for example, to love God for the sake of helping my neighbor. But the more important question concerns the appropriateness of ordering one virtue to another.

In the case of goods which belong approximately to the same order, either kind of relationship would seem to be possible. In the lives of the saints we can find clear-cut examples of the selection of quite different informing virtues. For example, there are the great penitents who ordered their manual work, their prayer, their efforts for the good of others to the purpose of satisfaction due in justice for past sins. The great contemplatives ordered their other activities to the spirit of prayer.

But even here there is reason in the subordination; there is always a reason for choosing the informing virtue, and it should never be pushed to absurdity. Can every virtue be subordinated, or is there one which by its nature should never be ordered to another? We can answer this question by considering the relationships of the various ends intended by the virtues. Now, we know that the end which is simply and without any qualification ultimate is God. In the order of ends, it might be conceivable but it certainly would be wrong to subordinate this end to any other— for example, a person loving God *because* he was going to profit by this love. If in a given case this were a real subordination, if a person really looked on God as having the function of providing satisfaction for himself, this would be absolutely and completely out of order. It is of course doubtful whether this ever happens, mainly because it is hard to see how someone could have any adequate idea of God and at the same time subordinate Him.[20]

We can also look at the same question from the point of view of the acts of the will. Is there any will-act which should never be subordinated to any other? It is possible to direct an act of the will immediately and simply to the last end, and this is an act of simple willing of the last end. It is not reasonable to subordinate this to any other act at all, and so it should never stand as matter in relation to any other act. It must always stand as form to matter.

We know from theology that in the present order the proper and proportionate act of the love of God must flow from a supernatural virtue, the infused virtue of charity. Consequently, just as the act of the love of God is always formal in any intention, so the virtue of charity is always the form of the virtues.

It is necessary here to digress for a moment on the informing role of charity as a guard against a misunderstanding. Neither physically nor morally is it necessary that a person explicitly love God in intending good acts. If he performs an act of justice because it is a good thing to do, this is a good, a virtuous act (and, if he is in the state of grace, he merits). Not every act need be actually and explicitly an act of the love of God. All we are saying is that if the love of God is consciously present, it can be present only as form.

Another kind of relationship between the virtues may be noted here. We have been considering the means-end relationship in the case in which they are simultaneously willed as a single complex object. Experience shows that there are also cases in which means and end are temporally distinct, the means coming first in time and producing the end as an effect. This of course is not strictly a composition of virtues, but rather an order between them. (Unfortunately, the same terms are used to express these quite different situations.) But at least there is this much similarity, that whatever restrictions are laid down about the means-end composition

[20] However, note that there can be what theologians call the "slavish fear" of Hell. Can there be an equally mercenary desire of Heaven? I think this would be quite rare. But spiritual writers sometimes fall into language which if taken literally would express a formally selfish desire for beatitude. On the different kinds of fear, see St. Thomas Aquinas, *In Ep. ad Romanos,* cap. 8, lect. 3.

of virtues will also hold about their causal relationship. For example, a person is both excessively attached to money and owes a debt. It can occur to him that if he paid his debt there would be no money to be attached to. So he can set up justice as a means for establishing a reasonable right order in the desire for money. He would practice an act of justice in order to practice temperance more perfectly.

There are really no new problems in considering these relationships, but there is too much careless language. People sometimes say, "Detachment from created things is important; one thing that will help is a great love of God." Or we read, "The love of God is a great help to chastity." Unfortunately, beginners tend to be literal and take this in the ordinary sense, according to which ends are more perfect than means. They get the idea that the greatest good is to be detached, or chaste. This is negativism, or a kind of spiritual pride which consists in thinking that the most important thing in the world is my own freedom from sin or imperfection. Surely no spiritual director means to say this. He is really thinking that when a specific virtue is lacking, a more general virtue may be made to do duty for it. He means to say, "Love God intensely and you will not yield to temptations against chastity and lose the love of God, but rather you will increase in the love of God." All this is good as a practical solution, if it is aimed at the acquisition of the proper virtues and at an increase in the love of God. But it is also important to keep our evaluations straight and to make our language correspond with the facts and the ultimate intentions.

We have already suggested that the means-end relationships are not merely arbitrary. One significant aspect of this intrinsic connection shows up in the problem of the adaptation of means to ends. If we considered this a merely subjective and arbitrary matter, then any means could work toward any ends—"The end justifies the means." This maxim is simple and obvious—and constantly misused. Of course the things which really lead to a given end are good if the end to which they lead is good, and bad if it is bad. And "intentions" have nothing to do with this real relationship. But if we mean that "a good intention" justifies any action—this is simply silly. When a politician helps the poor to buy votes, the evil end spoils the otherwise good means; and with equal force a means known to be evil spoils an alleged good end.

As soon as a person subordinates any act at all to an evil end, the entire act is evil. This is the sense in which it is truly said, "Every act of a sinner (i.e., as such) is a sin." As soon as an evil means, known to be evil, is accepted, alleged "good ends or intentions" no longer are real consequences of such means and no longer really inform the act.

We must distinguish this case from that of "mixed motivation." St. Bernard in his usual ingenuous way tells an interesting and illuminating story on himself. He started out to preach a series of sermons. After he had preached several, he became aware that he was doing very well and felt pleased with himself. Next came the thought that he was merely being vain in continuing the sermons. But then he drew himself up short: if he wished to avoid vanity entirely, he would also lose the good effect of his preaching. So he dramatically addressed the devil: "I didn't begin this work for you, and I will not quit it for you." In fact, mixed motives do exist, and it is a very difficult task to eradicate the evil motives while developing the good ones. A wise man, like St. Bernard, will not let the possible imperfections keep him from doing the good he can do, though he will try ultimately to eliminate all imperfect motives.

SUMMARY

In our examination of the habits which perfect man's various powers, we have discovered a number which are true virtues or vices, which involve moral goodness and evil. These are the mastery habits of the desiderative and aggressive appetites, the intellectual habits which control the conclusion-judgment of the act of choice and all habits of the will. Fine art involves virtue or vice because it includes as a necessary component of its group the virtue of veracity (or its contrary vice). Science is virtue in a secondary sense because, although it can be misused and so does not necessarily make the man as well as the operation of the power better, it still is ordered necessarily and intrinsically to truth which is a proper human good, at least in an inadequate sense of the term.[21] Wisdom is a virtue in the sense that it is a special kind of science including judgments of value. The other habits and habit groups we have examined are not in themselves virtues or vices; in themselves they are morally neutral, except in so far as they serve as material components of complex habits which are themselves virtues or vices.

Among the virtues there are a number of matter-form relationships. They can be classified thus:

1. within virtues: matter-substantial form (e.g., discursive estimation + prudence taken only formally = prudence taken adequately).
2. between virtues:
    a. each of which are properly virtues already distinct but which are combined as substance + form:
       1'. necessary (e.g., moral virtues and prudence)
       2'. contingent (ends-groups)
    b. only one component is a virtue by itself; the others are mastery habits or perhaps automatism habits (e.g., a complex such as virtuous friendship).
3. between virtues distinct and not combined but ordered one to another as in the subordination to ulterior and external ends.

Matter-form relationships are not univocal, but analogous. This means that each case must be considered in its concrete reality and its meaning found there rather than deduced from the philosophy of nature or from some a priori logical notion.[22]

SOURCES FOR CHAPTER FIVE

Aquinas, St. Thomas, *Summa Theologiae*, I-II, qq. 12-17 (on acts of intellect and will centering around choice); qq. 18-21 (on moral good-

---

[21] Truth is a proper human good only in an inadequate sense of the term, because proper human goods are moral goods. As such, they are objects of tendency which are suitable or unsuitable for man's free intellectual nature. Hence, science needs to be related to a free act (or habit) of the will before it acquires a moral goodness. St. Thomas speaks of science as a habit which gives man "a certain aptness for goodness" rather than actually making him good.

[22] The scheme given here is a slight variation on the diagram of the habits given above (p. 109). Some things are not shown here, and there is a little elaboration of detail.

ness and merit); qq. 55-60, 63-66 (on the virtues in general), q. 62 (on the theological virtues in general).

Boulay, Jasmin, "Quelques notes à propos des vertus morales," *Laval philosophique et théologique,* vol. 16 (1960), 20-52.

Couesnongle, V. de, O.P., "La notion de vertu générale chez saint Thomas d'Aquin," *Revue des Sciences Philosophiques et Théologiques,* vol. 43 (1959), 601-619.

Deman, Thomas, O.P., "Eudémonisme et charité en théologie morale," *Ephemerides Theologicae Lovanienses,* vol. 29 (1953), 41-57; a profound study showing how the two notions of love and happiness are related.

Deman, Thomas, O.P., "Towards an Objective Spritual Life," *The Life of the Spirit,* vol. 11 (1956), 148-157, 200-208; Translation by Kathleen Pond of an article in *La Vie spirituelle* (1944), also published as a pamphlet (Paris, Procure générale du Clergé).

Faraon, M. J., O.P., *The Metaphysical and Psychological Principles of Love* (River Forest, Ill., Pontifical Faculty of Philosophy, 1952).

Gelpi, Donald, S.J., "Artistic and Prudential Judgment," *The Modern Schoolman,* vol. 36 (1959), 163-178; the sense in which "art" can be considered a virtue.

Lofy, Carl A., S.J., "The Meaning of 'Potential Whole' in St. Thomas," *The Modern Schoolman,* vol. 37 (1959), 39-48.

Lumbreras, Peter, O.P., "Notes on the Connection of the Virtues," *The Thomist,* vol. 11 (1948), 218-240.

Mansion, A., "L'eudémonisme aristotélicien et la morale thomiste," *Xenia Thomistica,* ed. H. A. Scabó, O.P. (Rome, Angelicum, 1925), vol. 1, pp. 429-449; a basic study that has been overlooked very often.

Maritain, Jacques, *Creative Intuition in Art and Poetry* (New York, Pantheon, 1955); pp. 184-185, summary of his doctrine on poetic knowledge; pp. 238-240, poetic experience.

Mouroux, Jean, *The Meaning of Man,* A. H. G. Downes, trans. (New York, Sheed, 1952), pp. 100-102; on the meaning of the struggle with passion.

Pinckaers, Servais, O.P., "Le rôle de la fin dans l'action morale selon saint Thomas," *Revue des Sciénces philosophiques et théologiques,* July, 1961, 393-421; a detailed study of the function of the end in moral action.

Pinckaers, Servais, O.P., "Virtue is Not a Habit," *Crosscurrents,* vol. 12 (1962), 65-82; a careful and detailed study of the meaning of virtue and habit, rejecting the mechanical implications of the term "habit"; translated from *Nouvelle Revue théologique,* vol. 82 (1960), 387-403.

Rahner, Karl, S.J., *Theological Investigations,* vol. 1, Cornelius Ernst, trans. (Baltimore, Helicon Press, Inc., 1961), pp. 359-360; on the necessary acts of love and the imperfection that is present in them.

Schneiders, Alexander A., *The Anarchy of Feeling: Man's Struggle for Freedom and Maturity* (New York, Sheed, 1963); a psychological approach, with some excellent points on pleasure, guilt, inferiority, and discipline.

Sullivan, John L., S.J., *The Commandment of Love* (New York, Vantage Press, 1959); a more popular presentation of the place of charity in life.

"Symposium on Moral Development," *Catholic Psychological Record,* vol. 1 (1963), 7-44; the emphasis is on the "psychological roots" of this development.

Chapter Six

The Cardinal Virtues

At this point the great number of habits and virtues can begin to seem impressive and oppressive. Is there any way of getting some order into this vast scattered array of modifications? This question primarily concerns the *theory* of habit and virtue. We want to know how we can order and understand and reason about the virtues in a way that is more economical than dealing separately with every possible virtue.

But it is not solely a question of understanding; for a philosophical theory should not merely be economical, it should also be true. Hence the order and unity we are seeking should be an order of the virtues themselves. The question is not one of an order of *importance,* nor of dignity, nor of universality. Absolutely speaking, the most important act we perform is the one which puts us into the right relationship with the ultimate goal of our life (and in the present order this is brought about by the virtue of charity). Relatively speaking, the most important virtues are those which an individual most needs because of his special temperament, situation, and duties.

The virtues are habits whose objects are properly human goods. In view of these objects, the virtues in general can be divided into three major groups: (1) the supernatural virtues of faith, hope, and charity, whose objects are goods that are related to man and yet beyond the intrinsic constitutive ordination of human nature; (2) the virtues whose objects are human goods strictly as good, the moral virtues;[1] (3) the virtues whose objects are human goods but not precisely as good, the intellectual virtues (except pru-

---

[1] "Moral virtues" in English usually includes prudence; in the terminology of St. Thomas, *moralis* was limited to the virtues of the various appetites. The English usage is more advantageous, and so we will continue to call prudence a moral virtue.

201

dence). The first group is not directly within the scope of this book, and, even if it were, it would involve no great problems of classification and understanding. The third group contains habits which are virtues only in a qualified sense, as we have seen. Some general classifications can be given of these intellectual habits, but the complete analysis and ordering of these habits awaits an adequate theory of knowledge. This leaves for practical consideration only the virtues belonging to the second group; these are both more numerous and of greater practical importance than the intellectual habits.

The traditional approach to this problem has been the doctrine of the *four cardinal virtues*. What is meant by calling a virtue "cardinal"? This adjective is derived from the Latin word *cardo*, which means "a hinge." The first application of the adjective in a metaphorical sense seems to have been to the four directions. Thus, the ancients spoke of the "cardinal winds," and more recently navigators spoke of the cardinal points of the compass. In this sense, "cardinal" meant "a point of reference for an area." It will be best if we think of the *cardinal virtues* as "points of reference around which the virtues devoted to a certain area of activity are unified."[2] In these areas, the "points of reference" will be the basic, or fundamental, determinations of activity.

Now, how would we delimit the various areas of human activity in such a way that they can be unified around certain basic relationships? St. Thomas indicates two approaches: (1) by relating the activities to the power to which they are principally referred and (2) by analyzing the relationships between man, the agent, and the goods with which the virtues are concerned. There is no a priori reason why these two approaches should be completely identical, and indeed we shall see that they do not entirely overlap. Nevertheless, the fact that they do have a certain similarity gives us ground for formulating the following rule: we will use the term "cardinal virtue" only of such a virtue as is arrived at by *both* types of approach.

More in detail, the *first* approach looks to the powers whose perfections the particular virtues are. From our preceding analy-

---

[2] The dictionary definition of "cardinal" as "chief, principal" is therefore misleading when applied to the virtues.

sis, we know that there are four powers in which virtues (in the second sense given above) are found: the two sensory appetites, the will, and the intellect. Our investigation along these lines will thus give us four cardinal virtues. The *second* approach is the relation between the person and the goods of virtue. Man, in his free and deliberate activity, finds himself in a universe of goods and evils in common with other men. To act rightly, man must rightly judge and form his actions in these various relations. The knowledge must be correct, true, if the action is to be rightly ordered. The "true" here means practical truth, for only the strictly practical knowledge is necessary for activity. Since the correctness of this knowledge is ensured neither by the infallibility of our intellect nor the immediate evidence of things themselves, a virtue is needed to order our practical knowledge. Secondly, man as an agent must be rightly disposed in himself. This right disposition is of two kinds: (*a*) he must be rightly disposed toward the things which are attractive to him, to moderate or temper his relations to them; (*b*) he must also be rightly disposed toward the evils, so as not unduly to fear them or be repelled from doing good. Thirdly, in his external actions man comes into contact with his fellow man, directly or indirectly. Since there are objective relations between any individual and other men (and in these relations external objects are often included), right order needs to be established also in these operations.

THE CARDINAL VIRTUES AS WHOLES

If the cardinal virtues are to be "reference points" for an area of activity, then somehow they must include other virtues. A cardinal virtue then is a whole, in some way including other virtues. To see how this might work, we must remember that there are various kinds of wholes and parts. (1) There is an *integral* whole, made up of integral parts. The perfection of the whole is only in the whole as such, not in the parts. For example, an individual man is a whole, composed of various sorts of parts, for example, body and soul, or, head, trunk, arms, and legs. (2) There is the *universal* whole, such as a genus which is equally found in all its "parts," the species. Thus, "animal" is a whole genus. Each of the species of animal, such as men and brutes, contains completely the perfection of the whole, and each of them contains that perfection singly. (3) There is the *potential* whole which is midway between the other two. Like the integral whole, the perfection of the whole is not completely in the parts, and yet it is there in a secondary sense. Like the universal whole, the perfection is really in the parts, even though only secondarily. Thus, "knowledge" is found both in men and animals, but more perfectly in men, less perfectly in animals.

Another way of looking at these three types of wholes might consider the way in which they have or do not have common perfections. (1) The parts of an integral whole, as parts, do not have a common perfection at all. (2) The species which are parts of a universal whole all have a univocally common perfection. (3) The parts of a potential whole are analogously similar; they do not have simply the same perfection, yet they share a perfection to a greater or lesser degree.

In considering the various areas of activity, we must, then, ask whether an act of a given virtue is made up of other virtues like integral parts, whether it has specific virtues under it, and whether there are any similar virtues which are analogous to it. We need not suppose that every cardinal virtue has actually all three kinds of subdivisions, but in each case we can at least ask there three questions. In each case we will have to look at the activity with which we are concerned—there is no possibility of discovering either the cardinal virtue or its parts in any a priori fashion.

I. *The Desiderative Appetite*

This sense appetite is that by which man desires sensibly pleasing goods. Basically what is the virtue of this appetite? We can begin by considering the most common difficulty people have with regard to this power. Which is the fault people most commonly fall into, which is most necessary to eradicate in order to live a well-ordered life? Experience shows that the problem is that of excessive desire. In man, desires, left to themselves, become more voracious. Well-ordered desire with a view to right, reasonable use is restrained desire. Recall that the virtue of an appetite is the good *use of that appetite itself.* Therefore the point is not the eradication of all desire, but the building up of a desire that is intrinsically subjected to reason; in this appetite the subjection is restraint, or *temperance.*

The notion of restraint, control, moderation, must be correctly understood, and it will help to contrast two other notions. On the one hand, there is the notion of mere continence: the case in which a person has excessive desires, but does not allow them to determine his external actions; he overrides their demands by the "force of his will." On the other hand, there is the notion of repression: the attempt entirely to stamp out all activity of the sense appetite, which is approximately the same idea as that which the Stoics called "apathy." But we should note that the attempt to stamp out desire is usually not successful; what happens is that one denies that he has any such impulse, and so that impulse must disguise itself, must apparently have a different and admissible object, or no clear object at all. But control admits there is an impulse, and it is an intrinsic modification of that impulse, making it subject to the judgment of reason.

Of course, there is also a contrary fault, that of apathy, whose worst form is abulia—the almost total lack of any impulse to attain goods.[3] Laziness is sometimes lack of interest. But by and large the habitual deficiency of sense desire is not the major fault.

We can also look at the desiderative appetite positively. By its nature it tends toward sensible good, and as we know from experience there are no built-in limits to its activity. Unless its nature is modified, it continually moves towards pleasurable goods. Hence, from the very nature of its movement and its object, it is evident that the essential order needed is that of putting a limit to the outgoing movement of sense desire. Temperance thus is substantially a virtue of controlled desire. To illustrate this, we can consider the somewhat rare case of a person whose sense desires are naturally not very strong. And in the absence of unusual stimulation he would experience no violent or excessive desires.

[3] Apathy, and particularly abulia, are very often due to organic malfunctioning and in that case are not vices. Moreover, some apparent deficiencies (for example, frigidity in married persons) are much more likely to be due to bad habits of the discursive estimation and to repressions and other complications.

He would then have desires which are materially right, that is, which are of themselves conformed to a judgment of right reason, had one been made. So he could without any difficulty at all acquire the virtue of temperance. But he would not have this virtue until he learned to desire formally according to the measure of reason. The "restraint" he would practice would not involve any violence even in the course of acquiring the habit. Nevertheless, the order of reason even for such a person would be an "order of limit to desire"; for even his mild appetites have no inborn structural limitations.

Now, let us look at this same question, of desiring goods, from the second point of view, that of the formal relationship between man and goods. Goods are in the strict sense the goods of man when they are the "goods of reason," as we have seen in analyzing the notion of virtue. Now when we look at the goods which surround us, we can see that they are good for us to the extent that they help us. We see that it is definitely reasonable to use things which we need and which complete or perfect our nature. But we can also see that it is unreasonable to use them once this limit has been reached. Therefore, the right order in the case of all particular goods is an order of use-and-limit. When the particular goods to be used are sensible goods, then this formal relational analysis points to an order of limited desire for them. This approach then coincides with the analysis of the power of sensory desire. Consequently, the order of restraint or limit in sensory desire is a cardinal virtue, which is usually called *temperance*.

However, man's relationship to particular goods is not restricted to the desire for sensible goods. There are therefore other "virtues of control" which must be in some way assimilated to the cardinal virtue of temperance, and which we will have to consider when we take up the "parts" of temperance.

The Parts of Temperance: Integral and Specific Parts. We can first ask whether there are any *species* of temperance. In order that we can find distinct species, it must be the case that the good of the virtue is found in several distinct areas, each of which has in addition a special goodness to be sought for and a special evil to be avoided. Are there then classes of sensible goods which are sensibly good in different ways?

The goods which are *sensibly* good (that is, directly causing pleasure) can reasonably be considered to be of three kinds. The first is food. We know that when we are hungry or thirsty there is a pleasure in the eating and drinking itself.[4] Among these goods, there is one class which offers a different kind of pleasure: intoxicating drinks (and foods?), and this is the second kind. The third sort of directly pleasurable action is the use of sex powers.

Not only are there three kinds of immediately sensible goods, but each one of them has a different kind of moderation which makes their use reasonable. Thus, food and drink are necessities of life. The norm for rightly ordered desire is that amount of food (in quantity, quality, and so on), as will not only sustain life but will enable a person to enjoy his work, social dealings, recreation, and the rest. Intoxicants, on the contrary, are not necessary for life; but they can contribute to the enjoyment and best use of the meal with which they are taken, as well as to relaxation, the better functioning of social contacts, and so on. The use of the sex powers, also, is not a necessity of life, and in their case the norms for moderate desire are the purposes of married life (children, the fostering of mutual love, and so on).

Moreover, there are different kinds of failings against moderate use in these three cases. In the use of food, the excess is gluttony.[5] The excess concerns the same use but is unreasonable in quantity or manner. In the use of intoxicants, the excess is drunkenness.[6] Here the excess is mainly in quantity. In the use of sex, the chief fault is its use outside the marriage relationship (adultery, fornication, masturbation), and so the unreasonableness to be avoided is of a different kind.[7]

---

[4] Notice that there is not directly a question here of flavor and odor. To some extent the enjoyment of flavoring and aroma is learned. There is of course also a moderation of such pleasures, but they are not directly under a species of temperance.

[5] Not every fat man is a glutton; overweight may be simply a manifestation of glandular deficiency. And not even everyone who overeats is a glutton; some use food to compensate for failures in other areas (social acceptance, external achievements). This is a mixup in imagination and discursive estimation rather than a vice.

[6] Similarly, most alcoholics are not morally drunkards. There are cases of inherited sensitivity to alcohol, and most cases of alcoholism are due to neurotic tendencies and habits rather than to vice. See John Ford, S.J., *Man Takes a Drink* (New York, Kenedy, 1955).

[7] One should not imagine that chastity is the only virtue necessary for married life, not even the only one that governs the use of sex in marriage.

We conclude from these considerations that there are three distinct species of temperance, which we can call respectively abstinence, sobriety, and marital chastity.

We can next ask whether there are any *integral* parts (partactions) which taken together make up the whole action of temperance. St. Thomas points out that temperance involves an aversion from what is disgraceful in the use of sensible goods and an appreciation of what is suitable. Though a detailed discussion of these two aspects of temperance does not seem to be directly helpful in the understanding of temperance, a consideration of them will help us to locate it better in the overall picture of virtue.

Temperance is not the most important virtue from any absolute point of view. For some—perhaps many—persons it is one of the most difficult, especially in their early years.[8] But it is in a way a basic virtue for the establishment of rationality in a man. This is why people commonly say that a seriously intemperate person is "brutish." The faults against temperance are not only wrong; in their worst forms they, more than any other faults, are disgraceful or shameful. They offend not only against reason but even against refined sensibility, and from this point of view we say that they are "indecent." On the other hand, temperance confers a certain gracefulness to action, a certain attractiveness and beauty. It brings an interior harmony and opens the way for following the whole scale of tendencies.

The Parts of Temperance: The Potential Parts. We have seen that a potential whole consists of a principal part to which are attached by way of similarity (analogy) other secondary parts. These secondary parts have something of the perfection proper to the principal part, yet not the full perfection. (This relationship would not prevent a potential part from being a "higher" virtue in other senses.) There would be no reason why there might not be different ways in which potential parts could be related to the principal part.

One variety of potential part of temperance concerns itself with sensible goods, which however are not directly sensibly pleasant

---

8 Yet, in the training of children, care must be taken not to give a false emphasis and not to impose a Manichaean outlook. Nor should they be oriented solely to a life of celibacy.

in themselves. Here we might think of moderation in dress ("modesty"), in possessions ("thrift"), and in the use of flavorings in foods. For such sensible things there is not nearly the same intense desire; to some extent they are acquired needs. Yet it is clear that there is room for moderation. There is no doubt that some persons become unduly affected toward ostentation in dress and other means of personal display. The vice of avarice (and its opposite, prodigality) is unfortunately common enough. Fastidiousness in food is occasionally observable. So there is a sense in which moderation is necessary and appropriate even with regard to the desires for these particular goods.

A second kind of potential part of temperance agrees with temperance from the point of view of the formal relationship (restraint), but differs in that it is not substantially a virtue of the desiderative appetite. Thus, there is a restraint to be exercised in the case of the aggressive appetite and also in the case of the will.

An outgoing movement of the aggressive appetite which requires restraint is that of anger. The passion of anger, as we have already seen, is directed towards redressing some evil suffered, and it looks to the good of the restoration of justice. A certain anger at the presence of injustice is necessary if justice is ever to be established. Yet it is also evident that anger arises over fancied injustices to oneself, or exceeds all bounds (as when it leads to quarrelsomeness, to insults, to fighting, or to the more common "blowing off," or to resentment and bearing grudges). Consequently there is a reasonable anger which is a potential part of temperance.[9]

In the case of the will, there are also some excessive tendencies toward particular goods. In discussing the virtues of the will, we have already noted the virtue of humility and its opposite vice, pride. The formal order of humility is that of restraint on the tendency toward goods as *due to me*. It is therefore a potential part of temperance, inasmuch as there is the same formal kind of relationship; but, since the proper subject of this virtue is not the desiderative appetite, but the will, it is only a potential part.

---

[9] Obviously we could also classify this "virtue" under fortitude, if we were more concerned with the power in which the virtue is found than with its formal order. We will see other cases of cross-classification.

Another virtue that pertains strictly to the will is the virtue which is called "studiousness." Many people probably think that the desire to know needs encouragement rather than restraint; but, as St. Thomas points out, the desire to know is a natural one, and it does need ordering.[10] But knowledge is not a sensible good in any way, so the virtue directed toward its acquisition cannot substantially be a modification of the sense appetite. On the other hand, the vice of inordinate curiosity seems to be more than just a modification of the will; it seems to include habits of the discursive estimation and of the sense appetite, and so to be a composite habit rather than a simple one.

Finally, there are a number of acts and modes of life which are evidently connected with the matters with which temperance deals but which also differ in many points. They should be discussed in this connection, partly to avoid confusion, partly to locate them positively in the overall scheme of habits and virtues. Chief among these are three: the practice of fasting and of total abstinence from intoxicants, the life of voluntary poverty, and the states of virginity and celibacy. We can discuss them in order.

Fasting is the taking of so little food that some discomfort is felt. If a person does not feel any inconvenience, he is not fasting.[11] The mere feeling of hunger before meals is not a sign of fasting; if one never feels hungry at all, he is either overeating or he is sick. Now, what is the good of fasting, and how should we estimate it?

First of all, is fasting strictly a part of temperance?[12] Temper-

10 As is so often the case, the desire to know is present in all, but it may not manifest itself because of other desires which need to be governed by other parts of temperance.

11 On the other hand, the very thought that one is fasting makes a person sometimes notice hunger much more. The hunger therefore is sometimes not so much organic as psychological. As in so many other cases, too much attention to self is not good.

12 Some people say, "Fasting is certainly a part of the Christian tradition; therefore either temperance includes fasting, or it is a 'merely natural virtue' which a Christian must avoid under pain of sin." This is a lot of confusion. Temperance also does not take care of justice—is it therefore also not a virtue? "But when a Catholic is obliged to fast, the only good way he can use food is by fasting." True enough; all this means is that sometimes temperance is not practiced; we shall see later why this can be so. For the moment, this caution must be signalized: if we distort the notion of a virtue in order to make it

ance is substantially that perfection of the desiderative appetite which leads it to follow the judgment of reason in determining what is its suitable good. Prudence determines what is best here and now to realize, actualize the goal of temperance, which is to make the best use of pleasurable goods in line with their nature and man's. This goal, as we shall see more clearly later on, is presupposed for prudence and the exercise of temperance. This goal is spontaneously tended to by man and is set for him by the habit of first principles, "synderesis."

But we do not always have the simple case of man's nature confronted with pleasurable goods which are suited to serve his needs. Even reason by itself, and much more reason enlightened by revelation, may well find additional factors which must be taken into consideration. For example, suppose that a person finds he has committed many sins in the past, and that he cannot bring himself to an adequate sorrow for them by merely internal acts of his will. In that case, he may set as the goal the practice of penance to bring himself to the attitude that he sees is desirable.

Or another person may be so strongly moved by sorrow as to wish to express in concrete form his detestation of his past acts and may therefore practice penance in the form of fasting as a concrete expression of that sorrow. Or a person may wish to devote himself to the extended contemplation of God. The experience of all great contemplatives—even those in non-Christian lands—shows that this kind of intellectual and volitional activity is impossible except under the conditions of a "suprahuman" withdrawal from sensible things. This kind of life is not within the ordinary pattern for man; it is related to the ordinary life as acts of heroism are related to ordinary acts. The contemplative ought not to base his life on an error, namely, that sensible things are evil; and so even in his fasting he must continue to judge that the goal of temperance is good. If he judges that the strictly contemplative life is possible for him and that living it will not involve him in various sins of omission and commission, he then sets

---

cover acts to which it is not directed, we spoil it for its other acts. If we identify fasting and temperance, then all who do not fast are sinning; or, we have left *no criterion of the right use* of food at all. These consequences are both speculatively and practically very harmful.

a different goal. Still another kind of case can be considered: the "protest value" to one's self and especially to other men of the complete withdrawal from certain goods. As an example of this, we can take St. Benedict Joseph Labre. In his time, European culture set an absurdly high value on relatively trivial qualities: many were overdressed, overperfumed, while they neglected most of the important human values. Merely attacking this false judgment verbally was unsuccessful. But by flagrantly neglecting these niceties, St. Benedict roused a great many persons to a realization that there were more important things in life. Finally, in Christianity many other values are shown in the practice of penance: union with Christ in His sufferings, reparation for our own sins and those of others, suffering as a mode of prayer, and so on.[13]

Now, what sort of goal is intended in all this suffering and even self-infliction of pain? It is not a sensible good. To make pain sensibly pleasurable is precisely the perversion of natural tendency which is known as masochism. Indeed, if the pain became pleasurable, it would no longer be penance. The good is obviously an intelligible good: of sorrow, of intellectual activity in contemplation, of charity for others, of the love of God. Hence, it can be the object only of the will, not of the sense appetite. Hence, it is not a species of temperance, but a potential part.

The practice of total abstinence is quite similar, but with an important qualification. We have previously adverted to the fact that there are apparently constitutional alcoholics, for whom any use at all of alcohol leads at once to the formation of an uncontrollable automatism. Obviously, *for them* alcohol is not a good. They are in a situation where heroic virtue becomes necessary. For others, total abstinence may have a protest or encouragement value, or may function as reparation, and so on.

The practice of voluntary poverty ("detachment") is very similar. Again, under the ordinary conditions the possession of some sensible goods is not only allowable but necessary, as we shall notice also when dealing with justice. But, under special conditions, when the purposes of ownership (especially the develop-

[13] See, for example, the excellent though very brief treatment by Jean Mouroux, *The Meaning of Man*, A. H. G. Downes, trans. (New York, Sheed, 1952), pp. 86-89, 103-106.

ment of responsibility and also provision for the future) are taken care of in other ways, then voluntary poverty can be a good.[14] But again, it is not a sensible good, only an intelligible good. Hence, it is a potential part of temperance.

Thirdly, there are the cases of virginity and celibacy. Let us here begin with some standard definitions. Virginity is the state of never having had voluntary, deliberate experience of sexual pleasure. Celibacy is the state of being and remaining unmarried (to which can be assimilated the condition of a person who chooses to remain a widow or widower), without any implication concerning past experience.

When these states are thus described, there is no positive perfection implied in them, but only a negation. As such, they cannot be qualified as states of virtue. In fact, they would be quite compatible with morally wrong ends, as, for instance, St. Augustine ascribed the virginity of the Roman Vestals to pride. Or they may arise from physical or psychological defects, as in fact is the case with some perpetual bachelors and spinsters. (In the rest of the discussion, we will talk principally about celibacy.)

Taken in this negative sense, celibacy can be good only in the sense of a means. In his discussion of the vows of religion in his work *On the Perfection of the Spiritual Life*, St. Thomas states clearly that they are means, for they set up conditions in which the virtues which the religious life is intended to cultivate can be practiced more easily.

Furthermore, in this same negative sense, celibacy is not even a habit, nor does it have any acts proper to it. There is nothing to acquire, but only something to avoid. Celibacy, then, is simply not a virtue. It does nothing to make its possessor good.[15]

Since celibacy is negative, it cannot reasonably be intended for its own sake. If it were, this could be done only on the implicit

14 This condition must be stressed. For very many persons the only way they can learn responsibility is through material possessions (just as the only way they can learn true love and self-sacrifice is through marriage). If such persons fail to make use of these means, they remain permanently defective personalities. On the other hand, anyone who takes on voluntary poverty (and celibacy) is morally obliged to achieve the purposes of these means in other ways.

15 See St. Thomas, *Summa Theologiae*, II-II, q. 152 (virginity) and q. 155 (continence).

supposition that all use of sex is intrinsically evil, either morally or physically. And we have already seen a number of times that such an erroneous imputation of evil to physical, material reality is not conducive to virtue. To make it clear that neither virginity nor celibacy is a positive perfection, we need only suppose that in the life of a particular person, a brick fell on his head every time that a temptation to abandon this state of virginity or celibacy arose in his mind. He would be in the full sense a virgin or celibate though he had never performed a positive good act concerning his state.

One must have some goods and perform some good acts in order to have an acquired virtue, not merely be free of evils. Of course, a normal person must perform many actions in order to avoid all sins. For example, a person not in the married state may find in himself an inclination toward the use of sexual powers (or an act directly connected with such use). He cannot consent to this inclination, much less act on it, but he must try to get rid of it. But the acts he performs are not "acts of celibacy," though they are acts directed to the preservation of the state. These actions may well be acts of some other virtue or habit by which one restrains himself from giving in to sin. Certainly there are some habits of the imagination which a celibate must cultivate (in order to avoid other habits which are not suitable *for him*).

Moreover, the celibate must acquire certain habitual estimations of the discursive power. He should *not* judge sex to be evil in itself, or ugly, or repugnant. But he can build up an estimation that the use of sex here and now and in the concrete is not suitable *for him considering his state of life*. He needs to build up an imaginational ideal of himself as a perfect celibate, and to judge that for such a person the use of sex is not desirable. Thus, though continuing to judge that the use of sex is good in general for human beings, he slowly builds up another estimation under the guidance of reason in which he judges the use of sex as not good and attractive for him in his concrete situation. This complex picture and estimation is not strictly a virtue, though it is a good habit for him. If it can be completely achieved, he will no longer experience any inclination of the sensory appetite toward the use of sex. Until this is achieved, some inclinations of the appetite will appear, and they must be restrained when they do.

Is there any sense in which celibacy can be considered a virtue? Not simply in itself, as we have seen. But, like voluntary poverty, it functions as a means. Now, we also know that the goodness of a means depends entirely on the goal to which it is directed. Thus, if a person remains a bachelor because of repugnance to children or out of laziness, his state would not be praiseworthy.[16] Much less can it be considered good if the reason for practicing it is morally wrong: to make an impression on others, to propagate a false religion known to be false. But there can also be good reasons. We might consider the case of a scientist who remains unmarried in order to give his full time to study—this could in a particular case be a good reason. Or again, the service of the common good could be a valid reason in particular cases for remaining unmarried; this reason could hold for a nurse, a teacher, a statesman, a soldier, among others. Finally, the service of God can provide a reason for celibacy. Now, it must be remembered that God can be served in any state of life, married as well as unmarried. But St. Paul's suggestion remains true: in a certain sense married life can be a distraction from the service of God. Provided that the goods usually attained through marriage are provided for in another way, the life of celibacy, like the life of poverty, can be a shortcut to God. As such, it is not a "mere" means, though it does not become simply an intermediate end of the same kind as the sensible goods with which temperance, thrift, and so on are directly concerned.

To see in what sense there is an intrinsic good in what is directly intended by voluntary poverty and celibacy, we can recall that the purpose of all other creatures, as far as man is concerned, is to help him to reach God. Therefore, the overall attitude of a man toward all created goods is to use them in so far as they help

[16] However, if a person correctly judged that because of his particular temperament he could not successfully live a married life, his decision to remain unmarried would be good.

On the contrary, one sometimes finds people who enter religion on the assumption that only by remaining celibate can they avoid sin. This is usually a false premise (even when it does not rest on a Manichaean condemnation of sex). The chances are that after a few years they will discover its falsity and then will wish to leave the religious life.

him toward God and to refrain from using them in so far as they do not. This overall attitude we have already referred to as "detachment."[17] Now, creatures have a manifold use, and the use through external action is not the only one; there is, for example, the "use" which consists in their being known and in this way helping man to have a better knowledge of God. If we grant that for a particular person marriage would not get him to God as rapidly and directly as celibacy, and that the "rule of detachment" is what is directing this person's will in regard to all created goods, then celibacy will be a potential part of temperance.

But these virtues are potential parts in a special and limited sense. In order that *all* created goods be seen as under the "rule of detachment," some explicit intention of the ultimate end seems to be involved.[18] Secondly, they are not virtues of the sense appetite at all. Thirdly, they do not even have any corresponding "material part" in the sense appetites. At best, the most that can be achieved is that the sense appetite no longer is inclined toward the contrary object. But ordinarily there remains an internal conflict. Hence, the ease and pleasure derived from the practice of virtue are hard to find, because the conflict between sense desire and volitional tendency overshadows them. And it involves a certain difficulty, both in the long-range view that must be taken in order even to understand the relationship of all creatures to God as the last end,[19] and secondly, in the generosity of the will required to move so directly and selflessly to the ultimate good.

II. The Aggressive Appetite

The aggressive appetite is the one which is directed toward the elimination or overcoming of evils. What is its basic good modification as such a power? We can begin this question by considering what is the most disastrous fault in its activity.

There is a sense in which the most striking defects are those of

17 This is, I think, what St. Ignatius, in the *Spiritual Exercises,* means by the "indifference" he asks for in the "first principle and foundation."

18 For this reason, it seems to be advantageous to attach qualifications to their names; for example, we can speak of "Christian virginity," "religious or sacerdotal celibacy," "voluntary poverty."

19 This understanding is one the chief acts of the virtue of wisdom.

excess—the instances of violent anger. But most people are not continually angry, for the occasions of anger are relatively few (and if they seem to be many, the person is usually already in psychological trouble).[20]

There are two related faults of the aggressive appetite, cowardice and despondency. Cowardice in the face of death is not common because for most people the risk of death does not come up every day. But we have difficulties every day, and people are overcome by difficulties; they fail to do what they ought because difficulty is involved.

From the point of view of the harm done by the vice, the harm done by anger is often not very serious (though occasionally there is murder, mayhem, destruction of property). This harm is usually in the physical order, to persons or property—and note that it is done to another. The evil of anger to the person himself is that it is a disorder. The harm done to the coward by his cowardice and to the hopeless person by his despondency is only to himself; but this is not merely a disorder, for it prevents him from performing other acts of virtue, from gaining merit. These effects are much more serious than physical ones. More people are imperfect because they are cowardly or discouraged than because they are hot tempered. The harm cowardice and discouragement do extends very far, even to the life of prayer. In the sensitive order, there is an object for the aggressive appetite whenever there is a question of work to be done, pain to be suffered, opposition to be endured, human opinion to be withstood. Yielding to human respect is a kind of cowardice, for it gives way before the imagined evil of another's disapproval. Similarly, the refusal to take a particular sense pleasure often involves courage, because the imagined future situation (myself-deprived-of-this-good) appears to be an evil.

Looked at positively, the aggressive appetite has as its function getting us to tackle a difficult task, to meet evils head-on in order to obtain a good. Because of this, the most notable order of reason

[20] Psychologists indicate that concealed hostility may be rather common. From the point of view of formal object analysis, this would seem to be a very complex emotion, involving habits of imagination and discursive estimation, hatred (which is a passion of the desiderative appetite), and aggressive feelings such as irritation, resentment, anger, or revenge.

218 HABITS AND VIRTUES

is properly to direct the outgoing movement of the appetite against the evil.

What is the nature of this virtue (or virtues) ?[21] We saw earlier that there are two sets of passions of the aggressive appetite: (1) toward the difficult good, either hope or despondency; (2) toward an imminent evil, either daring or fear.

Some writers seem to think that the virtue of fortitude consists in not feeling any emotion at all before a future evil. This is akin to the Stoic view and simply fails to take account of man's sensitive nature. Others think that it consists in acting in spite of fear or despondency. But this explanation implies that the virtue is either in the external action or in the will, not in the sense appetite. Still others think that a brave man is one who fears, but only as much as a reasonable man fears. Now, it is true that there are some things a reasonable man fears, such as sin, the chance of an accident on a slippery road, and so forth. But these fears, reasonable as they are, are not acts of bravery, nor directly objects of an act of bravery. Indeed, in a given case, a man may have to act in a situation in which he really is afraid, and reasonably so. But in this case he acts like the continent man who forces himself in a given case to do what he knows he ought to do.

We can even say that in the process of acquiring bravery a person must moderate his fears. But ultimately, virtue does not consist in controlling fear. Rather, it consists in responding suitably to an object, with a response that is something like fear but also something like daring (or, something like hope and yet something like despondency).

True enough, from many points of view the positive response is much better—it contributes to psychological health, it leads to external effects, it makes people more pleasant companions and perhaps even appealing leaders. And, from the contrary point of view, as we saw earlier, it is by the "negative" or withdrawing passions of fear and discouragement that the most harm is done.

[21] Christians have on occasion become confused at this point in the analysis of the structure of the natural virtues. "Christian hope" properly so called is a virtue and a supernatural (infused) virtue at that. The reason, of course, is that the object of supernatural hope by itself is simply beyond the capacities of nature. But one should not confuse "Christian hope" with the passion of hope.

Perhaps, to show in what *direction* the good response of the aggressive appetite takes place, we could speak of *well-ordered* hope and daring.

But we must note that virtue does not consist in brushing aside the difficulty or danger. We should be fully aware of them, not ignore them or underestimate them. A fully realistic judgment about the danger or difficulty and our capabilities in the face of it is perhaps impossible to reach until we have at least begun to acquire some courage. Here, as in other areas, our responses are quite subtle: we tend to justify our fears by minimizing our own potentialities; we explain our failure to take action by suggesting that we really do not have any opportunities. In fact, fear and discouragement blind our vision, distort our judgment, and weaken our efforts if finally we do see something to do and decide to do it. Our appraisal of ourselves and of the objective possibilities of our situation is itself already "courageous," as is the objective norm by which we measure what our courage, our effort, and our achievement should be.

Though as simple passions hope and daring are different as experienced qualities and have a different object, namely, the difficult good and the imminent evil, their good order is the same: it is an order of stimulation, not of restraint. What precisely is needed in the aggressive appetite? That it be made to move according to its natural movement to the goal as rightly judged by reason. Otherwise, as we have seen, the appetite often falls short, slacks off, fails. The precise good order of reason lies in this—that the proper action be taken to face and overcome the evil, to reach out and acquire the difficult good. Actually, then, the virtue of the aggressive appetite is one and the same: that stiffening of the backbone which is often called courage, or bravery, or, more technically, fortitude.

Exactly how we respond in particular cases will depend on the particular aspects of the object, and this detailed consideration will arise from an investigation of the parts of this virtue.

The Parts of Fortitude. There are no *species* of fortitude properly so called; this will be clearer when we discuss the potential parts. As for the *integral* parts, we can consider that there are two aspects of fortitude: the attack and the sustaining. The reasonable attack on an evil involves both preparation and firmness in execution. The sustaining of evil involves firmness in the attack and endurance over a long period of time.

The *potential* parts of fortitude are divided according to the kinds of evils to be faced. This is because there is one evil that simply cannot be compared with any others, and that is death. Death has an absolutely special significance for man, and, no matter how great any other evil may be (and moral evils may well be greater than death), it is not an evil in the same sense. Hence, bravery in the face of death uniquely fulfills the perfection of fortitude and is therefore the principal part of fortitude.

The secondary parts of fortitude are divided according to the different objects. As we have already seen, fortitude can be divided into two integral parts, attack and sustention; the former is more active, the latter more passive in the face of evils inflicted.

The first of the secondary parts is confidence. This is the ordinary virtue of action. We have already mentioned that people are beaten down by the daily difficulties of life and become subject to fear. Now, confidence keeps us actively facing difficulties and prepared to overcome them.[22]

The second is sometimes called greatness of soul—we may say of a man that he has greatness of spirit. This virtue shows up more in action itself, in carrying a difficult task through. It is sometimes easier to begin a task than to see it through to the end. Hence, for any long-lasting projects involving difficulties, greatness of soul is a necessary virtue.

The third is patience, and this is the virtue by which we sustain ourselves in the actual presence of evil. Though the acts of sustaining are not so noticeable, patience is quite often necessary. Many problems that beset us cannot effectively be removed—from the small annoyances of the weather or a headache to great harm or suffering. But we need not give up, lose hope, stop working and praying, and so on. What keeps us going under difficulty is patience.[23]

[22] One of the pseudo virtues is the tendency to take on a great number of tasks, or to work beyond the reasonable limit of time, or to put in more energy than we can afford to give. This "overactivity" often masks a basic insecurity.

[23] Patience is quite different from the unyielding stiffness with which some people adhere to what they have determined to be the pattern of activity that

The fourth is perseverance, and this is the virtue which meets the special problems involved in evils that last a long time. "Man is an animal with a memory," said Aristotle, and undoubtedly the remembrance of the long time we have already suffered adds a new dimension to evils which could be easily sustained for a short time.

III. The Intellect

Since in the strictest sense there is only one moral virtue in the intellect, there is no need to inquire about which virtue of the intellect is cardinal. And the formal analysis of the relationships also points out the place of the formal order to be found in our actions toward the good. Hence, from both points of view prudence is a cardinal virtue.

The Parts of Prudence: Specific Parts. When we speak of prudence without qualifying the term, we mean the prudence of the individual by which he governs his own actions. But there are also other situations where the good involved is not an individual good, but a common good. In the governing of any society[24] (family, civil society, and so on), a special kind of prudence needs to be exercised.

The Parts of Prudence: Integral Parts. The integral parts are those parts (part-actions) which taken together make up the whole action. Often the division into integral parts is somewhat arbitrary: we can divide an integral whole into larger or smaller

---

they will follow. In religious orders, these people fix on the observance of the small rules and allow neither superiors nor fellow religious to influence them. These "independent" people are often hostile and aggressive, often have a basic mistrust of themselves, and so view everyone else as threatening them.

[24] These of course are the natural societies. There does not seem to be a special prudence required for free (arbitrary, conventional) societies or associations. Traditionally, three species of social prudence were distinguished: family, military, and political. I cannot see that there is a special military prudence in the present organization of human society. Possibly when military commanders were almost independent of civil rulers and had to make decisions involving more than military success, military prudence would have been a distinct virtue. On the other hand, I believe that there are natural societies besides the family and the civil society, such as social and economic groups, which involve moral decisions concerning a distinct sort of good and which are governed by a distinct species of justice. See the treatment of justice below.

parts, and the best division is the one that corresponds best to our purposes. So St. Thomas puts down eight integral parts. For our purposes we can perhaps do well enough with three larger sub-divisions.

Prudence can be looked on as involving a knowledge of the past, the present, and the future. We have already noted, in dis-cussing temperance, that the discovery of what is suitable here and now requires some experience. In general, it seems that the successful dealing with present reality requires some knowledge of the past, and in this sense we can say that memory pertains to prudence as its first step. Next, in order to deal reasonably with things, we must know exactly what the present situation is. This involves both our own direct perception and often enough infor-mation which we obtain from others. We must examine the situa-tion carefully in so far as it falls under our direct sense percep-tion. But often also we need to be prepared to see what others think. In fact, experience shows that in matters touching our-selves we are often blind to the facts or reluctant to admit them. Moreover, we often need information about things which we can-not observe ourselves, or we may need to rely on the specialized information which only an expert can obtain. Complete knowl-edge of the present, therefore, may require that we listen to others. Thirdly, we need to look to the future. Concerning the future we need to be aware of the various possibilities. Many people lack the imagination to think of more than one way to handle the situation; because so few possibilities occur to them, they do not have much choice. A person should, therefore, not be content with the first thing that happens to occur to him. By pausing a moment and asking himself what else he might do, he can develop his ability to discover more means. But it is not enough to be aware of various possibilities of action. One must also attempt to foresee the consequence of each one of them. The prediction of the likely result of a course of action depends partly on past experience, partly on a developed art of foreseeing conse-quences. And as we are making our predictions, it may be well to ask ourselves whether there are any additional "side" results of one or the other action which might make it less desirable. Fi-nally, when we have the time, it is good to review for ourselves the steps of the prudential inquiry to see whether we have over-looked anything. Once all these actions have been gone through, we can judge what in the concrete is best for us to do and make our decision to do it.

The conclusion-judgment (precept) of the prudential reasoning is such that the choice takes place. This does not destroy freedom, since it is the presence of the will-act throughout the reasoning which makes it effective. Does it ever happen that the precept is not followed by a choice? This certainly cannot happen often, since prudence is precisely destroyed by consistent contrary choices or by a failure to choose. In a single case, it could be considered to be a defect of prudence or a failure of some other virtue. For example, we might consider the case of a person who has not yet learned perfectly to regulate his irascibility. In situations where there is no violent provocation he practices prudence. But in a concretely irritating situation the flash of anger may distract the choice. For reasons like this we noted in an earlier chapter that the perfect exercise of one virtue requires the use of other virtues as well. Not only vices strictly so called can interfere with prudence—sometimes nonmoral automatisms, especially of the internal senses and sense appetites, prevent prudence from working properly.

Periodically philosophers and spiritual writers misunderstand prudence. They take it to be cold calculation, enlightened selfishness, as implying a lack of wholeheartedness and generosity. In the Aristotelian tradition, the term "prudence" designates the habitual application of reflective intelligence to action. The goals at which prudence aims, as we have seen, are the objects of the other virtues—the goals are set ultimately by nature, proximately by synderesis and wisdom. To jettison prudence is not a more generous service but an exaltation of blind impulse and therefore of sensory impulses, no matter by what noble name impulse is called.

The Parts of Prudence: Potential Parts. The conclusion-judgment is the most important knowledge-act in relation to the good. If it is not right, the choice cannot be right. Preliminaries (memory, observation of relevant factors, foresight) are neutral; and skill in them, not related to choice, is a useful ability but not a morally good one. Closer to the choice is the balanced judgment which weighs the goodness of the proposed possibilities in relation to each other and to the agent. Finally, there is the act by which the agent proposes to himself what he is to do. This "precept" is the proper act of prudence. Thus, prudence in a narrow and minimal sense is the virtue which makes the conclusion-judgment good, and prudence in this sense is the principal part of the cardinal virtue.

We have noted two subordinated movements in the movement of prudential reason. The first is counsel (not merely the information), by which we look to the concrete goodness of the various possibilities. The second is the judgment of what is best or better in the concrete. Thus, there are two potential parts of the cardinal virtue of prudence: good counsel and good judgment (sometimes called "common sense" or "good sense").[25]

We can sometimes observe the presence of these distinct virtues in distinct individuals. Some people are marvelous counselors; they are rich in ideas, and these ideas are practical. Other people have good judgment. They do not have many ideas of their own, but they listen with an open mind to others and have a fine sense for the better proposal. Still others firmly decide to choose and carry out concrete proposals; they may be lacking in the inventiveness and practicality of good counsel, and they may perhaps not have a very good judgment. But if these two are supplied for them, they are excellent in decision and execution. We might imagine, therefore, an ideal triumvirate: a counselor, a judge, and an executive. But in the final analysis, a man can ask for and get counsel from others, and he can even ask them for their judgment or recommendation. The one thing that no one can do for him is the precept itself. Only I can tell myself "I ought to do this here and now; I will do this."

At the present time, great emphasis is laid on counseling. Counselors are an important part of a school faculty; counseling services of various kinds can be obtained in most cities; there is a

[25] St. Thomas points out that good judgment in ordinary matters may still fail in extraordinary situations, and so he divides the virtue of good judgment into two kinds: ordinary (synesis) and extraordinary (gnome). On this last point, see also his quite strong statement in *In II Ep. ad Corinth.*, cap. 11, lect. 1.

method of psychological therapy known as "nondirective counseling." Is the counseling spoken of in these various cases identical with the good counsel which is a potential part of prudence? It seems necessary to make a distinction.

There is a kind of counseling which is largely informational. For example, economic and vocational counseling seem to be concerned with imparting the relevant information. As such, they would pertain rather to art than to prudence; they would of course presuppose speculative information.

Personal and marriage counseling often, at least in practice, get into the area of moral virtue. It is the truth about themselves that people often do not know. They experience difficulties in their personal activities or in interpersonal relations (for example, with their marriage partner). But they do not know what is wrong. They can be told what is wrong and what to do about it; this is more like imparting information. Or they can be helped to discover for themselves what is wrong; this kind of counseling looks as if it is essentially practical. Hence, it is a moral virtue in the counselor, and it is aimed not so much at solving a particular case as at developing the virtue of good counsel in the one being counseled.[26]

IV. The Will

The will is the rational appetite, which tends toward the good as known by (at the level of) intellect. In other words, the "nature"[27] of the will is to tend to whatever is good in so far as in any way it embodies the intelligibility of "good." The natural structure of the will is therefore sufficient to account for all willing of what is simply good (or is directly related to a simple good, as means to an end). The movement of the will toward the good is in general called "love," and the movement away from evil is "hatred."

[26] This seems to be especially true of nondirective counseling. Theoretically, in this kind of counseling, the counselor gives no explicit verbal advice (though undoubtedly he does communicate nonverbally something of his own outlooks and attitudes). By listening to the counselee and reflecting his statements and proposals back to him, the counselor helps him to gain an insight into his problems which is a true and sound judgment, at least partly objective.

[27] Recall what was said in Chapter One about intellect and will as "natures."

In contemporary writing by theologians, psychologists, and philosophers, there is a great emphasis on such terms as love, friendship, intersubjectivity. But there is good evidence that there is widespread semantic confusion. A few sources of this confusion can be pointed out with relative ease.

There is the historical fact that the theology of the supernatural virtue of charity has influenced the analysis of human virtue, sometimes without due attention to the complexity of the factors involved. According to the theology, in our present historical order, the basic orientation of the will to the actual ultimate end of all living is through the virtue of charity, and this charity has for its object not only God but also all men (all free rational creatures), for the sake of God. Charity, because it is an infused virtue resting on faith, reaches God as in His Divinity, that is to say, as transcendentally Other. Thus, charity is at one and the same time the basic orientation of the entire supernatural life and also immediately and necessarily a virtue, already perfect love, that is, the love of friendship, or "love of benevolence." There is a temptation to make a similar analysis of the very nature of the will, such that its basic act, "love," is at the same time its ideal act, "perfect love." A systematic theological effort has been made to establish this parallel between the natural love of the will and the supernatural virtue of charity.[28] But the basic orientation of the will as nature is not a virtue, but simply its structure as inclination, as "rational appetite."[29] Love, therefore, as a spontaneous volitional act is not a virtue, nor even virtuous.

Secondly, some more strictly philosophical positions have also caused some confusion. Some of the philosophies that are called "personalisms" have so extolled the dignity of the person and the primary importance of interpersonal relations that they have, apparently inadvertently, suggested that selfless love of others is natural. It is one thing to establish that the ideal, perfect rela-

[28] Gerard Gilleman, S.J., *The Primacy of Charity in Moral Theology*, André Vachon, S.J. and William Ryan, S.J., trans. (Westminster, Md., Newman, 1960). The more strictly theological part of this presentation is excellent. The epistemological and metaphysical bases for the analysis of the nature of the will are a priori and to many authors questionable. The parallel referred to above seems definitely to be mistaken.

[29] See St. Thomas Aquinas, *Summa Theologiae*, I-II, q. 63, art. 3 and ad 1.

tionship between persons is that of friendship; it is another to suggest that this act is the basic, defining act of the will. It is one thing to have noticed that for a group of philosophers the emphasis has been on particular obligations and external acts; it is another to suggest that love will be sufficient without any need to consider *what* is to be done.

Thirdly, some psychologists have discovered the primacy of love in human development. We should be grateful that "tender loving care" has replaced the mistaken ideal of antiseptic aloofness, but the impression is left that babies naturally love everyone and that they would be perfect human beings if they were not spoiled by society. Here the confusion arises between the instinctive recognition and love of other human beings on the one hand and real friendships on the other. The first is natural—in the sense that it is entirely spontaneous and predeliberate, and also in the sense that it is easy. The second, however, is neither automatic nor easy. The first is primarily a sense reaction (estimative judgment and sensory love), with acts of the intellect and will more or less passively conforming. The second is a freely acquired attitude. The first is self-centered, as sense appetite must be; it is in no sense a virtue, though under some circumstances it may arouse affection. The second is truly respectful of the other person as another person and is, if not a virtue, virtuous (as we shall see).

A way out of this semantic tangle can be found by a more detailed study of the formal object of the will. As a kind of "nature," the will has an object which specifies it. Abstractly, this object is "goodness as such," "the character or note of goodness wherever and however it be found"; and this abstract trait is what is technically called the "formal object." But of course there *are* no abstract objects, and no one desires them—they are objects only of knowledge. What then does man naturally desire as good? This question concerns *concrete* goods for man as a *concrete* existing individual, and so we must consider not only the natural orientation of the will to the good presented by reason, but also what goods are simply and spontaneously grasped by predeliberative knowledge.

Predeliberative knowledge is characterized by its concreteness and immediacy, in contrast to later abstractive, mediate (reasoned) knowledge. The goods which are known in predeliberative knowledge are the goods of the individual; and more accurately, the goods of his powers of acting and undergoing action; or, more simply still, the immediate satisfactions of his powers and that which is necessarily implied in them. Among such goods are food, sleep, free exercise of motor powers and of the senses, interaction with fellow humans, sexual relations, truth. (Admittedly, this very statement of these goods is quite beyond the predeliberative stage, but the point is nonetheless valid.)

Most of the goods mentioned in this list are sensible goods (and even truth can be indirectly sensible), and so sensory appetition is concerned with all of them. In addition, all of these goods are directly the goods of the individual. This level is necessarily involved with instinctual judgments, or in our more technical terms, with natural estimations. So, when the baby spontaneously reacts to the persons around him, he reacts on this sensory level. It is true that he reacts to people rather than to things, because he also is a human animal. But he reacts to them as *related to himself,* so that the love which he shows is not a love of the other person as other, but of the other as pleasing to himself. (When such a love becomes conscious and deliberate, it is often called the "love of concupiscence"; it is probably not far removed from what Freud referred to as the "pleasure passions.") We can add one more point. In this spontaneous reaction, a man loves himself and all that is necessarily connected with himself. Among the beings that are necessarily connected with oneself is God, Who is the principle and end of nature. Moreover, God is principle of nature precisely as greater than nature, and so as a greater good than nature itself. So it is possible to say that man naturally loves God more than himself, and yet to say that this love of God is self-centered, that is, it is God as principle of my nature that is implicitly loved by me. (This statement should not be taken to mean that every human being rises to an explicit love of God as above all things, but only that such an act is implicit in all spontaneous, natural loving, and that this implicit orientation grounds the remote possibility of a future actual act of love. Concretely, the obstacles to performing such an act may well be insurmountable.) Now, if all this is true, one can easily see why the super-natural virtue of charity is not just like natural love except that it is "greater"—it is radically different.

What has just been said must be taken precisely as it was said. We have been talking about the first response of the will in man, as it concretely happens. This is not a reductionist technique. True enough, people do use a reductionist technique often enough when they speak of the origins of something; for example, many Thomists say that all love of another is really love of one-self; some Freudians apparently try to say that pleasure remains the controlling motive no matter what reasons are alleged. But notice that a simple genetic account could be either reductionist or could suggest that a baby is a natural saint.

If we were to consider that all human love were a simple de-velopment and extension of the fundamental and primitive love as we have just described it, then a person would love all that he loves inasmuch as these objects are related to him. To some ex-tent, such an attitude is intelligible and basic. In a certain sense, children are extensions of their parents, husband and wife are one flesh, a friend is another self, fellow citizens and fellow hu-man beings are identical with the individual in citizenship and in species, and so on. Therefore we can truly speak of a simple, direct love of these objects. And for such love no virtue is re-quired, since it is merely an extension of the natural love one has for himself; by the same token it is a very imperfect love and is not virtuous in any sense. (It does not follow that it is vicious.)

On the other hand, perfect love respects the other as equal, as another person, a "Thou." In perfect love, the persons do not love each other in so far as they are identical, but in so far as they are distinct. This implies that the one beloved in perfect love is loved *as other*. To deal with another person as other is in some sense to be in the area of justice, as we shall see. Consequently, all vir-tuous love other than simple supernatural charity is related to justice.[30]

As a result of the preceding discussion, we can approach the question of virtues of the will, ready to see how the will can be-

[30] See St. Thomas Aquinas, *Summa Theologiae*, I-II, q. 60, art. 4; and II-II, q. 58, art. 8; q. 80, art. 1.

come more perfect. Our first question again can be the same as the question we asked about the other powers, namely, what is the most common fault of the will? Now, no one who is at all aware of contemporary problems can doubt the frequency or the seriousness of the injustices that are committed. Why should injustice be so widespread?

In the order of external, material goods, the "good of justice" can readily appear to be an evil, or at least it can be hard to will consistently and easily. For example, in giving to another what I owe to him, I deprive myself of its possession; in respecting the right of another to engage in the same occupation or industry, I must forgo possible opportunities for myself; in giving to another common utilities and the like, I deprive myself of culturally determined "grounds" for considering myself superior. Upon reflection, I can bring myself to see that these various actions are good, but this is a reasoned reflection, not a spontaneous, simple understanding. And I can bring myself to choose and to carry out in action what I have seen to be the just thing, but the spontaneous movement of the will tends to the simple possession of goods rather than to justice.

But is it not true that man is naturally social? Indeed it is. Man naturally tends to love others as united to him and to unite himself to them, as we have seen. But justice takes into account precisely the distinction and the otherness of persons. Justice is not "natural," because it is not spontaneous; it is, however, "natural" in the sense that it is suitable and even obligatory for man to have and practice.

We can also argue to the existence of a virtue of justice from the viewpoint of the formal order between an agent and the things that are good for him. The other two moral virtues have established certain orders; there is only one aspect left, and that is the relation between the agent, the goods that perfect man, and *other rational beings*. On the one hand, we have seen that all created goods are made to help man to reach his own goals of life. In regard to all subrational beings, this is true without any qualification. But in regard to other rational beings, we cannot simply say that they are *for* any individual. It is true, in a limited way, that other human beings can and do help me to become a better man. That, however, is not their sole nor their primary purpose. Quite the contrary. No human being exists primarily for another human being; as individuals, they are equally ordered to an end which is distinct from all of them.

Nonetheless, the relationships of equality and objectivity also need to fall under the rule of reason. "The good of another as other" is an irreducible good for man, arising from the communication of many individuals in one and the same rational nature, and from the immersion of all these individuals in one and the same world of interaction and objects. But the "good of another as other" is not directly a sensible good; it can be directly grasped as good only by intellect, though in a derivative fashion it can be grasped as good by the discursive estimation under the guidance of intellect. Therefore it can be aimed at only by a rational power, and only in a secondary, derivative sense, and therefore as a material part of a composite act, by a sense appetite. And, since we have seen that it does not flow from the spontaneous movement of the will, it must be a distinct, acquirable virtue. Hence, according to the formal analysis of the order of goods, there is a cardinal virtue of the will concerned with the good of another, and this is the virtue of *justice*.

The virtue of justice looks to a different kind of good than the other moral virtues. In the case of temperance and fortitude, the good is to be found in the proper dispositions of the agent himself, and in this sense we can say that their proper concern is with the passions of the subject. In these cases, the morality of the act is judged by studying the action and the agent. We could even say that temperance and fortitude are both relative and subjective: for the measure of temperance particularly, but also fortitude, is the concrete nature and needs of the subject. The norms of temperance and fortitude are not absolute (except within certain wide limits, as we saw earlier). St. Thomas says that in their case the "mean" or ideal is a mean of reason only.

In the case of justice we do not again look to the way in which the action flows from the agent—we have completely answered that question. What remains for consideration is an objective relation; the mean of reason in the case of justice is precisely the mean of reality. This mean, of course, is one that is known and willed, otherwise it would have no reference to morality at all. But, granted that it is known and willed, the judgment of right and wrong uses the norm of objective relations.

The Parts of Justice: Specific and Integral Parts. Justice is completely fulfilled when a man does the positive good called for and avoids the evil of injuring another. We can call these two aspects the *integral parts* of justice.

The *species* of justice, often said to be three or four in number, are not strictly species; yet, since the notion of justice is perfectly fulfilled in all of them, they can be considered as quasi-species. The kinds of justice can be more easily understood if we go about dividing it logically. Now, justice looks to the good of another as other. But the *other* in question can be a single individual entirely equal to me, or a member of a natural community as such. On this basis we can set up the following division:

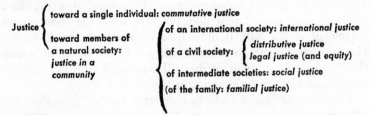

Commutative justice is apparently the first of the justice relations to be discussed and investigated, and it is probably the best known and most easily understood. Since it is a relationship between two individuals as such, it is characterized by strict equality. By the mere fact that there are two human beings both of whom are equally, and independently of each other, ordered to the same ultimate end of their nature, neither may make use of the other as a means. Justice first requires them to respect the rights of each other and to refrain from injuring each other. Particular positive obligations of doing something do not arise from nature, but from some additional, contingent fact. Thus, by contract two mutually corresponding obligations arise. Or, if another has been injured, in himself or his property, something must be done to repay him and "restore the equality." Finally, in another kind of positive fact, I may find myself in possession of the property of another (whether I stole it or acquired it innocently makes no difference here) ; justice demands that I give it back to its owner.[31]

Corresponding to commutative justice, there is a generic virtue, which I have called *justice in a community*. This is not merely a generic classification. Justice in a community refers to other people considered as a group. Since there are essentially different kinds of natural societies, there will be as many kinds of justice in a community as there are kinds of societies. Now, these distinct subspecies of justice work *within* an actually constituted and structured society—such a society we may call a *formal* society. But in several cases communities arise which as yet do not have a formal structure, and yet they already have common needs and common goods—this would be an unformed, or *material* society.[32] When a material society actually exists, there must be a virtue which impels its members to bring it into formal being as a society. Again, the virtue which supports the very existence of a formal society (not the obligations arising within it) , and which impels me to reform it if it is no longer functioning well, cannot be any of the subspecies, but must be the overall virtue concerned with the common good.

A further understanding of justice in a community can be derived by comparing it with commutative justice. Commutative justice looks to the equality between the agent and another person, and its most distinctive act is *restoration* if the equality has been disturbed. On the other hand, justice in a community looks

[31] It seems that the third case is the only one where the contingent fact that brings about a positive obligation of justice need not have been brought about by a human act. In the other cases, it seems that a human act is needed to bring about obligation. Suppose I think something is my property and destroy it, and in fact it was not; it does not seem that restitution is obligatory. But suppose I think it is Smith's when in fact it is Jones's; it seems that restitution is obligatory—the ignorance here is not substantial.

[32] This distinction makes it possible to combine two views of the origin of civil society. The arguments which show that a society as such can arise only through moral activity, and that the authority in civil society comes from the consent of the governed, all bear on the *formal society*. But the arguments which point to the needs and goods which arise often as unforeseen consequences of activity or through natural causes, and which urge that there *are* *some obligations* arising from circumstances, bear on *material societies*.

Moreover, not all things can be reduced to law; some relationships thus remain unformalized. That is why there are courts of equity as well as of law.

rather to the equality of all in relation to the common good, and its most distinctive act is the *contribution* of each member to the whole. Whereas in commutative justice the avoidance of some actions (refraining from injuring others) seems to be primary, and the respect for the rights of others the primary intent, in justice in a community the primary acts seem to be the positive acts of cooperation and contribution.

Concerning the subspecies of justice in a community relatively little need be said here; we will content ourselves with commenting on the particular goodness intended and comparing some of its features.

The natural society which most clearly exemplifies the justice relations is the civil society. In civil society there are two kinds of justice: the justice of the governor and of the governed. The governor has the obligation of distributing the benefits and burdens of civil society equally to all the members.[33] The governed in turn have the obligation of equally supporting the society and of obeying its laws, and this is called legal justice.[34]

In the family, ethicians do not ordinarily speak of justice. Yet it seems reasonable that some justice relationships subsist between the adult members of a family, especially between husband and wife. It is true that there is not a complete "otherness" between husband and wife, and between parents and children. But it also seems that we can legitimately insist that the members of a family are persons, not merely "parts" or "possessions" of the father. In Roman law, the father could dispose of wife and children almost at will; he had, for example, the power of life and death over his children, and he traditionally married off his children as he pleased. This does not seem to be an entirely valid conception.

[33] Ethicians point out that the equality in commutative justice is mathematical, the equality in civil society is proportional. This distinction is obvious.

[34] Obviously this is fully true only under a *just* government, and those who are directly obliged by legal justice are the citizens. If a government is unjust, it may still be necessary to provide for common safety and to keep internal order —this would not be from legal justice, but from the generic justice in a community. A noncitizen is not a member of the society, yet as long as he stays he is bound to the laws which maintain order, and he may be bound partly to support it, as by paying taxes; it would seem that he is not bound to military service and the like.

We can well grant that the relationship between parents and the children who are not yet adults is certainly not comparable to commutative justice. Yet the parents are bound to act for the good of their children, not merely for their own good. And the whole point—the ultimate goal as it were—of bringing up children is that they may become distinct, responsible adults, capable of founding families in their own turn. The nonadult status of the children means that certain types of decisions are not within their competence and that in these matters the parents act *for them*.[35] Yet even when the parents act for, and, as it were, will and choose in their stead, they are bound to consider the best interests of their children as distinct. Similarly, husband and wife are not simply two distinct individuals in mutual relationships of equality. From some points of view, there is an equality, and it seems that these situations are simply governed by commutative justice. But between husband and wife there is also a complementarity, and this is a special relation. Moreover, there must also be a seat of authority in a family. These considerations show that commutative justice is insufficient to govern all intrafamilial relationships. "Love" in the family will be discussed below.

The other two "societies" are as yet not fully structured, and it does not clearly appear what their precise functions are. That an international society ought to be established seems quite clear, but its nature cannot be clearly specified. Negatively some points can be made. First, it seems that the international society ought not to be simply one of the existing civil societies expanded to take in the whole world. Secondly, it does not seem that we ought to think of a superstate which would be a new state but of exactly the same kind. This would imply necessarily that our existing states would cease to exist except as departments of the one state. Positively, it would seem best that we work steadily but perhaps slowly toward a world organization whose nature will appear more clearly as we get closer to the goal. There are some encour-

[35] Ethicians say that the authority of the state is legislative, that of the parents dominative. Law goes further (it is general, has power of life and death, and so on), but it supposes that the subject has an independently acting will. The dominion of the parents is more limited, but it can nullify the effects of attempted decisions of children (as in the making of contracts and so on).

aging signs: the cooperation among a great number of nations in the control of the dope traffic; the World Health Organization. In another direction, the United Nations itself and the various regional organizations, such as the European Free Market, show the possibility of concrete cooperation in well-organized forms.

The other "society" is in one way more amorphous, since it seems to include several unrelated goods. At present, the goods spoken of are economic and sociocultural. Economic opportunity for all men is one of the goals; it embraces living wages for workers, but also such things as trade and manufacturing together with the production, distribution, and market price of farm products. In the sociocultural area, the emphasis is on the removal of injustices: racial and other discrimination in education, cultural opportunity, housing; segregation; civil inequalities. By and large, the concern for these various objects is assigned to a virtue most often called *social justice*. But just as the social reality is amorphous, the views on social justice are conflicting and often unclear. Many writers, assigning these and more specific tasks to social justice, also give to it the functions we have assigned earlier to our generic justice in a community. Perhaps social justice as it is spoken of has no unity beyond the identity of name, and perhaps a much more formal analysis ought to be made in terms of the *kind* of good that needs to be accomplished in each area.

The Parts of Justice: Potential Parts. A potential part, it will be recalled, is one that in some way possesses the perfection of the whole (or the principal part, as the case may be), yet not completely, not according to its full nature. Justice is concerned with the good of another and with some kind of equality that is to be established or maintained. A potential part can be so called if the "other" is not simply viewed as other; or if equality is fundamentally lacking; or, finally, if there is no specifiable norm in the equality. Thus, there is a whole family of virtues relating to others.[36]

In the first class of potential parts we may put truthfulness. The obligation of telling the truth and avoiding lying is not sufficiently explained by speaking of the *right* of the listener to be

[36] On the "natural love" or "natural charity" of men for each other, see above.

told the truth. It is only rarely that a questioner has a right to a particular truth; that is, only rarely would withholding it leave him in the kind of ignorance that would bring harm to him. But the obligation of truthfulness goes much beyond that and includes all communication between persons.[37] But there is a common good served by truthfulness, the confidence that we must place in other human beings in order to live and make progress. In regard to this common good, the person to whom we communicate what is in our mind is not looked on simply as other; rather, he is looked on as sharing with us the good of mutual confidence and trust. And yet, if he were not another person, we could not communicate with him. So, the common good of mutual confidence and trust is found among persons, and it is impaired by any lie, even a trivial one.

Similarly, in friendship we do not find a strict relationship of justice; and yet, as we have seen, friendship does involve a kind of "otherness" between the friends. An examination of friendship as a potential part of justice will help to understand both better.

Friendship has been classified in many ways,[38] and the three varieties which are proposed here for consideration are chosen only because of their significance for our purposes.

Historically speaking, the most broadly based kind of friendship used to be called "civil friendship," in so far as it was thought to hold between fellow citizens. In past ages, it would have seemed unreal to talk about real interactions between all

---

[37] Ethicians have a number of theories about the ground of this obligation and a great deal to say about lying and its malice as well as the right to keep secrets.

[38] The best known of these is the Aristotelian division into three kinds:

a. The friendship of usefulness, such as might be found between two business partners who maintain a community of goods and interests in their business, but in no way beyond. This friendship is ethically neutral and very conditional.

b. The friendship of pleasure, found between persons who take pleasure in one another's company for various reasons; thus, gangs of boys may have such friendships; much "love" between boys and girls may be of this sort. This friendship of itself is also ethically neutral, conditional, unstable, and can be very selfish.

c. The friendship of honor, based on the mutual respect of the friends for the virtuous goodness found in each other. This friendship is always morally good, unconditional, stable, unselfish.

men. But modern conditions of communication and interaction make it both possible and necessary to talk of relations between all men throughout the world. We will, in our discussion, retain the term "civil friendship," but understand it as including all the "citizens" of that "international society" which should be in the process of formation.

In civil friendship, there is equality not only of nature but also of concrete relationship; there is a mutual regard for each other's dignity as fellow man; there is a mutual love of each other's good in that a man does wish the good of every man he knows and is prepared to wish the good of any other man who comes into contact with him as fellow man. On the other hand, there is very little known mutuality of knowledge, regard, and love; there is no possibility of shared memory; there is ordinarily no sensory component. But it is not merely a possibility of relationship; it does have an act, and that act consists essentially in a state of preparedness to meet any fellow man on the basis of civil friendship. This act has sometimes been singled out as the essential "friendliness" that every man owes to every other man.[39]

What is called "friendship" in the strict sense seems to be a very complex affair. It is required as a condition that the persons involved be equal in some real way. There is an essential act of the will, by which the friend is loved "as another self," that is, for his own sake, "as an end," in no way subordinated to me. This means on the one hand that he is regarded as a distinct individuality, but also one that is joined to me in a mutual willing of each other's good. There is a second, essential act, a habitual knowledge of the friend's return of love and knowledge.[40] Thirdly, usually but not necessarily, there are shared memories,

[39] St. Thomas uses to describe this the term "affability," but he means much more than the mere external approachability which is indeed its sign; see *Summa Theologiae*, II-II, q. 114, arts. 1 and 2.

[40] St. Thomas does not call friendship a virtue. There seem to be two reasons for this. (1) The term is applied to the "friendships of utility and of pleasure," which are morally neutral. (2) The reciprocity rests on two really distinct persons and therefore is not an intrinsic perfection of either one without qualification. He will say that it is "an ornament of virtue." Yet there seem to be good reasons for considering friendship virtuous, even if we cannot call it simply *a* virtue. And see also *Summa Theologiae*, II-II, q. 101, art. 1, obj. 3 and ad 3.

involving imaginational habits. Fourthly, also usual but not necessary, is a component of sensory affection. These last two habits
pertain to the substantial wholeness of friendship, though only
on the material (determinable) side of the composite habit group
which is friendship. According to this analysis, then, there are
two essential features of friendship in the strict sense: the quality
of the love and the knowledge of the mutuality of the knowledge
and love. The second of these two requirements is not difficult to
understand.

The quality of the love in friendship in the strict sense is somewhat more difficult to analyze. Traditionally, it has been called
"the love of benevolence." As we have said, it can be described
as that act by which we wish good for another person. That such
love can be found among men would seem to be undeniable; it is
most strikingly demonstrated in cases where the good of the other
cannot be gained except at a great cost to the lover (for example,
when one risks his life to save the life of another). A problem
seems to arise when we try to explain this act in terms of the
various "objects of the will."

We noted earlier that the formal object of the will is "goodness
as such" and that the very notion of good implies some relation
to the one who responds to it. Good, we can agree, means a suitability, an appropriateness, a perfection for the one for whom it
is good. This suitability can sometimes be an advantage, a benefit
accruing to that one. If this were taken as the unique and essential meaning of good, however, then problems could arise concerning the very possibility of a love of benevolence. If, on the
contrary—recalling that the good which is the object of the will
is the good as understood by reason—we define the good as what
is in any way appropriate for a reasonable nature, then we can
easily see that an act of unselfish love may be the most suitable
act that a man can perform at a particular time.[41]

Another problem that arises is the relation between the concrete objects of the will when viewed in terms of means and ends,
and the love of benevolence. When we consider the nature of

[41] St. Thomas warns us that we ought not to consider human love as if it
were primarily sensory love. Human love is most importantly rational love;
see *Summa Theologiae*, I-II, q. 4, art. 2 ad 2.

moral activity, we discover that moral goodness is a value which is absolute, at least in its demand upon us. When we consider human activity in terms of the ultimate orientation of human nature, we find that God is the ultimate end for man, to which everything else must be ordered. When we examine the kinds of love which man can exercise, we find the love of benevolence as a perfect act. With respect to the last two points, there is really no problem, if we recall that God also is a Person and that other persons participate in the perfection of personality. With regard to the first of these objects, moral value, the problem is quite different. Moral value is not a being, as persons are; it is not even an action like loving or paying one's debts.[42] It is a formal quality of objects as they are presented for our rational choice. Now persons are themselves moral beings, so that the love of benevolence, wishing their good, must consider their good as moral beings. If this is kept in mind, then what is the true good for another cannot be in conflict with any moral demand. The good for another can seem to be in conflict with a moral requirement only if the good belongs to some nonmoral order of goods, such as health, money, pleasure. But any nonmoral good is, as such and without further consideration, not a properly human good. Therefore, the "devotion to the ideal of moral activity" is not an act of love comparable to the love of benevolence. It is rather the sort of volitional act that gives the ultimate meaning and direction to the totality of one's actions, including the love of benevolence, and also including the acts of all the other virtues.[43]

A third kind of friendship that can be considered for its illustrative value is that of marital or conjugal love. We must of course bear in mind that marriage is marriage whether or not conjugal love is present; that the act of entering into the married state with someone has some contractual aspects and that the married state itself is a kind of society; that therefore there are justice obligations of a stricter sort and also other aspects of justicelike

---

[42] St. Thomas, *Summa Theologiae*, I-II, q. 26, art. 4, says that love of a person is love without qualification, *amor simpliciter;* love of a formal goodness is love in a qualified sense, *amor secundum quid.*'

[43] This volitional act follows upon a judgment of synderesis (or wisdom, as the case may be), and belongs to the class of "intentions" rather than to the more particular acts which are divided into the kinds of love.

virtues, such as familial loyalty ("piety"). But whether or not
man and wife always love each other, it seems possible that some
husbands and wives love each other with the highest kind of love
of benevolence and at the same time are fully aware of the known
mutuality of their love. In this case, we could with complete pro-
priety of language speak of a marital friendship. This friendship
has a kind of perfection which cannot be shared by any other
human relationship, for the selflessness of love is expressed in an
inimitable way in the self-giving of sexual intercourse. If and
when such a friendship is reached, it is probably the most perfect
human relationship: and in that sense it can be a springboard for
the highest human perfection, or sanctity.[44]

The second group of potential parts is one in which the notion
of equality is verified only very indirectly. Most prominent among
these is the virtue of religion. St. Thomas understands this virtue
to be that which governs the service of God, especially the worship of God in ritual and prayers. Now, the relation of creature
to God is altogether unique; not only do we receive our existence
from Him, but any act by which we recognize our dependence
and His greatness or express our gratitude and devotion is equally
a gift from Him to us. Hence, not only is there no equality between the acts of worship and their object, but there is not even
any equality between these acts and what we as creatures owe to
God. The particular acts of the virtue of religion have been
amply discussed by others.

The third sort of potential part of justice is a secondary part
because there is no specifiable norm in the equality sought. Typical examples are gratitude and liberality. In gratitude there is no
specified act or thing which is to repay the donor. Indeed, the
whole idea of repayment is repugnant to gratitude. Nevertheless,
gratitude is a "return" to the giver, at least a return of recognition and acknowledgment, often also of appreciation, and under
some conditions even a return of gifts. Liberality is primarily an
attitude of the will by which a person who has an abundance of
possessions is disposed to give them to other men who have less.

[44] Mystics have very often tried to describe their experience of God in terms
of human married love. Compare the analysis of this conjugal friendship with
what was said earlier about celibacy as a state of perfection.

But it is not just any desire to give—not prodigality, not ostentation. Liberality keeps in mind that material things are made *for man* before they are the possession of any individual man and that other men are his fellows, equal to him in nature and personal dignity. When, then, the liberal person sees someone in need, he has mercy on him; when he sees a good that can be done with his money, and most of all if it is a good that will extend to many, he is prepared to give. Thus, liberality is concerned with what we now often call the "works of mercy," or "charity," or "good works." Most commonly, liberality is concerned with the giving of money, but it will also include the giving of time. Yet if we attempt to ask how much a truly liberal person gives, we find we cannot specify a definite amount, either absolutely or relatively. On the one side, we know that a person may not so give away his money as to neglect other obligations; on the other, liberality is possible and in place even if a person has only a quite moderate and common "abundance" of material goods. No one can specify beyond this: the good inclination of the will as guided by prudence will determine what is to be given.[45]

Legal justice also has a potential part. For in addition to the various natural societies, there is also a supernatural society, the Church. This society owes its existence to a supernatural fact, the delegated authority of the Church, which she receives from God. Thus there is real authority in the Church, but not one arising from the consent of the governed; and so there is real virtue in the subjects, but neither the "otherness" nor the "equality" of legal justice are to be found in it. Moreover, the good at which the Church aims is in a way "common" (the salvation of all men), but it is not an external common good distinct from the subjects; it is "common" in that it is to be possessed individually by each individual.

Because the good at which this society aims is an intrinsic perfection *of the subject,* it can directly command the internal act of a virtue.[46] This means, for example, that it can command the

[45] This is again an example of a "moral debt" or of "what is owed because it is the honorable thing to do."

[46] Legal justice can command the act of any virtue if conditions call for it. However, legal justice primarily demands the performance of the external act rather than the interior virtue; obedience in the Church primarily intends the

subject to perform an act of temperance or of religion. Now, in order to obey completely, the subject must perform the act prescribed not only because of the authority of the superior; he must do it as a formal act of temperance as well, because of the proper goodness of temperance itself. In this way, religious obedience can cause all other virtues. Consequently, it can be called a "general virtue"; not because it has some supposed "general formal object," but because of its causality.

SUMMARY

We have seen that the moral virtues can be divided into four major areas, each centering around one cardinal virtue. In the intellect, the cardinal virtue is prudence, by which man concretely determines for himself what is the good thing to do. Associated with this principal virtue are the steps in the prudential determination and the secondary virtues of good counsel and good judgment. In the desiderative appetite, the cardinal virtue is temperance, by which man rightly tends to the goods which surround him. Associated with this virtue are its species (such as abstinence, sobriety, and marital chastity) and its potential parts (modesty, clemency in the aggressive appetite; humility, celibacy, poverty of spirit, and fasting in the will). In the aggressive appetite, the cardinal virtue is fortitude, by which man attacks and resists the evils which hinder him from the good and sustains himself under the impact of evil. Associated with this virtue is the principal virtue of bravery in the face of death and the secondary parts of confidence, greatness of soul, patience, and perseverance against lesser evils. In the will, the cardinal virtue is justice, by which man gives to another his due, thus relating himself not only to goods and evils but also other persons. Justice is divided into the quasi-species of commutative justice in his relations with individuals and of justice in a community (subdivided into legal and distributive justice, and social justice, together with other less clearly developed virtues). Associated with justice are its

interior virtue and secondarily the external act. In a particular case, religious obedience could aim also at external acts, for example, if the community were in real physical need.

potential parts: truthfulness, friendship, religion, obedience, and
gratitude. With these major lines of organization delineated, the
entire scope of the moral virtues can be seen as a harmonious
whole with its various parts having their own value and mutually
supporting each other.

SOURCES FOR CHAPTER SIX

General Sources

Aquinas, St. Thomas, *Summa Theologiae*, I-II, q. 61 (the cardinal virtues).

Bond, Leo M., O.P., "A Comparison between Human and Divine Friendship," *The Thomist*, vol. 3 (1941), 54-94.

Carpenter, Hilary, O.P., "Natural Virtues," in *Moral Principles and Practices,* G. J. MacGillivray, ed. (New York, Sheed, 1933).

Crowe, Frederick, S.J., "Complacency and Concern in the Thought of St. Thomas," *Theological Studies,* vol. 20 (1959), 1-39, 198-230, 343-395.

Gilson, Etienne, *Wisdom and Love in St. Thomas Aquinas* (Milwaukee, Marquette University Press, 1951).

Guitton, Jean, *Essay on Human Love,* Melville Chaning-Pearce, trans. (New York, Philosophical Library, 1951).

Henry, A. M., O.P., *Virtues and States of Life,* Theology Library, vol. 4 (Notre Dame, Ind., Fides Publishers, Inc., 1957); quite uneven.

Johann, Robert O., S.J., *The Meaning of Love* (Westminster, Md., Newman, 1959).

Johann, Robert O., S.J., "A Meditation on Friendship," *The Modern Schoolman,* vol. 25 (1947), 126-131.

McGinnis, Raymond R., *The Wisdom of Love* (Rome, Officium Libri Catholici, 1951).

Mary Emil, Sister, I.H.M., "Teaching and the Person," *Sponsa Regis,* vol. 32 (1961), 306-313; on the acquired virtues.

O'Brien, Patrick, *Emotions and Morals. Their Place and Purpose in Harmonious Living* (New York, Grune & Stratton, 1950).

Philippe, Paul, O.P., *Le Rôle de l'amitié dans la vie chrétienne selon saint Thomas d'Aquin* (Rome, Angelicum, 1938).

Wade, Francis C., S.J., *Teaching and Morality* (Chicago, Loyola, 1963).

Fortitude and Temperance

Adam, August, *The Primacy of Love*, E. C. Noonan, trans. (Westminster, Md., Newman, 1958); a rhetorical attempt to relocate chastity; well-intentioned but not profound.

Aquinas, St. Thomas, *Summa Theologiae*, II-II qq. 123-170.

Carlson, Sebastian, O.P., *The Virtue of Humility* (Dubuque; Wm. C. Brown Co., 1952).

Chastity, Lancelot C. Sheppard, O.P., trans. (Westminster, Md., Newman, 1955).

Chereso, Cajetan, O.P., *The Virtue of Honor and Beauty According to St. Thomas Aquinas* (River Forest, Ill., Aquinas Library, 1960); explains why temperance is an especially beautiful and honorable virtue.

Garrigou-Lagrange, Reginald, O.P., "Humility According to St. Thomas," *Thomist*, vol. 1 (1939), 2-13.

Graham, Dom Aelred, *The Love of God* (New York, Longmans, 1939); temperance is well treated in this book.

Hildebrand, Dietrich von, *In Defence of Purity* (New York, Longmans, 1931); eloquent and often useful.

Pieper, Josef, *Fortitude and Temperance*, Daniel F. Coogan, trans. (New York, Pantheon, 1955).

Plé, A., O.P., "The Virtue of Chastity," *Theology Digest*, vol. 5 (1957), 13-17.

Poverty, Lancelot C. Sheppard, O.P., trans. (Westminster, Md., Newman, 1954).

Suenens, L. J. Cardinal, *Un Problème Crucial: Amour et maîtrise de soi* (Bruges, Desclée de Brouwer, 1960).

Valentine, Ferdinand, *Apostolate of Chastity* (Westminster, Md., Newman, 1954).

Wolff, Harold C., "What Hope Does for Man," *Saturday Review*, vol. 40 (Jan. 5, 1957), 45; an enthusiastic presentation, using "hope" in a loose sense.

Justice

Aquinas, St. Thomas, *Summa Theologiae*, II-II qq. 57-122.

Barker, E., *The Political Thought of Plato and Aristotle* (New York, Dover, 1961), pp. 235-237; has a fine treatment of civil friendship.

Martinez, Marie Louise, R.S.C.J., "Distributive Justice According to St. Thomas," *The Modern Schoolman*, vol. 24 (1947), 208-223.

Newman, Jeremiah, *Foundations of Justice* (Cork, Ireland, Cork University Press, 1954).

Obedience, Lancelot C. Sheppard, O.P., trans. (Westminster, Md., Newman, 1953).

Phelan, Gerald B., "Justice and Friendship," *Thomist,* vol. 5 (1943), 153-170.

Pieper, Josef, *Justice,* Lawrence F. Lynch, trans. (New York, Pantheon, 1955).

Rahner, Karl, S.J., "Reflections on Obedience," *Cross Currents,* vol. 10 (1960), 363-374.

Smith, Raymond, O.P., "The Virtue of Docility," *Thomist,* vol. 15 (1952), 572-623.

Prudence

Aquinas, St. Thomas, *Summa Theologiae,* II-II qq. 47-56.

Augenque, Pierre, *La prudence chez Aristote* (Paris, Presses Universitaires de France, 1963).

Dempsey, Bernard W., S.J., "Prudence and Economic Decision," *Thought,* vol. 35, (1960), 16-36.

Gerhard, William A., *Infra-Rational Knowledge and the Intellectual Virtue of Prudence* (Notre Dame, Ind., University of Notre Dame Press, 1948).

O'Neil, Charles J., *Imprudence in St. Thomas Aquinas* (Milwaukee, Marquette University Press, 1955).

Pieper, Joseph, *Prudence,* Richard and Clara Winston, trans. (New York, Pantheon, 1959).

Intellectual Virtues

Brennan, Sister Rose Emmanuella, *The Intellectual Virtues* (Washington, Catholic University Press, 1941).

Chapter Seven

Conclusions and Correlations

Even though we have seen how the many possible virtues can be ordered and correlated through the notion of the cardinal virtues and their various kinds of parts, the overall impression is still that the problem of moral perfection is an extremely complicated one. How can an ordinary person deal with this problem? Should every person have all the habits and virtues? And if not, can any principles be discovered which would make selection possible and intelligible?

PEOPLE DIFFER

We all subscribe to the proposition that people differ. Yet it is extremely easy to have just a few stereotypes which in fact we use to classify people. Ethical and ascetical writings are filled with various kinds of oversimplified classifications,[1] so that it is really worthwhile to delay for a few moments to consider the kinds of differences that can be found and to try to realize that these may be very far reaching.

Most obvious of all differences is that between men and women. Surely it would be absurd to deny this difference or to suppose that it is of no importance. It is quite another matter to deter-

---

[1] A widely accepted division is that which divides people according to their "dominant passions" into the proud and the sensual. Besides the fact that some people show both the supposedly contrary passions, we find that others have no single dominant passion, no single flaw of character but several of equal gravity. In addition, the aggressive types are overlooked. So this division is of no use.

Another variety is division according to the "four temperaments": the choleric, the sanguine, the phlegmatic, and the bilious. This psychological theory is an extension of the biological theory of the "four humors," which was rejected centuries ago. Since the basis of this theory has been shown to be incorrect, there is no reason for a contemporary writer to make use of it.

mine the origin of the differences which we find in the people
with whom we have to deal. And it is still another matter to consider whether differences that arise only within a definite culture
(for example, in Western civilizations) are good or bad, reasonable or to be rejected and corrected.[2] But there are some general
considerations which may be of value in concrete circumstances.

Let us first consider the human person concretely, in regard to
concrete and detailed action.[3] Surely, the quality of a man's courage or love is different from that of a woman. This is bound to be
the case, if we admit the unity of the human person and the unity
of his activity. Therefore, there is a sense in which sexuality enters into every activity of a person, intellectual, moral, religious,
as well as bodily. Thus, when we are giving advice or direction, it
makes a great deal of difference whether it is a man or a woman
who is being considered.

But there is also the analytic consideration of human activity
based upon the distinction of formal objects.[4] Does sexual differentiation enter in at this level? Evidently it does not enter into
the purely intellectual virtues, such as science. Nor does it enter

[2] Older views perhaps stressed these differences too much. Thus, Janet
Erskine Stuart, *The Society of the Sacred Heart* (San Francisco, San Francisco
College for Women, 1914), pp. 82-83, strongly insists on the differences and
seems to consider them entirely innate. See also her *Highways and By-ways in
the Spiritual Life* (New York, Longmans, 1923).

Psychologists and anthropologists tend on the other hand to insist on the
likenesses between men and women and on the great variation of psychological
traits in various cultures. But patterns which are acquired from the ambient
culture are just as real as if they were innate and may be almost as hard to
change. The present point, of course, is that such differences are *there*.

There is a third question, *should* boys and girls be brought up to act differently as men and women? Again, older views here tend to be rigid, and
from our contemporary point of view excessively rigid. See the *Catholic Psychological Record*, vol. 2 (1964), 87-121, for three views that are considerably
different.

[3] Much contemporary literary treatment, and also philosophical treatments
which are influenced by existentialist points of view, very strongly insist on
these concrete differences.

[4] Experimental psychology, as a scientific discipline, also deals with human
activity abstractly. Consequently, masculinity and femininity are considered
by it in themselves; they are found to be clusters of psychological traits,
and these traits in turn are found to be independently variable.

It is important to note that there is no quarrel between these distinct points
of view.

into prudence. *What* a person has to deliberate about will be different, depending on whether it is a man or a woman deliberating; but that choice should be guided by the best deliberation a person is capable of in the light of the moral goods at stake—*this* is equally necessary for men and for women. Similarly, justice must intend the good of another; in so far as there are material components in the composite act by which a person in fact *performs* a just act, the sexual differences will show up, but they will not affect the essential quality by which this act is precisely a just act. So, too, temperance and fortitude are formally what they are for both men and women, though here the differences of objects and of material components loom larger than they do in the other virtues.

Sometimes the concrete actions required by virtue may differ much more than their formal constitution as virtuous actions would seem to indicate. This is perhaps most clearly shown in the case of temperance.

At the level of those mastery habits which are not virtues (in the discursive estimation and imagination), as well as in many of the automatisms, the differences between men and women may be essential. These differences are, generally speaking, well treated by psychologists, and to that extent need not be discussed here.[5]

Psychologists and educationists have also pointed out that boys and girls develop at different rates and that there are quite complex differences in physical, psychological, emotional, and social development at various points. Often enough boys and girls themselves are unaware of these differences; indeed, all too often grown men and women remain ignorant. Much of this material is very easily available, and its significance for education and counseling has also been indicated with sufficient clarity.[6] Consequently, no more need be done here than to indicate, as has just been done, where this material fits in relation to the rest of the analysis.

We need not admit hereditary determinism[7] to see that people

[5] Books on individual psychology, counseling, and developmental psychology are readily available and have a great deal of practical information.

[6] In the past, religious counselors seem to have failed to make use of all the available books.

[7] One should not dignify racism by even discussing it.

250 HABITS AND VIRTUES

already differ according to their biological heredity. No doubt, these differences have a greater or lesser significance: the color of the eyes or the straightness of the hair of themselves make very little direct difference in the quality of activity, whereas congenital deafness would obviously make a great deal of difference. Unfortunately, though we know that there are very many differences in almost every organ and in most of the basic functions, we are not at all sure precisely how these differences affect the various kinds of personality that we do find.[8] In very many cases, these differences are not indivisible qualities; it seems best to consider individual differences as lying along a continuum with an indefinite number of variations between extremes.

On the whole, there do not seem to be any simple and unmistakable clues to personality. There is a long history of attempts to find such clues: physiology, morphology, phrenology, graphology, palmistry. The best of them have been accorded only a minor place; the rest have been completely discarded.

---

[8] One kind of difference is of very great significance, and that is the way in which persons vary in the quality of their sensory functions. This is a very broad kind of difference and does not seem to be capable of exact measurement; it seems to have been largely ignored. Bodily differences of function of individual organs, such as sight, hearing, taste, and smell, can easily be discovered. However, these differences by and large do not imply any general physical or psychological qualities. On the other hand, differences in the functioning of the sense(s) of touch seem to be connected with general qualities, mainly because touch is the basic sense of an animal and involves almost the entire organism. This correlation was first pointed out by Aristotle; there is some immediate evidence for it, but mostly it is concluded from the very close dependence of mental functions on the body and of intellectual knowledge on sensation, especially internal sensation.

Thus, a delicate or highly sensitive touch implies a very delicately balanced body composition and so also a very responsive central nervous system (internal sense). As a result, persons with a very fine sense of touch are more likely to have a good intelligence. Similarly, the strength or liveliness of sensory appetency (strong emotional response) is connected with the excellence of the sense of touch and the nervous system in general. Keen intelligence and strong volition are often to be found in connection with lively emotions.

From this point of view, it is clear that the distinction sometimes assumed to exist between the intellectual and the sensualist is not one of basic or native temperament. The person who has a vivid imagination and a very lively experience of sense pleasure can also be the one who has the capacity for high intellectual achievement. There can be native differences of interest, but of much greater importance is the learned, habitual channelling of both interests and activities into one direction.

Some authors who agree that heredity is not a completely determining factor have attempted to relate all differences to "environment." This controversy raged quite violently a few generations ago, but now there is rather general agreement that it is incorrect to think of heredity and environment as completely opposed. What should be said is that a mature person is a product of heredity *and* environment *and* his own activity. Heredity accounts for the basic physical possibilities and the psychological possibilities that develop from them. There is a certain latitude in the qualities and relations of the physical organism, though the limits of this latitude cannot easily be drawn. Within these limits variations are of comparatively slight importance compared with environmental factors and acquired modifications. Certainly, differences in education bring about very important differences in adults.

People also differ as to the obligations that concretely fall upon them. Circumstances of general culture may require that a good man act habitually in a way that otherwise he might not have to conform to so explicitly. For instance, because of the unjust distribution of economic and cultural goods in the United States today, a person not having direct dealings with anyone thus deprived may still have to go out of his way to involve himself in the bettering of these conditions. Therefore, he may have to practice the virtue of social justice to a much greater extent than would be necessary in his own immediate contacts. Again, more particular circumstances of state of life may create obligations. For example, the father of several children may have to refrain from otherwise legitimate but expensive recreations, thus practicing temperance in a way that would not have been incumbent upon him had he not married. And even more particular circumstances of commitment to a particular task may involve added obligations. Thus, because two men have joined in a business partnership, one may have to practice patience if the partnership is not to be dissolved at a time when one of the partners would suffer loss.

Finally, even when there are no determinants that bring about or demand particular actions, people find themselves with likes and dislikes that they not only can but should consult. It may well be that when all exigencies have been considered, several courses of action remain open, at least in principle, and yet that one of them seems totally unattractive. In a particular case, it can definitely be the part of wisdom to stay away from a course of life for which a person has pronounced dislikes.

In general, it may not be practically very important to notice how culture determines both ideals and patterns of behavior. For any depth of theoretical understanding, of course, a considerable knowledge of sociology and anthropology is necessary. For example, the precise role of husband and wife in a family and the ideals of masculinity and femininity are known to be partly determined by the particular culture. Generally speaking, the male infant grows into the boyish behavior that is presented as fact and as ideal around him, and the boy into manliness; the girl grows into her corresponding patterns. In addition, there may or may not be special patterns for occupations, social levels, and the like. Provided that these cultural patterns do not hamper natural possibilities, it is usually not necessary to pay much attention to them. However, in some individual cases, and in cultures which are under stress or are in rapid change, the roles may be ambiguous or in conflict. If, for example, a little boy is treated as a little girl by his mother, he will usually experience a great deal of difficulty. As another example, there may be a discrepancy between the factual role and the ideal that is at least verbally presented, or the role presented within the family circle may be widely at variance with that of the peer group. In such cases there is great likelihood of trouble of some kind later on. Surely, no well-informed person is ignorant of the stresses and tensions present in American culture and of the changes that are going on both in behavior and in ideals. Under these conditions, an inarticulate, merely passive acceptance of ideals and externally imposed patterns of behavior is radically insufficient. A much more conscious choice of ideals and a much more explicit understanding of ascetical theory is certainly desirable, if not necessary.

One of the consequences of these individual differences is that there must be individualized direction. True enough—and we shall consider this point shortly—there are many things in common. But even the common things are affected by individual differences. Thus, each man has the same set of powers (within limits) ; yet, as we have seen, there are differences even at the level of the external powers, such as the external senses or the motor powers. The differences grow as we consider the more human and personal powers, such as the appetites, the intellect, and the will.

Moreover, the beginning steps are more likely to be common, since individual differences at that point tend to be the passive ones. But as progress is made by the person, it is made largely because of his own activity, so that the differences of his ability become multiplied in their effect upon himself. Consequently, the more advanced a person is, the more individualized must be the advice and direction he is to be given.

From another point of view, these differences must be recognized when we try to understand any particular individual. Again, there is a certain sense in which whoever intends to be temperate must intend a rational control of his desires. But he cannot intend this abstractly and in general. Concretely and for him, they are *his* desires which have to be controlled, precisely in their particular intensity, their particular variation to be moved by some sensible goods rather than others, their interrelation with other appetitive responses, and so on. In the same way, the control and moderation the person has to achieve is his control, in the way in which his understanding and judgment see the goodness of such control, and in the way in which he chooses to determine the particular level he will reach. That is why temperance never looks quite the same in two perfectly temperate people.

In addition, we have seen that various virtues can be grouped together in various ways. Now, some of these groupings are contingent, that is, are able to be structured in different ways. These are structures, not just juxtapositions. In our technical terminology, the component virtues will be related as matter and form. Consequently, they will be modified according to the special structure in which they concretely exist. Naturally, they will also express themselves in different ways in harmony with the special position which they have in the given individual.

As students of human perfection, therefore, we should not expect to find uniformity. Nevertheless, careful use of formal object analysis makes it possible to discover common elements. We must guard ourselves—repeatedly—against the "post-analytic fallacy," of thinking that what we isolate by analysis exists separately, and of projecting back to the real order the conditions of what is understood abstractly.

If we are directing others, we should not aim towards stereotypes. We must constantly remind ourselves that each individual must develop his potentialities. Not only that: no matter how detailed the patterns we are justified in proposing to another, there remain matters of free choice. We have seen this in theory, and we have seen that many of the precise determinations and fine structures are matters of free decision. This theory must guide all direction. Yet direction remains possible as long as there are principles that everyone must use.

COMMON NEEDS

Are there any general things that can be said about the need for special habits? We can begin with motor skills. To some extent, of course, a child cannot live long without acquiring some motor skills, unless his basic needs are cared for entirely by others. One of the first things to be learned is the regulation of physiological activities at spaced intervals. The infant has no control over these functions, but sleeps, wakes, eats, and so on, as the functions proceed. Our kind of civilized life cannot be lived in this way, so haphazard spontaneity has to be replaced by regulation and control. Because this control is somewhat indirect, it is gained only slowly; but to some extent it is a condition for future progress. At a second level of development, particular motor skills are more important. In childhood, coordination of bodily activities is very important, but many children do not have sufficient opportunity to develop this coordination. Athletic skills are a partial fulfillment of this need, but they do not seem to be sufficient by themselves. Ability with needle and thread, with penknife or screwdriver, are not only useful in taking care of simple material needs, they have significant repercussions in overall bodily control and in psychological development.[9]

[9] This is an instance in which cultural patterns seem to be seriously deficient. Yet if children have no work of any kind to do, either at home or in

Secondly, there must be some development of particular habits of the internal senses. Obviously, there are the practical necessities of learning a language (or several languages) and of retaining a considerable amount of factual information. This, however, is not enough. As far as the imagination is concerned, particular modes of artistic imagining need to be acquired, or there will be a corresponding impoverishment of personality. Early adolescence seems to be the most important period for the development of such habits of imagination.

Moreover, we have seen that the human estimative power is innately determined only for a very few and very simple judgments. Adult life requires a very great number of these, varying from matters of tact to appreciation of art to the material side of prudence. Very many basic estimations are acquired in very early infancy, at an age when language is not the primary means of communication. Particularly significant are those estimations which concern interpersonal relations. Infants need to learn that other people are basically friendly and concerned with their welfare; they must therefore be treated with love and attention but also with strength; recent studies have strongly emphasized the need which young children have for finding firm boundaries for behavior. But the love and attention must be really felt, not merely spoken of. Put in another way, children need to experience in a concrete sensible way what *good* is. Deprived of this experience in early childhood, they seem to restrict "the good" to their own personal satisfaction. As a consequence, they are unable to view their relations with other persons and with external things in the light of moral good; it would seem that such a personality approximates the so-called "psychopathic personality," who is said to have no grasp of moral good and evil. At a somewhat later period, probably in early adolescence, literature and art are very significant means for the development of culturally modified and harmonious estimations. The presence or absence of such estima-

---

school, it is hard to see how they are to develop diligence, perseverance, a sense of responsibility, and so on.

Perhaps the Montessori methods have a special value where children do not have and perhaps cannot have the experiences of handling and perceiving sensible things.

tions seems to be the difference between refinement and crudity, between a liberally educated person and a narrow-minded one.[10]

Thirdly, there need to be habits in the sensory appetites. In this group of powers, the formation of habits can be avoided only on the condition that behavior be so inconsistent that no pattern of emotional response occurs. Ordinarily this is not the case; and so in fact habits of these powers will be formed almost from the beginning. What is important in the area of appetitive habits is that *good* habits be formed, otherwise almost inevitably bad ones will be developed. As we have noted in considering the habits of the sensory appetites, there is a double possibility: (1) mastery habits (the virtues of temperance and courage or their contraries) and (2) automatism habits (attitudes and feelings toward other persons, toward the structure of society, toward oneself). In both cases, these habits are intimately connected with habits in the internal senses and the intellect. Thus, in the very early stages of life, good or bad habits are formed toward members of the immediate family and also toward self (as for example, self-confidence, right evaluation of one's place in the scheme of things, and the like). In adolescence, emotional responses become stronger and affect new areas of relationship, especially those involving other persons in their sexual differentiation, and in turn oneself. Hence, new and more specific attitudes need to be developed; in addition, the rapid rate of physical and psychological change makes the functioning of the habits of childhood quite unsatisfactory. In this connection, motor skills (and again: not merely athletics) are quite important in providing concrete grounds for attitudes of self-confidence and poise in relation to others. It should also be noted that other types of achievement are now possible and that the necessary generalization from success in one field to a general confidence is made much easier by achievements in several particular areas.[11]

[10] On the importance of a good humanistic formation, see "Knowledge and Action," in *Christian Wisdom and Christian Formation,* J. Barry McGannon, S.J., (New York, Sheed 1964), pp. 43-45, 49-51, 53-57, 59-60.

[11] It is not psychologically healthy that the success be illusory. For this reason, the practice of some schools of not grading students' achievements is not a good solution for the problem of enabling everyone to find some success. It is much better, because more realistic, to provide other opportunities for success (manual skills, athletics, dramatics, social relations, and so on) and also to gear teaching levels and standards to varying levels of pupil possibilities.

Fourthly, some intellectual habits must be developed. As far as practical intelligence is concerned, some intellectual habits will be easily brought about, though they will not necessarily be good ones (imprudence, for example). In the order of speculative knowledge, some opinions probably will also arise without much forethought and planning. But the intellectual virtues cannot be gained without deliberate and distinct attention and effort. Prudence is necessary for everyone—at least the minimal prudence which judges that advice is to be sought. Good sense is not simply innate, though some people may find it harder to become prudent than others; however, there is good reason to think that parental example is most significant. But prudence is so important that it deserves to be worked for all through life. Other intellectual virtues are not universally necessary, but they may well be necessary —in a culture where they are important—for given individuals in a state of life where their absence would lead to serious error, or for particularly talented individuals.[12]

Fifthly, some habits of the will are also necessary. It is hardly conceivable that an individual should live so alone that justice would never be called for. Action which concerns other persons almost necessarily comes into everyone's life, and so justice and its associated virtues must be worked for, or else injustice will inevitably be developed.[13]

UNITY IN MULTIPLICITY

In addition to the several distinct elements which go into a personality structure, there is the structure itself. We have seen, as far as the habits are concerned, that structure is combination ac-

---

[12] It is not superfluous to state again that well-educated persons need to have an equally mature, that is, scientific, knowledge of their faith.

[13] Finally, in the supernatural order which is our present historical state, the supernatural and infused virtues of faith, hope, and charity are necessary in order that actions which are unqualifiedly good may be performed.

The fact that this book to a large extent prescinds from these virtues is not meant to imply that they are incidental or unimportant; the supernatural virtues complete, perfect, and crown the natural structure, which is, *concretely* speaking, defective without them. And yet the natural structure does have an intelligibility and internal order that needs and deserves study for its own sake.

cording to the various matter-form unions. Now, the first point to be noted is that this structure will be different as the concrete goal actually intended differs. It is clear that persons live for various ultimate goals; and in the concrete historical situation of mankind, they are ordered to these goals by virtues or vices: supernatural charity or selfishness or political loyalty and so on. Next, we must recall that even when all the habits needed for a completely developed personality are present, they can be arranged and ordered differently under the supreme and most formal habit. The differing importance and scope of various habits depend on this order. It is of course possible and often happens that a complete order is never achieved, or only slowly brought about. To the extent that complete order is lacking, a personality will lack unity and integration.

To work our way into this point slowly, we must note first that even though in fact an individual person *is* ontologically a strong unity (technically we call this a per se unity), neither his consciousness nor his external behavior automatically manifest this unity. Rather, certain particular points of unity have to be developed. We shall look at some of the more significant factors in turn.

First of all, a person must have a grasp of himself as one. It would not be significant to think of this merely abstractly or in some merely verbal way, as if one were only to say to himself, "I am one being." It is rather a matter of how he concretely imagines and evaluates himself, and these images and estimations will constitute a complex habit group, perhaps even a set of habit groups.

This grasp of one's self is very, very important. Let us recall that the person as knowing-tending being is necessarily grasped by himself in every human act, though obviously not in the same way every time. Though ordinarily we isolate an object to which we primarily intend and attend, and talk about it as if it were the sole content of our consciousness, that object is not abstract in that way. Of course, one of the things we learn as we grow up— if we do—is that some aspects of our experience are irrelevant for some purposes. "Total attention" would not only make any kind of generalization impossible, it would most probably immobilize us; not even "stream of consciousness" writing comes near to representing all the submerged items of awareness. As a result, we abstract. But abstraction is not ordinarily complete; some people are rather absentminded, but cases of complete "abstraction from the senses" are abnormal.

Next, for human action, our judgment of what is good is decisive. "Good," as we have seen, is a relational term, and a great number of goods are estimated by us in relation to ourselves. Therefore our judgment of good depends essentially, if only partially, on our evaluation of ourselves. That is why, in the order of action, it makes so much difference how a person grasps himself.

It is clear that our knowledge of ourselves is not automatically and immediately complete and true. On the one hand, we cannot help perceiving ourselves as agents; on the other, it takes time and effort to know ourselves, both in the concrete as the kind of person we are and in the abstract as the kind of nature we have. So our knowledge of ourselves must be built up out of experiences, judgments, analyses, and even feelings and actions. Or, we can state it this way: our knowledge of ourselves is a composite of sensation, thought, estimation, feeling, and volition. Or again, we can consider our knowledge at any point as a composite of memory and immediate consciousness. Or, in still another way, our knowledge of ourselves is a knowledge of ourselves both as subject of our activities and as object of some sensations, thoughts, feelings, and actions.

Psychologists have written a great deal about these various facets of knowledge. Some of the more significant discussions have singled out "my body," the "body-image," the "self-image" or "self-concept," and the "self-ideal." Anyone engaged in counseling or directing others must have at least a general acquaintance with the basic discoveries in these areas.

In addition, psychologists and sociologists have studied the mutual relations between person and society. From these studies have come such notions as that of the "social role" and its relation to the individual personality, the social causes of delinquency, and many other insights which are helpful not only for understanding deviations but also for directing and counseling a perfectly normal adolescent or adult.

THE FUNCTIONS OF THE SELF-IDEAL

The self-ideal is often discussed from purely psychological points of view. There are certain aspects of this ideal which have a particular value for us here. We are not interested in what people say their ideals are; by the self-ideal we mean that idea-image complex by which we represent to ourselves what we would like to be and to do. However, it is very hard to pick an ideal self which is both within the bounds of possibility and enough beyond our present actuality to be both an encouragement and a spur.

When the self-ideal is held unrealistically high, there seem to be two possibilities. One is self-deception, wherein the force of the ideal leads the person to overestimate the present self so as to reduce the discrepancy between that ideal and the actual self. The other reaction is frustration. An ideal set so high that no achievement can come up to it (at least practically speaking, in view of the actual endowments of the self) leads to almost continuous dissatisfaction with regard to every action. Now a person can afford to fall short sometimes, or in some areas; but if he always fails in his own estimation, then his drives (appetites) are without any object. This situation we call "frustration." The frustrated person has several possible reactions, frequently appearing alternately in the same person. One is the cynical one, depreciating all ideals so that the failure to reach an ideal is of no importance anyway. Another is the "humility with a hook," putting the actual achievement so absurdly low that others—and perhaps even oneself—by way of reaction overrate the achievement and so bring it closer to the ideal. Another is censoriousness, finding comfort in the equal or "greater" faults of others. A fourth is the "persecution" or "evil fate" escape, which blames outside influences, people or things, for the failures to reach the impossible ideal. Among the things thus to be blamed is sometimes one's own nature, so that an excessively high self-ideal can paradoxically lead to self-contempt. These mechanisms are usually not entirely successful and can join hands with the frustration to develop complicated defenses.

One of the complicated reactions that can result is scrupulosity: the tendency not merely to find faults and imperfections where they do not exist or to exaggerate them, but also to keep on looking for such faults in a ceaseless reexamination of past activity. This obsession has several results. First, it enables the frustrated person to toy at least in thought with forbidden objects (often in the sexual area) under the "justifying" guise of looking for possible faults in previous behavior, and thus to obtain some covert satisfaction at a lower and unacknowledged level. Secondly, the alleged urgency of repeated reexamination of past actions makes it unnecessary to perform the other actions which would normally urge themselves on the person. Thirdly, the very excesses of scrupulosity lead others to react to reassure the scrupulous person that his actions were not so bad: and apparently this same reaction is somewhat obscurely going on in the scrupulous person himself.[14]

On the other hand, the defensive mechanisms to cover up frustration can be much less "successful"; there is likely to be a violent reaction. Sometimes the final result is the rejection of all ideals in some severe crisis which may occur at various times of life, not infrequently during adolescence. Another is periodic indulgence followed by periods of remorse: the periodic "binge" seems often to be a part of this pattern. Still another is repression of the notion of failure, with the consequent disorganization and, often, psychosomatic illnesses.

The opposite extreme is to set the self-ideal too low. The direct psychological consequences of this mistake are not as bad, but it is not a good solution, either. First, there is the fact that relatively little effort will be brought to bear and much less will be accomplished than would have been possible. However, there are other, more dangerous results. One is that the person with a low self-ideal finds very little challenge in life, and so he often finds life very boring. When a person can very easily reach all his goals, there is very little satisfaction. Thus a low self-ideal can indi-

14 We have pointed out in an earlier chapter the very great difficulty of overcoming scruples and other anxiety reactions. Direct action is not only not successful, it usually makes matters worse. Long-range solutions are the best: readjustment of self-ideal and self-concept, rebuilding of confidence.

rectly lead to frustration or to refuge in sense pleasures without order or reason.

But the fact that the self-ideal must be both realistic and a bit beyond reach makes it necessary that it be constantly revised. This means that we actually need two sets of ideals. The first is that of ideal human perfection, toward which we can revise our own ideal.[15] The second is that of the person I could and should be now. Failure to differentiate these two ideals can lead practically either to an unrealistic self-ideal or to an inability to revise our self-ideal upwards; speculatively (i.e., as an explanation of human behavior) it can lead to relativism or to a misunderstanding of what actually motivates behavior.[16]

Properly understood, the self-ideal is open to further development. Virtue does not consist in any given action or any given level of excellence; it is an excellence according to the norms of reason.[17]

PERSONALITY AND A WORLD VIEW

Often, one finds controversy about the relation between an integrated personality and a world view (a "philosophy" of life, *Weltanschauung*). Is a certain world view necessary for a well-balanced personality? A number of distinctions must be made. First, a formally elaborated, scientific, speculative philosophy is as such not necessary for every human being. Second, a purely speculative and abstract view of reality has little influence on action and so is barely connected with personality. Third, we must distinguish between a psychologically integrated personality and an integrally good personality; the latter involves moral as well as psychological considerations. Fourth, realizing that in the real or-

[15] To be more accurate and concrete, the ideal human perfection is a reflection of the life of Christ. But we cannot simply transpose downward from Christ's level to our own; the "imitation of Christ" gives a *direction* to our efforts, it does not tell us concretely what we should do.

[16] Many psychologists consider "rigidity" a fault. Unfortunately, some of them include in this notion not only a lack of prudence and an inability to deal with differing circumstances and people, but also an understanding and an adherence to first principles—which is something quite different.

[17] As some people "materialize" prudence by trying to substitute a set of mechanical rules, others "materialize" moral virtue by aiming at completely concrete external action as the goal.

der absolute, well-rounded perfection is a rarity, we must be ready to accept less-than-integral perfection and to rest content with the least damaging deficiencies.

Now, in the sense of a practically effective view of the universe, does a particular view of life affect personality? All that can be said, apparently, is that certain gross errors, easily recognized to be at variance with common sense, can seriously damage personality, morally or psychologically. (I mean errors which are not merely asserted, but believed, at least in the sense of confusion.) For example, a consistent solipsism, a complete denial of the total possibility of knowledge, the belief that all events happen entirely by chance, the total denial of the difference between right and wrong, the view that life is to be lived simply and totally for immediate sense pleasure, the view that reality and life are totally devoid of value[18]—these views seem to be incompatible with a sound personality.[19] Other views are damaging to some aspects of personality, for example, practical atheism, the notion that morality is limited entirely to actions involving other persons, the notion that religion is a matter of literal observance only without any inner spirit, an extreme dualism which holds that matter and sense are evil. In this broad sense, a well-ordered personality is one that has a sound philosophy, and an adequate theory of personality rests on a more explicitly elaborated philosophy.[20]

A somewhat similar question asks whether virtue can correct neurotic behavior. Neurotic behavior is behavior that is nonfree; compulsively consistent; motivated by fear, anxiety, or some similar emotion; not rationally successful in solving a problem, though concretely effective in reducing psychological needs. Once

[18] It is my view that Jung's stand for the necessity of a "religious" view of life is to be understood in this extremely broad sense.

[19] Obviously none of these crude positions have been held by philosophers, and it seems to me that not even many psychotics accept one or all of them.

[20] It is my opinion—as the approach of this book clearly shows—that a Thomistic realism (or, more completely named, a Thomistic Christian naturalism), is the best speculative framework for an understanding of human action and human personality.

The "naturalism" is stressed, because of its positive value, but not so as to exclude the supernatural order. In the limited perspective chosen, philosophy functions as the principle of order. A complete analysis would proceed from theology—but it would not deny or eliminate anything that is found from the analysis of nature and natural perfection.

it has become habitual, there is much less opportunity to practice virtuous behavior. Even if a virtue can be developed, there remain additional factors of induced modifications, automatisms. Changing the environment will not cure the problem, for such a change only removes some stimuli, and so some responses may cease; yet the faulty personality structure remains. But suppose the environment has been changed and a certain amount of re-education has taken place, so that the person comes to see personally that there are other ways of solving his problem; then he is a position of being able to help himself, and perhaps then he can also begin to acquire virtue.

But virtue can more effectively prevent neurotic behavior. Through temperance, one's desires are not excessive and his impulses are controlled. Through courage, he can face his failures instead of hiding from them; he can remain calm under difficulty and so solve his problems in an objectively, rationally successful way.

MOTIVATION

We mentioned earlier that one of the factors bringing about a unification of actions and habits is the goal or end we have in mind in our actions. Some of the terms used in discussing this point are confusing and need clarification.

"Motive" is a very common term that is hard to identify; at best it is often vague; at worst it is equivocal. It has three meanings: (1) an ulterior and external goal—"the goal of the agent himself"; (2) the act (object) itself viewed as good—"the goal of the work"; (3) the formal part of a composite virtue.[21]

1. *Motive in the sense of an external goal.* For example, a man does not want to overeat because by doing so he will get fat and

---

[21] The "goal of the agent" is the *finis operantis;* it is the goal which the agent intends over and above the intrinsic worth of the action itself. "The goal of the work" is the *finis operis;* it is what the act is or produces in itself. When the agent intends the goal of the action itself, we need not make the distinction. (Sometimes people mistakenly refer the *finis operantis* to prudence, the *finis operis* to art. This would restrict prudence to the intention. But more accurately, prudence looks to the moral goodness of the action, art to its physical goodness, or effectiveness. Both the action itself and any added intention the agent may have are governed by prudence.)

so be despised. In this case, the desire for food will remain but will be overridden by the fear of disapproval.[22] The external motive in this sense does have in itself the characteristic of goodness or evil, but it does not communicate it to the action in question. Take another example, that of studying. When people speak of "motives for study," they are often thinking of things like parental approval, later success in business, God's will, and the like. As long as such goals remain external to the action, the person is functioning like the continent man. Then an act done for a motive carries no attractiveness in itself, but is like a pure means.

If one assumes that the action he is doing is worthless, and good only because of something else, he is not directing his life wisely. True enough, external motivation can keep a man from committing sin (for a time) ; it can enable him to perform the external act or to get a single act done; but if one has used only external motivation, he will never have performed the acts of the virtue and so will not acquire it. At best, it might keep him from the added evil of the external act, and thus he would not acquire the contrary vice in its fullness.

In imitating Christ, people often do not see the good of the virtue itself. But as St. Ignatius warns us, we should not omit the reasons for fear and hope.[23] For, when people try to act from external motivation alone, often the motives which they think move them (e.g., zeal, love of Christ) do not really move them very much, whereas others, quite unknown to them, are effective.

In attempting to work from very lofty ultimate motives, a person must go at the thing rightly. His intellect must pick out the proper intelligibility (and, if it is a moral virtue, the proper intelligibility of sensible good to be sensibly known and desired).[24] External motives will give a different slant to virtue; as many particular virtues are ordered under this or that ulterior goal, the whole structure of the moral life will look different.

[22] This situation is just like the one described by writers as "servile fear." Servile fear (e.g., of getting caught) does not remove desire (and so the interior disorientation of the will remains). Therefore it does not imply love or true sorrow for sin.

[23] St. Ignatius addresses this warning to people who think they are great saints and so can neglect what they deem "lower motives."

[24] To *acquire* a virtue, one must grasp the intelligibility at least specifically; the generic intelligibility is necessary for *transfer*.

2. *Motive as the act-object itself.* The important thing in the acquiring of virtue is that the action in question become an intermediate goal both in knowledge and in intention on all levels that are possible and pertinent; there should even be a sensible pleasure coming from the performance of the act. If the action-as-goal ("the goal of the work") does not get into the performance of action X (e.g., eating moderately), a man will not acquire virtue X (temperance), but something else. It is not easy to make sure that the proper intention is present. It is obvious that one cannot be satisfied with saying, "I want to be temperate," since this is only a wish. Neither is it enough to say, "I desire this food temperately"; talking to oneself is a pleasant occupation, and it may even help to convince oneself of the importance of a particular act, but it is not the practice of that act. A man may announce a motive to himself, but the real question is: How much is this motive actually *moving* him? Because he says to himself that he has a given intention, this is not enough to prove it.[25] But it may perhaps be a step on the way.

3. *Motive as the formal part of a virtue.* As we saw, virtues are composed of a formal part in intellect and a material part in some other power. For example, temperance has its formal part in intellect, its substantial part in the desiderative appetite. When we speak of stressing the motive of temperance, we may mean that we should have the intellectual awareness and volitional intention of what we are doing as well as having a desire (for the latter without the former is an automatism habit). In this sense of the term "motive," we always need to have the right motive if we wish to practice virtue.

THE ORDER OF ENDS

Ulterior ends which are merely extrinsically attached to actions do not help to acquire virtue or to unify life and action. On the other hand, correctly and formally to intend the intrinsic goods

[25] Moralists warn of the "masked intention." Self-knowledge about intentions is not easy; self-deception is unfortunately very easy. But a careful attention to our intentions will gradually bring about a better self-knowledge and make the right intentions more effective. Probably most people act a good part of the time from mixed motives.

that are immediately concerned with action here and now does bring about the acquisition of virtue, but it does not help to unify action and virtue. Nor will formally virtuous action be unified if it is subordinated to the ultimate end alone, even if this is done quite consciously. It is necessary to connect the immediate objectives with the ultimate end. We know, of course, *that* actions are so connected, but this abstract knowledge is insufficient.

Obviously what is needed is to become aware of intermediate ends and to acquire habits concerning them. We may call these "broadly generic" habits and virtues in order to distinguish them from the immediate generic virtues like temperance.

Some studies have been made of the broadly generic habits: all of them seem to be habit groups, though they can be distinguished by what is most noticeable about them. Thus, there are traits which are largely cognitive, such as curiosity, tendency to analysis, dominant imagery; and yet is also clear that some general attitudes are connected with these. Then, there are other traits which are more like attitudes; they have been called "generating themes" (Mounier) and "intentional characteristics" or "Leitmotivs" (Allport). Among these attitudes are those such as persistence, flexibility, control, practicality, introversion-extraversion, confidence, dominance-abasement, autonomy-conformity, aggression-affiliation. These general habits, however, seem to include both some habitual modifications of knowledge and also action. A third sort of generic habits seem to involve external expression, such as style, fluency, poise; yet these also seem to involve cognitive and emotive habits.

Some of these attitudes, obviously, exclude others, but this is far from being a general rule. In addition, we must note that some goals can be taken up into higher and more inclusive ones, or left at their own level. An example of this inclusion is the scale of motivation given by Maslow: physiological needs, safety needs, love and belonging needs, esteem needs, the self-actualization need, and the desire to know and understand. In this scale, the "lower" (immediate) needs are not denied nor left unfulfilled; but, on condition that they are satisfied, cease to be the principal motivation and are integrated into a more extensive order of goals.

When we come to the broadly generic virtues, we find that less has been done to analyze them and clarify their relationships. We have already noted that the ultimate goal is not enough. If we were to suppose that a series of intermediate goals were perfectly harmonious, we could imagine a series beginning with the more ultimate and coming down to touch the immediate goals of the particular virtues. We have then, first, the ultimate goal. What man must do is order himself to the possession of the good which is his ultimate perfection. And he must in some way have some concrete view of what that possession is. Next, he must find the concrete way in which *he* can live this goal. The closer we come to immediate goals, the more necessary it is to consider the person in his concrete actuality: his special abilities and his special circumstances. Only in the light of such particular determinations is it possible to see how this particular individual can embody an ideal in a way that is apt and suitable for him. Thus the distinctive life patterns of different saints, for example, are set up.

Most people do not so radically and single-mindedly establish the series of interlocking goals. In actual practice they seem to work from both ends, now bridging back from more ultimate goals, now working up from concrete circumstances. The result is that full coherence and harmony is attained only late in life, or perhaps never reached. Sometimes intermediate goals are decided on, and then it is found that they are not mutually compatible; this of course is an unsatisfactory state of affairs. Sometimes also an ultimate goal is held (or at least projected), but not very firmly; in the meantime an intermediate goal (for example, a professional career) is firmly decided on. Then, if the ultimate goal can be superimposed on the intermediate one, well and good; if not, the ultimate goal is changed to fit that proximate goal which the individual desires most intensely. (Cases like this seem to be reasons why many psychologists disregard ultimate goals in their analysis of personality.)

Nevertheless, the concrete vision of an ultimate goal does influence the total personality to some extent, even when it is not totally consistent with other goals. Since it is connected with a particular "view of life," it manages to give a direction to choices, or leads to a characteristic similarity of concrete action. It does not seem to be operative in very small details or to influence choices between courses of action which would be equally compatible with the goal. Yet occasions will arise when the goal will influence choices, and these occasions will be significant ones. One ordinarily does not ask about the character of someone who is performing a temporary service, but he should be concerned with the general outlook on life of anyone whom he admits to a close relationship with himself. The Roman poet Horace bitterly commented that his contemporaries were careful in the choice of a trainer of their horses, but casual in engaging a tutor for their children.

For a Christian, the way of concretely seeing the overall goal of his actions in this life is the "imitation of Christ." But even this goal needs further determination. Every man must find a way in which he can carry out this imitation of Christ.

An interesting series of such ways of conceiving an ideal is offered by the various so-called "schools of spirituality" in the Catholic Church. There are, first of all, the very broad differences between the Greek traditions and what may in general be called a "Latin" tradition. Within the Latin tradition, writers commonly speak of the Benedictine, Dominican, Franciscan, Jesuit, and Oratorian "schools," and there are others which can be characterized in similar ways. According to ascetical writers, the Benedictine spirit emphasizes the regular pattern of communal prayer and manual work as a way of imitating Christ. The Dominican spirit imitates Christ in meditative prayer, study, and preaching. The Franciscan spirit views the imitation of Christ in terms of "poverty," the Christian detachment from worldly goods and pleasures. The Jesuit spirit stresses the readiness to undertake any task and to do it in whatever way promises to be most effective for the greater glory of God. The Oratorian spirit sees the "humanity of Christ" in prayer and work.

These various "spirits" are not abstract and formal schemata. In each case, an outstanding man became a founder of a religious order. He gave to a lofty abstract ideal an imitable concrete expression. Hence, adequately to understand a "religious spirit," we need to know not only its rules and its abstract formulations, but also its founder, its important leaders, and its traditional concrete expression.

A very similar reason seems to account for the practice of the veneration of saints. Many of us more ordinary people have considerable difficulty in translating ideals into action. Sometimes we lack imagination; more often, perhaps, we seem unable to adapt intermediate goals without losing ultimate ones. Acquaintance with a number of outstanding individuals opens our eyes to possibilities, and for a beginner who wants to make progress in virtue this is most helpful. Then, when we come to see that ideals can be concretized in various ways, we begin to find a measure of freedom and a notion of how we ourselves can reach an ideal that lets us be ourselves and yet also enables us to do what we see ought to be done.

CONTINUING EFFORT

Supposing then that a person has discovered what virtues he needs and has worked hard to acquire them; can he then finally relax and just live according to the virtue he has acquired? Or, granted that we must continue to live at a level of attention and deliberate intention in order that our actions be really human, free, and virtuous, can we at least expect that we need not apply additional effort? We would like to think so, and yet experience shows that this is not the case. Why should this be so?

One very important reason is that perfection for a man is not a suddenly acquired and indivisible state, but rather the high point of a continuous process. So, if a person could say at some given time, "I now have enough justice, all things considered," what has brought him to this sufficiency is a very recent acquisition. Our previous investigations have shown that in most cases virtue is not acquired by a single act, but needs repeated exercise. The initial and relatively quite imperfect level of virtue has therefore had a lot of exercise, and so is deeply ingrained; whereas the final and perfecting increase is not yet so completely acquired, has not yet taken deep roots in the person. In addition, as we have also seen, full virtuous human activity requires complete rational control.

On the other hand, the instinctive responses and those coming from automatisms operate easily without rational control. Therefore, there is a kind of "drift" in human nature to the more primitive, the more imperfect, the less controlled, in a word, toward mediocrity. And, as a consequence, some effort is necessary even to continue on the level which one has already reached.

Another factor in the disintegration of an acquired virtue is our own change of activity. It often happens that what was once a means becomes a goal sought for its own sake. For example, a teacher may first try to maintain discipline as necessary for teaching and in time come to make discipline itself a goal. So, too, a person takes a job to support himself and his family and after some years puts the requirements of his job ahead of the needs and advantages of his family; thus also many a businessman makes his business into his main preoccupation. The mechanism here is easily intelligible, but it is none the less very effective. It is this. In order to achieve my goal, I must be successful in the activity to be done here and now, and so I pay close attention to what is immediately before me. This is good and even necessary. But if now I attend to the means alone time and time again and do not refer them to anything beyond themselves, I equivalently, unintentionally, but effectively deny to myself that they *are* *means*. Consequently also my intention toward them changes: I now intend them as goals in themselves. This development has been called the "functional autonomy of motives" by Gordon Allport. Thus, by repeated activity, entirely new habits are built up, and some of the old ones are indirectly destroyed.

This process may explain otherwise startling "collapses in adult life." It can happen that a young person undertakes a difficult and complex task out of very high motives, and partly because of his very generosity (though without the guidance of prudence) pours out his entire attention on the immediate activities of his task. After years of what had seemed continued generosity and virtue, the same person suddenly abandons one or more of his original motives (for example, his faith). Of course, such a change is not sudden; the reorientation may have gone on for years along the lines suggested, until the original motive "no longer meant anything."

A third reason is that life simply will not let us alone. Perhaps there still are simple patterns of living in which a person can locate himself as a child and remain there unchanged to his dying day. But it seems impossible that this be true of the majority of people who live in a Western culture. And, as one emerges from one pattern to another, habits and virtues that were suitable to the prior often are no longer suitable to the later pattern, and so they must be changed at least to some extent. This means that there will be periods at which effort will again be necessary to acquire the new habits which we need for the changed situations.

THE CRISES OF GROWTH

Connected with this last point are the changes that take place within ourselves. What this connection is, is not quite clear, but for our present purposes we need not examine it deeply. It is sufficient to know that these changes do take place.

There is general agreement that there are periods of accelerated change and of instability which are now called "crises"; there is also somewhat general agreement on the kinds and the locations of these crises. As to their precise character and their exact causes there is very little agreement; however, such a detailed understanding is again fortunately not necessary for our present purposes.

From several points of view, one can say that there are three crises or groups of crises: in childhood, adolescence, and adulthood. Each has its own characteristics, its own needs, and therefore its own sort of solutions. When a crisis has been successfully resolved, the person is ready for a period of more or less stable growth.

The childhood crises are described in several different ways. Apparently there is some difficulty for the child in determining his (her) relationships to father and mother, though this difficulty is most often resolved by accepting a clear-cut role. With the physical possibility of freer action and the usually concomitant beginnings of discipline, there is a conflict between initiative, activity, self-direction on the one hand, and passivity or guilt and shame on the other. With the awakening of reason comes the conflict between the rule of reason and reality (and God) as against the following of immediate pleasure and impulse. If these crises are successfully passed, the child has accepted his own moral responsibility, has learned to control himself somewhat, has begun to see the relationship between means and ends, and has also to some extent come to trust his parents and others who stand in a similar relationship to him.

The adolescent crisis comes more or less with the awakening of sex. The child withdraws more from the home and turns to his peers; and so there is on the one hand something of a turning away from authority, tradition, and religious faith, and a turning to personal rights, personal choices, and development of the individual. However, at the same time, there may be a problem of acceptance by peers and a problem of what the adolescent is to become. If the adolescent problems are successfully solved, there is a new rise in confidence and a strong desire to undertake a definite kind of life, to choose and to follow out a vocation.

The adult crises are usually frustration crises. At some point, the youthful enthusiasm begins to wear out, and the person begins to realize that he will not reach the level of success that he had planned for himself. This very realization, of course, implies that the person is both somewhat idealistic and also somewhat introspective. A person who has never aimed for very much may well be satisfied with what he achieves, and an imperceptive person may not notice an even rather wide discrepancy between his ideals and his accomplishment. This problem can be well solved if the entire set of goals is carefully reevaluated so that it is more in line with what the individual can realistically expect to accomplish, and yet is challenging enough to give him something worthwhile to work for. The value of firmness, or perseverance, needs especially to be stressed. Otherwise, there can be merely a ceasing of all real drive, or perhaps even despair. It is perhaps at this third level that the role of virtue will be most prominent, because adult crises seem to rise more to the level of rational awareness, and for their solutions they need well-guided choices.

In addition to the chronological viewpoint, these crises can be looked at in other ways. Earlier, we referred to the fact that the environment can serve as a framework for patterned living and that a major change in such a framework can lead to very great changes in behavior. This experience of losing a support or bulwark can also arise in other ways—in a severe disillusionment with some person who had been an ideal, in the loss of a supporting friend by death or separation. This kind of experience can occur in connection with the other crises, and in that case it will give a special coloration to them; or it could conceivably occur by itself. In any case, personal activity, personal commitment, and intrinsic motivation are called for if the crisis is to be passed successfully.

Another source of conflict, and therefore of a possible crisis, is the discovery that faith (or any similar commitment to an outlook and a way of life) involves action and refraining from action, under conditions in which the action is (or seems to be, promises to be) difficult, or in which the refraining from action seems to be too great a sacrifice of pleasure. This conflict cannot be solved without moral virtue, and to the extent that moral virtue is acquired, the tension ceases.

From this, we can conclude that not all crises directly concern virtue. Some of them seem to be more biosocial, others more strictly social. On the other hand, some crises possibly occur because virtue is not adequate for a new situation; others cannot be solved except by the acquisition of virtue; still others make much greater virtue possible. It is to the extent that some crises do involve virtue that we have been interested in considering them.

SOURCES FOR CHAPTER SEVEN

General Sources

Allers, Rudolf, *Character Education in Adolescence* (New York, J. F. Wagner, 1940); applies Adler's theories in a very helpful way; can be quite useful.

Allport, Gordon W., *Becoming* (New Haven, Yale, 1955), pp. 46-47; on the function of an ideal self—highly recommended in general.

Allport, Gordon W., "The Personality Trait," in *Psychological Theory,* Melvin H. Marx, ed. (New York, Macmillan, 1951), 503-507.

Arnold, Magda B., *Emotion and Personality* (New York, Columbia, 1961), vol. II, pp. 209-308; on the self-ideal.

Cruchon, G., S.J., "Genèse et structure du moi humain à la lumière des sciences bio-psychologiques modernes," *Nouvelle Revue Théologique,* vol. 73 (1951), 364-384; perhaps not always aware of the constructural character of scientific theories.

Dobzhansky, Theodosius, *Mankind Evolving* (New Haven, Yale, 1962); the nature-nurture controversy is covered, pp. 42-46, 51-75, 76-99, 322-327.

Erikson, Erik H., *Identity and the Life Cycle* (New York, International Universities Press, Inc., 1959); a formal statement by one of the leading theoreticians.

Evoy, John J., S.J., and Christoph, Van F., S.J., *Personality Development in the Religious Life* (New York, Sheed, 1963); a number of good practical points on direction and development.

Geiger, L. B., O.P., *Philosophie et spiritualité* (Paris, Les Editions du Cerf, 1963), vol. I, 217-238, vol. II, 289-373; a number of important theoretical points.

Gillet, M. S., O.P., "Les éléments psychologiques du caractère moral," *Revue des sciences philosophiques et théologiques,* vol. 1 (1907), 74-98, 217-238; still a basic study, highly recommended.

Godin, A., S.J., ed., *Child and Adult before God* (Brussels, Lumen Vitae Press, 1961); on the development that is necessary both in knowledge and attitudes.

Guardini, Romano, *Faith and the Modern Man* (New York, Pantheon, 1952); a Catholic's view of the various crises that can happen to a man.

Hagmaier, George, C.S.P., and Gleason, Robert W., S.J., *Counselling the Catholic* (New York, Sheed, 1959); good on the interplay of various levels of motivation and the influence of automatism habits.

Heaney, John J., S.J., *Faith, Reason, and the Gospels* (Westminster, Md., Newman, 1961); good on the contemporary views of the interrelation between faith and reason.

Hildebrand, Dietrich von, *Christian Ethics* (New York, MacKay, 1953); though this book practically rejects the natural order and particular virtues, it has an excellent treatment of the importance of the involvement of the whole person and of having overall goals.

Horney, Karen, *Neurosis and Human Growth* (New York, Norton, 1950), p. 64; on the idealized self.

Jersild, Arthur T., *The Psychology of Adolescence* (New York, Macmillan, 1957); an outstanding text on this subject.

Kelly, Gerald, S.J., *Guidance for Religious* (Westminster, Md., Newman, 1956); also practical points on direction, bringing out the idea that there must be a continued growth toward self-direction.

Lindworsky, Johannes, S.J., *The Psychology of Asceticism,* E. A. Heiring, trans. (London, 1936; reprinted, Baltimore, Carroll Press, 1950).

Lindworsky, Johannes, S.J., *The Training of the Will*, A. Steiner and
E. A. Fitzpatrick, trans. (Milwaukee, Bruce, 1929); both of Lindworsky's
works are excellent on the function of ideals; unfortunately he has
only a mechanical notion of habits and so rejects mastery habits of the
will.

McLaughlin, Barry, S.J., *Nature, Grace, and Religious Development*
(Westminster, Md., Newman, 1964); applies Erikson's theories to the
special case of the religious.

Maslow, A. H., *Motivation and Personality* (New York, Harper & Row,
1954); excellent on motivation and on the hierarchy of motives.

Masserman, J. H., *Principles of Dynamic Psychiatry* (Philadelphia, Saun-
ders, 1954); good on motivation.

Moustakas, C. E., *The Self: Explorations in Personal Growth* (New York,
Harper & Row, 1956); good on motivation.

Nebraska Symposium on Motivation, ed. Marshall R. Jones (Lincoln,
University of Nebraska Press, 1954); a classic source.

Oraison, Marc, *Love or Constraint* (New York, Kenedy, 1959); the contrast is perhaps somewhat rhetorically exaggerated, the evils of motivation through fear are well delineated.

Pikunas, Justin, and Albrecht, Eugene J., *Psychology of Human Development* (New York, McGraw-Hill, 1961); perhaps the best book on
developmental psychology by a Catholic author.

Religion in the Developing Personality (New York, New York University Press, 1960); a symposium with some excellent papers.

Research in Religious Psychology (Brussels, Lumen Vitae Press, 1957);
some excellent survey articles.

Rogers, Carl R., *On Becoming a Person* (Boston, Houghton Mifflin Co.,
1961); stresses the self-direction; perhaps overstresses the ability of the
natural powers to effect cures; stresses the need and advantage of being aware of motives and views.

Royce, James E., S.J., *Personality and Mental Health* (Milwaukee, Bruce,
rev. ed., 1964), pp. 94-96; on the self-concept.

Stein, Maurice, Vidich, Arthur, and White, David, *Identity and Anxiety*
(New York, Free Press, 1960); a collection centering on themes of
growth and crisis.

Zilboorg, Gregory, "Love in Freudian Psychoanalysis," in *Selection II*,
Cecily Hastings and Donald Nicoll, eds. (New York, Sheed, 1954), pp.
159-179; good treatment of the importance of love.

Maturity

(Most of the books already mentioned, especially the ones on developmental psychology, contain sections on maturity. Some few additional titles can be added.)

Allport, Gordon W., *Personality, A Psychological Interpretation* (New York, Holt, Rinehart and Winston, 1937), pp. 213-214.

Arnold, Magda B., and Gasson, John B., S.J., eds., *The Human Person* (New York, Ronald, 1954).

Schindler, John A., *How to Live 365 Days a Year* (New York, Prentice-Hall, 1954); very much at a popular level of presentation, full of usable examples.

INDEX

Abstinence, 140, 207-208
  total, 212
Abstraction, 258-259
  must be deliberate, 158
Abulia, 205
Accident-substance relationship, 109, 113-114
Act of virtue, meaning of, 158
Action, virtue of, 220
Activity, complex, 105-106, 110-111
  control of, 16-17
  control by knowledge, 107-108
  immanent (vital), 11, 107
  instinctive, 36-37, 38
  motor, 15, 25, 96
  reflex, 133
  transient, 11-12, 107
  unconscious, 77-78
  See also Behavior; Operation
Adam, 245
Adatation, 20
  of means to ends, 196-197
  mechanical, 99
  physical, 9
Addiction, *see* Drug addiction
Adolescence, 256, 273
Adolescent crisis, 273
Adult crisis, 273-274
Aesthetic exerience, 119
Affability, 238
Affective link, 36
Aggression, 221
Albrecht, 276
Alcoholism, 207, 212
Allers, 274
Allport, 267, 271, 274, 277
Ammons, 73
Analysis, 23
  formal object, 12
Anger, 58, 59, 115, 209, 217
  controlled, 141
  reasonable, 209
  violent, 217

Animal, 18, 28-29, 35, 36-37, 40-41, 49, 75, 78, 82
Anxiety, 59, 84
  free-floating, 83-84, 86
  reaction, 261
Apathy, 56, 59, 205
Appetency, 86
Appetite, aggressive, 48, 56-60, 243
  desiderative, 48, 50-56, 243
  and virtue, 204-206
  sensory, 41-42, 48-50, 66-67, 95, 96
  and consciousness, 88-89
  habits of, 141-142
Appetition, 37, 49-50
  sensory and intellect, 107-108
Appetitive powers, losing habits of, 147
Appreciation, 241
Apprehension, simple, 65
Aquinas, Saint Thomas, 2, 14, 28, 41, 71, 96, 99, 101, 106, 124, 126, 128, 131, 137, 140, 141, 164, 165, 172, 176, 183, 184, 190, 191, 192, 195, 198, 201, 202, 208, 210, 213, 224, 229, 231, 238, 239, 240, 241, 244, 245, 246
Aristotle, 54, 108, 119, 139, 221, 223, 237
Arnold, 73, 274, 277
Art, 62, 118, 144
  as complex habit, 117
  creative, 118
  fine, and virtue, 183-184, 197
  and imagination, 119
  and intellect, 119
  manual, 77, 118
  and meaning, 118
  mechanical, 17
  non-representational, 120
  not a virtue, 183-184
  useful, 118, 120
  as virtue, 199